THE PHOENIX INDIAN SCHOOL

The Phoenix Indian School

Forced Assimilation in Arizona, 1891–1935

by Robert A. Trennert, Jr.

UNIVERSITY OF OKLAHOMA PRESS
NORMAN AND LONDON

By Robert A. Trennert, Jr.
Alternative to Extinction: Federal Indian Policy and the Beginnings of the Reservation System, 1846–1851 (Philadelphia, 1975)
Indian Traders on the Middle Border: The House of Ewing, 1827–1854 (Lincoln, Nebr., 1981)
The Phoenix Indian School: Forced Assimilation in Arizona, 1891–1935 (Norman, 1988)

Library of Congress Cataloging-in-Publication Data

Trennert, Robert A.
The Phoenix Indian School: forced assimilation in Arizona, 1891–1935.

Bibliography: p.
Includes index.
1. Phoenix Indian School. 2. Indians of North America—Arizona—Cultural assimilation. I. Title.
E97.6.P4T74 1988   303.4'82'09791   87-40560
ISBN 0-8061-2104-1 (alk. paper)

The paper in this book meets the guidelines for permanence and durability of the Committee on Production Guidelines for Book Longevity of the Council on Library Resources, Inc.

Copyright © 1988 by the University of Oklahoma Press, Norman, Publishing Division of the University. Manufactured in the U.S.A. First edition.

For my father,

ROBERT A. TRENNERT, SR.

Contents

Preface	xi
1. Introduction: The Sword Will Give Way to the Spelling Book	3
2. An Oasis in the Desert	12
3. Marking Time	33
4. A School for Many Tribes	57
5. Stability in an Era of Change	85
6. Student Life	112
7. Education Under Duress	150
8. End of an Era	182
9. Conclusion and Epilogue	206
Notes	215
Bibliography	245
Index	253

Illustrations

Girls' Building, Phoenix Indian School	30
Hospital Building, Phoenix Indian School	44
Phoenix Indian School Band	80
Boys' Washroom, 1914	107
East Farm Sanatorium, Circa 1918	108
Phoenix Indian Drill Corps	116
Women's Officers	117
Sewing Class, 1914	121
Free-Hand Drawing Class, 1900	122
Girls' Basketball Team, 1903	129
Chicken Yard, 1903	130
The Mature Campus, Sometime After 1900	152

Preface

IN MARCH 1982 the U.S. Department of the Interior suggested closing the Phoenix Indian School. It was not the first time the government had threatened to shut the institution, but on this occasion the opposition of the Indian community was enough to cause the Reagan administration to back down temporarily. The plan to close the school, however, created a flurry of interest in the institution's history. During the succeeding discussion, it became evident that neither Indians nor white residents knew much about the school or how it fit into federal Indian policy. Hardly anyone remembered that the Phoenix Indian School had once been an important part of city life and played a key role in the nation's now discredited program to "Americanize" the Indian population.

The Phoenix Indian Industrial Boarding School was founded for the specific purpose of preparing Native American children for assimilation. During its first forty years, the main goal was to remove Indian youngsters from their traditional environment, obliterate their cultural heritage, and replace that background with the values of white middle-class America. Yet the definition of assimilation was repeatedly revised between 1890 and 1930, and the changing educational policies of the federal government forced the school to shift emphasis from time to time. In this sense, school operations were subject to national trends and philosophies. It is the changing concept of assimilationist education and its application to the Phoenix school that forms the basis of this book.

The story of Indian education during the assimilationist period is broad and complex. There were many kinds of schools and many programs. Some scholars in the field, such as Francis Paul Prucha and Fred Hoxie, have looked at the larger picture. Yet no one has studied, in any detail, the way national educational policies operated in a typical school. Carlisle School in Pennsylvania and Hampton in Virginia have been studied, but those institutions were far from ordinary. The Phoenix school, on the other hand, represented the nonreservation institutions that dominated the school program. Although it would be naïve to maintain that Phoenix was similar to all nonreservation schools, it was quite representative. More than day schools or reservation boarding schools, the off-reservation facilities presented a full range of educational programs. Phoenix was an important member of this group, and a detailed study of the institution contributes greatly to our understanding of federal education as it actually worked.

A study of this nature permits one to test some of the assumptions of those who analyze federal policy. One quickly sees that some of the federal actions described by scholars did not work on the local level. The western schools developed a personality of their own; they were affected by pressures and circumstances not recognized by policymakers and thus did not always follow national trends. This by no means implies that national issues had no impact on Phoenix and similar institutions. Philosophical, racial, and educational theories affected the West as they did the rest of the United States. But these issues must be considered in the light of local conditions to evaluate the successes and failures of the educational system.

A case study also permits the consideration of questions that are glossed over in national studies. It provides an opportunity to look into the activities of school administrators, for the most part professional bureaucrats who did not always see the administration of Indian schools in the same light as national policymakers saw it. Too, studying a specific school enables us to analyze the relationship between the school and the local community. Nonreservation schools were intentionally established near centers of white population, and interaction between the two peoples was an important part of the assimilation program. But why white citizens welcomed the schools and how they treated Indian students have yet to receive adequate attention. Finally, the study of a specific institution provides the chance for an in-depth look at the effect of assimilationist education on Indian children. Any rounded view of the Indian schools must consider the Indian perspective to analyze how the federal programs affected individuals. It is too often assumed that the schools were bad because of their obviously racial perspective. As this book shows, such conclusions can be misleading. Given the stated purpose of Indian education and the reaction of Indian children and parents, the schools have had a more favorable impact on Native American cultures than might be expected.

The book is organized chronologically, centering around the school superintendents. These administrators dominated school life: they implemented federal policy, reacted to community pressures, and provided inspirational guidance. In a general way, their terms of office coincided with the major philosophical changes in federal Indian policy, thus making the impacts of these changes more visible. Because such an approach makes it difficult to incorporate the Indian perspective, a separate chapter on the Indian students deals specifically with school life.

The book ends in 1935, when the assimilationist approach gave way to the ideas of cultural pluralism. During its first four decades the school functioned much as it had been designed in 1891. It was dedicated to assimilationist education in an off-reservation environment, and many of the basic approaches changed little. By the 1920s times were changing; the nonreservation industrial boarding schools had fallen from favor, and the survivors were evolving into Indian high schools. This transformation was largely completed during the first years of the New Deal. By that point, the Phoenix Indian School had changed forever; the old assimilation format was dead.

Like all other such scholarly endeavors, this book could not have been completed without the assistance and cooperation of a good number of individuals and institutions. I owe a great debt of gratitude first and foremost to Robert M. Kvasnicka, of the National Archives, for helping locate all the documentary material related to the school. Mrs. Susie Sato, of the Arizona Historical Foundation; Ken Rossman, of the Federal Records Center at Laguna Niguel; Mary Fry and Virginia Renner, of the Huntington Library; and the staffs of the Arizona Collection at Arizona State University and the Arizona Historical Society Library, in Tucson, also deserve recognition.

I am also indebted to a number of my students who took their time to help the project. In particular, I wish to thank Roxie McLeod, Julie Campbell, Georganne Scheiner, Betti Arnold, Susan Jacobowitz, Evelyn Cooper, and Gilbert Gonzales. I owe a special debt of gratitude to my colleague Kathleen Sands for her advice and help in procuring oral interviews. Additionally, I am grateful for the cooperation of former Phoenix Indian School students Tony and Hazel Dukepoo, Helen Sekaquaptewa, and Peter Blaine for permitting me to talk to them. To Beth Luey, Karen Dahood, and Margaret C. Szasz my thanks for being available to discuss those thorny problems that inevitably crop up. Finally, I wish to express my appreciation to the office staff of the History Department, at Arizona State University, particularly Dee Anne Marsh and Eunice Brown, for their help and kind understanding.

Some of my research was sponsored by grants from the National Endowment for the Humanities and Arizona State University. I am deeply indebted to these institutions. In addition, a few ideas presented in this book were introduced in the following articles: "Peaceably if They Will, Forcibly If They Must: The Phoenix Indian School, 1890–1901," *Journal of Arizona History* 20 (Autumn 1979): 297–322; "'And the Sword Will

Give Way to the Spelling-Book': Establishing the Phoenix Indian School," *Journal of Arizona History* 23 (Spring 1982): 35–58; and "From Carlisle to Phoenix: The Rise and Fall of the Indian Outing System, 1878–1930," *Pacific Historical Review* 52 (August 1983): 267–91.

ROBERT A. TRENNERT, JR.

Tempe, Arizona

THE PHOENIX INDIAN SCHOOL

1
INTRODUCTION: The Sword Will Give Way to the Spelling Book

DURING THE 1880s the United States committed itself to incorporating the Indian population into the mainstream of American life. Having finally defeated the Indians militarily and settled them on reservations, national leaders believed that the time had arrived to make good on the centuries-old pledge to exchange native lands for "the gift of civilization." Although this promise meant little to Native Americans, the reformers of the late nineteenth century felt honor-bound to carry it out. True to the spirit of the times, they saw reservations as incompatible with the ideals of American society. Confinement could be justified only if it was used to promote the ultimate good. And what greater good could be accomplished than lifting a race of people from the depths of "savagery" to the enlightenment of modern "civilization"? The Indian reform organizations of the 1880s thus dedicated themselves to devising a process whereby the reservations might be slowly abolished and their residents assimilated. One of the most effective methods of accomplishing this transformation seemed to be education. Many sincere people believed that the time had come for the sword to give way to the spelling book.[1]

The idea that education could be used to promote assimilation was hardly new. From early colonial times white Americans had been attempting to school Indian youngsters in the ways of European civilization. In the years before the American Revolution this task had been entrusted to religious societies and private charitable groups, neither of which had the funds or the organizational ability to make significant headway. As a result, only a handful of Indians had received what might be called an education by the end of the colonial period. The United States government became involved in Indian education in 1819 when Congress created the "Civilization Fund." This subsidy to religious schools, combined with treaty provisions requiring the use of tribal annuities for schools, produced added interest in Indian education but very little success. During the 1840s considerable emphasis was placed on "manual labor schools" which were expected to provide "education in Christianity." This program floundered badly before the Civil War as religious societies charged with operating the schools proved unable to overcome the problems resulting from the increasing tempo of warfare and relocation caused by national expansion.[2]

The end of the Civil War signaled the beginning of direct federal involvement in Indian education. Such investigative groups as the 1867–68 Indian Peace Commission recommended that "schools should be established" as an effective method of resolving the "Indian problem." In 1870, Congress responded to such suggestions by increasing its financial support to religious schools; by the late 1870s the government was moving toward a school system of its own. This trend was accelerated by the establishment of the reservation system and the organization of humanitarian reform groups dedicated to the principle that the Indian must eventually be assimilated. As the reformers began to champion the cause of a comprehensive program of federal education, most of their energies were directed at the boarding school, which they regarded as superior because it promised to separate children from their cultural background, enforce discipline, and provide a controlled teaching atmosphere. By the end of the 1870s federal day schools and boarding institutions had been opened on many reservations.[3]

Until 1878 educators gave little attention to locating boarding schools away from the reservation. It took the visionary efforts of army officer Richard Henry Pratt to add a new dimension to Indian education. Pratt was the father of the nonreservation industrial school, which emerged in the following decade as the most popular type of institution in the federal school system. Because of his achievements, Captain Pratt became the most significant force in Indian education. His school at Carlisle, Pennsylvania, was a showplace, and its apparent success convinced the public that schools were capable of solving the "Indian problem."

Pratt's interest in educating Indian children developed as the result of an assignment to supervise a group of Indian prisoners confined at Fort Marion, Florida. Convinced that "civilization" provided an answer to the national dilemma of race relations, he undertook to transform his prisoners into model citizens. He removed their chains, gave them responsibilities, and put them to work in nearby Saint Augustine. The success of this experiment convinced Pratt of the beneficial results that might accrue from direct Indian contact with white society: disciplinary problems could be reduced, the Indians would be able to earn spending money, and association with white citizens would encourage them to feel comfortable in American society. Partly because of these observations, Pratt reaffirmed his conviction that Indians could be civilized by removing them from their traditional environment and transplanting them into surroundings that would cause them to work for a living, learn English, and develop into productive citizens.[4]

In 1878, when the government decided to return the Fort Marion prisoners to their reservation in Oklahoma, Pratt mounted a campaign to implement his ideas. He persuaded the U.S. Indian Office to allow him to retain seventeen of the younger male inmates in the East, where they would be schooled at Hampton Institute in Virginia. There, at that previously all-black school supervised by General Samuel C. Armstrong, Pratt began his educational career. In line with most other reformers of the day, Pratt and Armstrong agreed that any plan for schooling the Indians should focus on assimilation. The basic objectives of these pioneers of Indian industrial education thus centered on teaching the English language, the work ethic, Christian moral principles, and the responsibilities of citizenship; Indian students were to be "Americanized."[5]

The first year at Hampton saw Pratt and Armstrong develop several significant programs—all aimed at eventual assimilation. One of the most important, the "outing system," sent students to live with farm families in hopes that they would adopt the Anglo work ethic, improve their language skills, and develop a desire to live like their white neighbors. Another device involved dividing the school day into two segments, the mornings being concentrated on academic work and the afternoons given over to vocational training. The boys worked on the school farm or learned to be blacksmiths and carpenters, while the girls received instruction in household skills. The practice of educating women along with men, although not a new concept, was favored because it would produce a "civilized" family unit. Finally, in an attempt to instill the personal discipline necessary to succeed in the white man's world, students were forced to conform to a rigid military-type routine.[6]

Pratt was pleased with the progress the students seemed to be making at Hampton but objected to educating Indians at the predominately black school. He therefore broke with General Armstrong over the race issue and demanded that the Indians have a school of their own. In 1879 he went to Secretary of the Interior Carl Schurz and asked to be allowed to open an Indian school in the East. A major part of his argument centered on the proposition that Indians needed a chance to participate directly in American life, that they could be useful citizens only "through living among our people." Schurz concurred, and in the summer of 1879, Pratt was authorized to open a school at Carlisle Barracks, Pennsylvania.[7] General Armstrong, meanwhile, continued to develop his own program at Hampton.

The Carlisle Indian School rapidly became the nation's leading center of Indian education. Not only did it surpass Hampton in the number of students, but it attracted the strong interest of a public willing to provide considerable moral and financial support. At Carlisle, Pratt implemented the most advanced ideas of his generation regarding Indian assimilation.

His school was a self-contained unit that shut out all traditional Indian influences. Each year his agents recruited as many students as possible from western reservations. Although Indian parents were often reluctant to send their children away from home, Pratt effectively used his personal influence to keep the classrooms filled. In the years after 1880, Carlisle regularly enrolled children from scores of tribes. By mid-decade the school was home to more than five hundred Indian students.[8]

Once the school was established, it became obvious just what Pratt expected Carlisle to accomplish. He had great faith in the Indians and believed that with proper help they could be fully assimilated into American society; he did not relegate them to an inferior position. Carlisle was designed to transform the Indians by placing them in direct contact with American society. The masthead of the the school paper perhaps most succinctly stated Pratt's outlook: "To Civilize The Indian; Get Him Into Civilization. To Keep Him Civilized; Let Him Stay." To the innovative schoolmaster, returning a child to a tribal home was counterproductive, negating the basic purpose of his education and destroying individual initiative by placing him under the "communistic government of the tribes."[9]

Pratt saw the nonreservation boarding school as a place where Indians could be shorn of their cultural heritage. A key feature of his school was the "industrial," or vocational, aspect. The headmaster wanted his students trained in useful mechanical skills. "Industrially," he stated, "it has been our object to give direction and encouragement to each student of sufficient age in some particular branch." Carlisle therefore concentrated on teaching such trades as shoemaking, tinning, tailoring, harness making, steamfitting, and blacksmithing, assuming that Indian boys would eventually find jobs in white communities. Girls received instruction in such domestic tasks as cooking, washing, laundering, and sewing. The academic branch at Carlisle was geared to support the industrial program and played a secondary role. Most "literary" emphasis was placed on learning English and such useful subjects as mathematics and economics. Students who completed the full course of study received the equivalent of an eighth-grade education. Most pupils, however, stayed in school for three or more years but were not pushed to complete the academic program.[10]

By the mid-1880s, Carlisle was hailed as an outstanding success. Although its accomplishments were more illusory than real, the school's reputation led the Indian Office to consider opening additional nonreservation institutions. Such expansion fit well with the government's attempt to create a comprehensive school system for the Indians. Although interest in reservation schools remained high, the apparent progress of Carlisle and Hampton, combined with Pratt's aggressive lobbying, convinced reformers and politicians alike of the superiority of the nonreservation boarding school. Guided by this belief, the government began opening industrial schools in the West. A small facility had been established at Forest Grove, Oregon, in 1880, but it required four more years to get any meaningful expansion under way. Congress supported this effort and proved willing to increase appropriations and provide other inducements. In 1882, for example, the legislators authorized the Indian Office to acquire abandoned military posts to be used as schools. As a consequence, a burst of construction in the mid-1880s saw nonreservation industrial schools established in several locations: Genoa, Nebraska; Chilocco, Indian Territory; Lawrence, Kansas; and Albuquerque, New Mexico.[11]

The western nonreservation schools were patterned after Carlisle and Hampton, employing a two-tier program consisting of vocational and academic instruction. Students followed a routine of discipline, moral training, and work similar to that used at the eastern schools. But even more than their eastern counterparts, the western institutions emphasized manual labor and farming. By the late 1880s, some of the western schools were even attempting to implement an outing system, although there was seldom an urban white population capable of taking Indians into their homes, or willing to do so.

The new schools generally found favor with government and

civil leaders. Although the schools were usually situated near a major reservation, the idea of separation remained supreme, and students were discouraged from direct contact with their relatives. Meanwhile, a few congressional leaders had begun to question the effectiveness of Carlisle, especially since most of its students had chosen to return to their reservations rather than enter white society. If this trend continued, some suggested, the cause of assimilation might be more effectively served by training the Indian children to return home and lead their people into "civilization." Regional nonreservation schools seemed well adapted to this purpose, and they were more economical to operate. It is no wonder, then, that Carlisle was not duplicated, while the number of western facilities increased.[12]

The western industrial schools generally received high marks, although a number of problems limited their effectiveness. Several of the school sites were selected to please local politicians, and they were not well situated to serve Indians. School programs were also hampered by the inadequate government allowance of $167 a year for each pupil. Suffering a chronic shortage of resources, the schools were forced to rely on student labor. Therefore, instead of receiving a full-time education, Indian pupils were pressed into service making school uniforms, doing the laundry, serving as cooks, and providing other menial labor. By the end of the 1880s this pattern had become institutionalized, and students were playing an increasingly significant role in maintaining the schools. Unfortunately, the drudgery discouraged students, many of whom ran away. Even those who remained at school acquired few usable skills and quickly returned to the ways of their people once their school days ended.[13]

By the late 1880s the nonreservation industrial schools were well established in the federal school system. They received an additional boost in 1889, when Thomas J. Morgan became Indian commissioner. Morgan, an ordained Baptist minister, possessed considerable educational experience. His writings and membership in the National Education Association had earned him a great deal of respect among reform groups. In many ways he represented the archetypical humanitarian reformer: dedicated, devout, enthusiastic, and sure of his course of action.[14] Although Morgan disagreed with Pratt's total commitment to off-reservation education, he nevertheless saw the nonreservation school as a significant part of his assimilation program. Fully believing that the American public school system had succeeded in absorbing foreign immigrants into the mainstream of national life, he saw no reason why the same approach would not work for Native Americans. "It is no longer doubtful," he wrote in 1889, "that, under a wise system of education, carefully administered, the condition of the whole people can be radically improved in a single generation."[15]

Supported by the reform community, Morgan sought to formalize the federal education program. Arguing that the reservations must inevitably be abolished and their residents taken into American society, the commissioner hoped to create a "public" school system "which will convert them into American citizens." Compulsory education for Indian children appeared the most effective way to accomplish this goal. Morgan proposed using three levels of schooling, beginning with primary instruction at the day schools and advancing to "grammar and high schools." Although he did not believe that most Indian students would rise beyond the grammar school level, he placed his greatest hope in the high school, where a "worthy few" might receive "a liberal and professional education." Contemporary nonreservation schools, of course, were not operating at such lofty levels, but Morgan clearly saw them developing the advanced programs he desired. He envisioned a typical high school as a boarding and industrial facility situated in a farming community, remote from the reservation, and preferably near a city so that students could mingle with "civilization." Morgan thus expected the nonreservation training school to sit atop his educational pyramid.[16]

The commissioner knew that his dream could not be realized overnight. In 1890 he noted that the existing nonreservation schools needed upgrading. "These institutions," he wrote, "are not universities, nor colleges, nor academies nor high schools. In the best of them the work done is not above that of an ordinary grammar school, while in most it is of the primary or intermediate grade." Part of the problem arose from the fact that nonreservation schools took untutored children directly from the reservations. The schools, consequently, spent most of their energy providing rudimentary training. Another difficulty centered on the lack of a systematic approach to Indian learning. To rectify this deficiency, Morgan developed a basic set of rules to govern the course of study at all government facilities. These rules attempted to ensure a uniform methodology. With such regulations in place, the Indian Office expected to perfect its "public" school system.[17]

Morgan's ideas and proposals produced inconclusive results. Still, optimism prevailed; the new commissioner placed his confidence in a future where the nonreservation schools would advance the cause of assimilation. In his annual report for 1890, Morgan succinctly summed up his hopes for off-reservation education. "These training schools," he remarked,

> removed from the reservation, offer the pupils opportunities which can not by any possibility be afforded them in the reservation schools. The atmosphere about them is uplifting, they are surrounded by the object-lessons of civilization; they are entirely removed from the dreadful down-pull of the camp. If the entire rising generation could be taken at once and placed in such institutions, kept there long enough to be well educated, and then, if such as chose to do so were encouraged to seek homes among civilized people, there would be no Indian problem.[18]

The Indian Office thus viewed Indian education as a mainstay of the assimilation program and sought to expand it. Under Commissioner Morgan's direction, new schools were opened at localities that had been underserved. One of these areas was central Arizona, where, it was presumed, all the wisdom of federal policymakers could be brought to bear on the local Indian population.

2

An Oasis in the Desert

WHEN THE PHOENIX INDIAN SCHOOL opened in September 1891, it stood as an example of the government's commitment to educate the Indian children of America. The school was established for reasons similar to those advanced for all of the non-reservation institutions created during the educational fervor of Morgan's regime,[1] and it was intended to play a key role in bringing Indian youth under federal tutelage. Thus the school was expected to concentrate on assimilation, develop a vocational program, and fit within the federal school system at the highest level. Because of unforeseen circumstances, however, the Phoenix school was destined to stray from the ideal and develop a character of its own. Like other western schools, the institution would be hastily rushed into operation; it would prove to be unable to fully implement national policies and thus demonstrate the gulf between idealism and frontier actuality. The conflict between pragmatism and romanticism produced some unique adjustments as it became evident that the realities of operating an Indian school did not always conform to theory, and local political, racial, and economic interests played a much greater role in school affairs than reformers anticipated.[2]

Interest in building a major Indian school for the Indian population residing along the Gila River in central Arizona developed during the 1880s. The Pima Indians, combined with a small group of Maricopas, made up the bulk of this population, which numbered about five thousand during the latter half of the nineteenth century. Generally peaceful in nature, these people prided themselves on friendship and cooperation with white Americans. Indeed, many of their men served as army scouts during the Apache wars. Both tribes practiced extensive agriculture, lived in permanent villages, and possessed a well-established cultural heritage. A deeply religious people, they had always impressed visitors with their friendship, hospitality, and generosity.[3]

Despite admiration for these hard-working people, Anglos demanded they be "Americanized." To outsiders, their traditional culture seemed valueless, their life-style immoral and degraded. Beginning in 1858, the government sent agents to encourage the "civilization" of the two tribes. A decade later a reservation of some 145,000 acres located along the Gila River (about forty miles south of Phoenix) was set aside for these people. About the same time, a school was opened by the Reverend C. H. Cook, known locally as the "Apostle to the Pimas." Unfortunately for the civilization program, Cook's early educational efforts were hampered by inadequate resources and the reluctance of Pima parents to send their children to school. Attempting to rectify this situation, the government opened a boarding school at the agency town of Sacaton in 1881, but this facility proved incapable of providing for more than a handful of students. As a result of the poor educational facilities on the reservation, several of the more promising children were sent to Carlisle and Hampton. In the late 1880s most of these students were transferred to the newer industrial schools at Albuquerque and Genoa. A few additional children were sent to Tucson, where the Presbyterians opened a small contract school in 1888. Including a small number of children enrolled at Roman Catholic institutions, perhaps a hundred Pima and Maricopa youngsters were attending school in 1890.[4]

To reformers, the haphazard educational system in central Arizona needed attention. As early as 1883, eastern philanthropists meeting at Lake Mohonk, New York, recommended that an industrial school be located in the Gila valley. Federal Indian agents in Arizona also favored a centralized school. Reservation schools, suggested one agent, hampered the educational effort by leaving Indian children too close to their parents. As soon as Indian children returned home, he noted, they "drop back into their old filthy ways." The agents also correctly surmised that Indian families were reluctant to send children to distant schools where they might not be heard from for long intervals and were subject to deadly diseases. The solution to these problems seemed to be in building an industrial school close enough to the reservation to appease parents yet distant enough to provide a break from the home environment.[5]

When Thomas Morgan became Indian commissioner in 1889, one of his first priorities involved expanding the federal school system. Believing that assimilation could be achieved in a single generation, he wanted to ensure that schools would be available and hastened to build as many as possible. In order to compile information on current deficiencies, Superintendent of Indian Schools Daniel Dorchester was sent on a tour of western reservations. A prominent minister and advocate of industrial education, Dorchester used his travels to recommend new schools. In the spring of 1890 he visited Arizona, asking questions and admiring the ability of local peoples to survive the torrid climate. Expressing concern about the primitive living conditions of most Arizona tribes, the federal official was quick to recommend the construction of a nonreservation industrial school in the central part of the territory.[6]

Dorchester hoped to establish the school at Fort McDowell, a military post located in the desert some thirty-two miles east of Phoenix. He took an interest in the site as a result of the activities of post commander Captain J. M. Lee. By 1890, McDowell had outlived its usefulness as an army post. Knowing of the government's desire to open new schools, Captain Lee wrote his superiors in February 1890 that the fort would make a fine school when abandoned by the army. With a few minor repairs the buildings could be put in shape to care for three hundred children. Moreover, the site, located on the Verde River, was touted as being one of the healthiest places in Arizona. "The only drawback is the heat of summer," he noted, "but Indians who have lived along the Gila and Salt Rivers could not find this objectionable." Lee thus urged the government to take advantage of this great opportunity to educate the Indian children of central Arizona. He did caution, however, that many local citizens were opposed to providing any benefits to the Indians and might be expected to oppose the school because "they want the land for their own advantage."[7]

Captain Lee's suggestions were forwarded to the Indian Office, which in turn sent the information to the Reverend Dorchester when he arrived in Arizona. Accordingly, the federal superintendent visited Fort McDowell on March 11 and 12, 1890. He could hardly have been more impressed as Captain Lee escorted him around the grounds. He found the fort located in the middle of "the most beautiful valley in Arizona," relatively close to transportation, with buildings in fair condition. Situated on 24,750 acres of land, the post would provide plenty of room for farms and gardens. Despite the excessive heat, Dorchester proclaimed the site perfectly healthy (a major consideration since many Indian schools were plagued with disease). At the conclusion of his tour he recommended that Fort McDowell be converted into an Indian school. There seemed to be several specific advantages. It already had irrigation works and fields under cultivation; it was located close to, but not on, a reservation; and it could ultimately attract students from the entire territory. In addition, it seemed better to educate Indian children in their accustomed climate. Dorchester closed his report with an appeal for immediate action: "The Indians of Arizona, long under the tutelage of a Mexican civilization, are now exposed to the no less debauching influence of Mormonism. Now is the fit time for the Government to render them its best service. This golden opportunity should not be allowed to pass unimproved."[8]

Dorchester had little difficulty selling his proposal to Commissioner Morgan, who was eager to get Indian children into the schoolhouse. Upon completing his visit, he wrote his superior several enthusiastic letters, cautioning only that "the small politicians of Arizona" should have no say in school operations. Dorchester was convinced that public sentiment in Arizona was hostile to Indian education and he wanted professionals running the school. On the basis of these letters, the Indian Office moved quickly to secure the desired site. When the army authorized abandonment of Fort McDowell on April 10, 1890, the commissioner requested that the buildings be transferred to his jurisdiction for use as a school under provisions of the Act of 1882. By May 2, 1890, the secretary of war had approved the request and it seemed that within a few months a school would be opened at the former cavalry post.[9]

Establishment of a school was guaranteed when Wellington Rich of Omaha, Nebraska, was appointed superintendent. Rich fit the profile of the professional educators being introduced into the Indian service during Morgan's administration. Before his appointment, the new headmaster had served at the Yankton Agency Boarding School in South Dakota. Although successful in his work among the Sioux, Rich yearned for greater responsibilities and better pay. He was induced to accept the McDowell appointment when Morgan sent him the highly favorable reports of Dorchester and Lee. Agreeing to the position on May 12, Rich wrote: "I have become deeply interested in Indian School work. I enjoy the work and desire to continue in it—so long as my labors may prove beneficial to the young people under my tuition and care.... I would like to have charge of an establishment in which I might enjoy a larger degree of freedom in the administration of its affairs than I can exercise in an agency school."[10] Little did he realize in the rush to open a school in Arizona that no preparations had been made for his arrival.

Rich made plans to open his school without any firsthand knowledge of conditions in Arizona. He knew nothing about the Indians he was supposed to educate or the area where the school would be situated. What he did know was how Indian schools were supposed to work in theory. Therefore, when it came to selecting a staff, he was guided by Commissioner Morgan's desire that teachers have a high degree of moral fitness and a "positive religious character." "You will be called upon," he was told, "to train pupils who, for the most part, if not positively pagan or heathen, are at least those who have had little or no religious training." In recruiting his staff, Rich drew upon career people like himself. The appointment of a matron, industrial teacher, and clerk, all former colleagues from South Dakota, indicated that the schoolmaster planned to run the institution in conformity with prevailing ideas.[11]

In July, Rich visited Morgan in Washington to discuss the school and its mission. Ever aware of political considerations, Morgan wondered if the superintendent's appointments might be taken as an insult by Arizona politicians and suggested that one or more territorial residents be added to the staff. Rich rejected the idea; by the time he returned to Nebraska, he had concluded that the necessary professional help could not be secured in Arizona and stuck to his original choices.[12] At the end of July, Wellington Rich gathered his staff together in Lincoln, then bravely set off for the Arizona desert, unsure of the reception awaiting him.

It took the party almost ten days to reach Arizona. Consequently, a somewhat tired group recuperated at the Mills House in Phoenix before continuing on to McDowell. While Rich was in Phoenix, a reporter for the *Arizona Republican* interviewed him. Optimism prevailed. The schoolmaster predicted that classes would begin in a month with an enrollment of one hundred. He foresaw little difficulty in obtaining students because "they can always be seen by their parents." Rich also gave some hints about his approach to Indian education. In contrast to the commissioner, he expressed doubt that the Indian could be quickly civilized. His task at McDowell therefore would be a patient attempt to train Indian youngsters in "the superior methods of the white man." While not neglecting the English language and simple branches of learning, the main goal would be to teach them to work. He postulated that the new school would prove a great success.[13]

The staff arrived at Fort McDowell on August 12, 1890, to discover that not all was in order. Captain Lee had departed a few days earlier, leaving the post in charge of a dozen men. No furnishings, goods, or supplies had been sent in advance, and the school employees had to round up their own cookstoves, utensils, furniture, and bedding. Moreover, although the soldiers realized they were to turn the post over to Rich, they received no orders to do so. All that could be done under the circumstances was to make a survey of the facilities, which were found to be in less than perfect condition. "The Post is not in so good condition, nor nearly so attractive a place as I expected to find it," a disheartened Rich wrote Morgan on August 15. Some of the buildings were in reasonable shape, but the three largest ones were "quite dilapidated" and had been left full of dirt and rubbish by departing soldiers. The parade ground looked "very much like a newly formed Missouri River sand bar." With daily temperatures ranging between 104 and 110 degrees in the shade, the superintendent's illusions faded rapidly.[14]

Communication problems with the army compounded his woes. The soldiers finally turned the post over to the Indian Office on September 15. They would not, however, hand over any additional property, including stores of hay, barley, and medicine, a steam boiler, cord wood, and some old army stoves, without an agreement to pay the original cost of the items plus transportation. Because many of the goods were in poor condition, not required by the school, or priced too high, Rich refused to receive them. As a result, they were sold at auction by the army. More important, Superintendent Rich began to realize that Fort McDowell was unsuited for an Indian school. After a thorough survey of the facilities, he concluded that Dorchester's report was completely misleading. Instead of a few minor repairs being required, Rich estimated "that to make the alterations and repairs necessary to adapt the buildings for school purposes, and then render them fairly comfortable, and decently attractive in appearance, will require the judicious expenditure of fully $15,000." He found the fort located too far from the nearest railroad station, in the middle of a hostile desert, and completely unfit for an Indian school; the land was not as good as pictured, the heat too intense, and the post buildings ill placed for educational purposes. Moreover, repair rates were as much as 50 percent higher than in Phoenix. All this disagreeable information was communicated to Commisioner Morgan.[15]

As it became obvious that Fort McDowell would not work out, the residents of Phoenix began to take an interest in having the school located near their city. Just twenty-three years old and supporting a population of no more than three thousand, Phoenix did not have a particularly good record in dealing with Indians. Those natives who came to town to sell their handicrafts, to deliver wheat to millers, or to purchase such necessities as calico and thread, were treated with scorn and ridicule. In an attempt to control access to the city, a municipal ordinance was passed in 1881 requiring all visiting Indians to wear "sufficient clothing to cover the person" and to leave at sundown. After that time white citizens seem to have considered the Indians who congregated on city streets during daylight hours a public nuisance and often expressed the opinion that such transients were giving Phoenix a bad reputation.[16]

Phoenicians thus welcomed the opportunity to secure the Indian school from the perspective of economic gain more than any humanitarian benefit. By 1890 the city was dominated by a group of energetic boosters who envisioned a great commercial future for the Salt River valley. These ambitious entrepreneurs were involved in real estate promotion and canal building; they had invested heavily in valley enterprises and were looking for every opportunity to promote the town. Several projects designed to enhance business prospects had already been successfully completed in 1887; and in 1889 local boosters engineered their greatest coup when they persuaded the legislature to place the territorial capital in Phoenix.

Colonel William Christy and William J. Murphy, more than anyone else, wanted the Indian school in Phoenix. These two speculators were actively promoting the development of the city and had played a prominent role in moving the capital from Prescott to Phoenix. Together they ran the Arizona Improvement Company, an organization described by one historian as the "most significant agency for the promotion and development of Phoenix and the valley in the 1890s." Christy and Murphy controlled large sections of land and all northside canals, were active in developing the valley's first citrus orchards, and were well aware that a federal facility could enhance the value of their holdings. A strategically placed Indian school promised to encourage real estate development, while students from the school could provide cheap labor for the adjacent orchards through the outing system.[17] Moreover, the institution did not seem to threaten existing racial relationships; the Indian students would be closely controlled, permitted to interact with townfolk only under regulated conditions, and posed no danger of becoming a nuisance.

With such possibilities in mind, Christy, Murphy, and several other prominent citizens decided to induce the Indian Office to locate its school just northwest of the city limits on a triangular tract of public land reserved for school purposes. Not accidentally, the school section lay adjacent to the Maricopa Canal and the lands of the Arizona Improvement Company. Unfortunately for the promoters, the proposed site was occupied by several families of squatters, some of whom had lived on the land for a decade. Upon receiving word that their farms might be taken for the school, the settlers immediately petitioned the Indian Office, stating that certain parties had acquired large tracts of land adjacent to their farms and were atempting to eject them. Calling themselves "pioneer settlers," the petitioners asked that there be no arbitrary decision regarding the school site.[18]

Town boosters ignored the grumbling settlers when it was announced that Commissioner Morgan would visit Arizona as part of a major tour of western schools. Morgan arrived in Phoenix on October 9, 1890, and was immediately besieged by a citizens' committee composed of Acting Governor Nathan O. Murphy, Colonel Christy, and a half dozen other leading citizens. It took little effort to convince the commissioner that Phoenix offered many advantages. His main concern was that moving the school from Fort McDowell would cost the government additional money. After preliminary discussions, Morgan indicated that he might consider Phoenix if local residents donated the necessary land. Before agreeing to such a proposition, Governor Murphy took the commissioner on a tour of the city that managed to end at the proposed school site. Here the visitor was informed that citizens were willing to provide an eighty-acre parcel of land, but that the only available locations were some distance from the city. Murphy recommended instead that the government use the plot of public land spread out before them. The squatters were pictured as trespassers who were under orders to leave. Morgan accepted this explanation and came away convinced that the school section was indeed an excellent location. The *Arizona Republican,* which gave full coverage to the visit, reported on the benefits to be reaped from the school. As much as $50,000 annually would be added to the local economy by a facility for two hundred pupils, and "in a few years our lands, now being so extensively planted with fruit trees and vines, would give employment to many of the pupils."[19]

With a favorable impression of Phoenix in mind, Morgan proceeded to Fort McDowell. It took him only a short time to confer with Superintendent Rich and decide to abandon the military site to "the bats, skunks, rattlesnakes & Gila Monsters, scorpions, centepedes, and other uncomfortable creatures with which this place abounds." Officially Morgan decided against the post because of its distance from Phoenix and railroad connections, the dilapidated condition of the buildings, the heat, and its location far from the civilizing influences of modern society. Having thus concluded that Fort McDowell would be impractical, Commissioner Morgan faced the task of making arrangements in Phoenix. To that end, he and Superintendent Rich returned to town on October 12, and with the help of Governor Murphy, called a town meeting at Patton's Opera House.[20]

On the evening of October 12, Morgan presented a talk on Indian education before "as large an audience as ever greeted a lecturer in Phoenix." During his introductory remarks Governor Murphy noted that while most Arizonans preferred removing the Indians to Oklahoma, the government was committed to "educating and elevating" them within the territory. Commissioner Morgan then mounted the platform, and using the theme that it was "Cheaper to Educate Indians Than to Kill Them," spelled out the philosophy of reform groups and government leaders regarding industrial schools. Uneducated native children were pictured as obstacles to progress, while those with training would become producers and wage earners contributing to the general prosperity. As he explained to the audience, "education is a cheap method of converting aliens, enemies, savages into citizens, friends, and honorable intelligent men and women." Whether Phoenicians really believed Morgan is problematical, but they applauded his talk and indicated a willingness to support the school.[21]

General Morgan could not remain in Phoenix long enough to complete arrangements for the school. Before he departed, however, he wrote a long letter of instructions to Assistant Commissioner R. V. Belt, describing Phoenix as an admirable location. Morgan was particularly impressed with the leading citizens. Deep in his heart he surely knew they were more interested in profits than Indian education, but because they "showed a very lively interest in the school and are very anxious to have it located there," their enthusiasm could be used to good advantage in getting what he wanted. The commissioner was also impressed with the school site he had visited and asked that the secretary of the interior authorize the use of this land. In the meantime, he suggested that the government rent the unoccupied two-story West End Hotel (located at the corner of Seventh Avenue and Washington Street) for use as a temporary school. All local arrangements would be left to Superintendent Rich, who "has already secured the confidence and respect of the best elements of the community."[22]

Rich hoped to open the school immediately, and at first everything seemed to go well. On October 14, the Phoenix newspapers endorsed the institution. The *Daily Herald*, whose publisher, N. A. Morford, had been a member of the citizens committee to greet Morgan, was especially enthusiastic. Using a quote from Governor Murphy, Morford reminded his readers that "from a pecuniary standpoint ... it would be worth to this valley what ten Capitols, Universities or Normal Schools would be." The same day, Superintendent Rich reported that every influential man in town endorsed the project and an eighty-acre tract would be offered if the school site could not be obtained. Everyone obviously preferred to use the government's land, however. Governor Murphy wrote the secretary of the interior urging him to set the parcel aside. William J. Murphy, who took Rich on a tour of the city, promised his help in securing the school. When the headmaster contacted the owner of the West End Hotel, he learned that the building and adjacent adobe structures could be rented for $100 per month.[23] Pleased with these developments, Rich returned to Fort McDowell to await orders.

Shortly after Morgan's visit, the squatters, having received no response to their petition, wrote directly to President Harrison. Stating that an "outrage" was about to take place, they asked not to be dispossessed. Their improvements, including a schoolhouse, were noted, but the main thrust of the argument was that Christy and Murphy, "parties who have already acquired title to more of the Public Lands than was ever intended by all the acts of Congress," were out to evict them. The letter closed with a reminder that the good of the Indians had nothing to do with the sudden interest of leading Phoenicians in an Indian school. The Reverend Dorchester unwittingly bolstered the argument of the settlers. Miffed that Fort McDowell had been rejected, the federal school superintendent wrote a bitter letter to the commissioner on October 28, 1890, refuting point by point Morgan's argument for abandoning McDowell. He maintained that the fort was no more remote from civilization than most other Indian schools, that roads to the place were reasonable, and that the buildings were usable. Although conditions at the location might be more uncomfortable than in Phoenix, this too was seen as typifying such institutions. Dorchester believed that landgrabbers wanted Fort McDowell, and closed his letter by implying that Morgan had been hoodwinked by Governor Murphy and the prominent citizens of Phoenix.[24]

Interior secretary John W. Noble studied both sides of the controversy before handing down a decision on November 29, 1890. Quite possibly because the Indian Office had been criticized for dispossessing white settlers elsewhere, he refused to authorize the use of the government plot for a school. In an even more surprising move, Noble also declined to authorize the leasing of the West End Hotel, maintaining that the reasons for deserting Fort McDowell were insufficient and that Phoenix did not provide a proper environment for Indian education. On these grounds, the secretary informed Morgan that he would take no steps to open a school in Phoenix.[25]

Neither Phoenix boosters nor the commissioner were ready to concede defeat. Morgan asked Noble to reconsider, and after an intense lobbying session, convinced his superior that he knew more about the matter. Noble backed off, approving a school for Phoenix. Since he would not permit the use of public lands, however, Morgan was required to secure a donation of land from Phoenix citizens. As a result, on December 11, the Indian Office instructed Superintendent Rich to return to Phoenix and obtain a written pledge of no less than eighty acres.[26]

To accomplish his task, Professor Rich held a public meeting at the courthouse on the evening of December 16. Speaking before a large crowd, he emphasized the financial benefits a school would bring to the community. In a few years, he said, the school could be expected to spend as much as $125,000 annually. Moreover, its establishment would provide "cheap and efficient" labor for the production of fruit and cotton. Local businessmen were implored to take advantage of this opportunity and reminded that if no guarantee was forthcoming the school might be established elsewhere. Some unexpected fireworks erupted when some members of the audience questioned whose land would be purchased. Several speculators apparently wanted to make the sale profitable, and this touched off arguments. The *Herald*'s representative was so worried about the divisiveness that he reminded the principals that "the advantages of the school near this city will indeed be many and far reaching, and our citizens cannot afford to let the thing go somewhere else simply because one man's land or another's is not bought for the purpose of the school." At the conclusion of the meeting a committee was selected to secure pledges for the purchase of an unspecified plot of land and the audience signed a document promising to furnish the government title to eighty acres at a cost not to exceed $4,000.[27]

Immediately following the meeting, Rich visited two potential school sites, one located some three miles north of town, the other about a mile southwest of the city limits. Both were agricultural plots complete with water rights. Although the sites were deemed acceptable, the superintendent hoped that competition between real estate men might produce an even more desirable location. In the meantime, he informed Commissioner Morgan that the West End Hotel was still available. Armed with this information, the Indian Office took steps to formally establish a school. On December 29, 1890, Morgan asked Noble to authorize the hotel rental and requested a congressional appropriation of $30,000 to open an industrial training school in Phoenix. Before the secretary would approve the request, he asked Morgan to comment on an angry letter just received from Arizona. Written by Charles D. Poston, the letter objected to the establishment of a school. Poston characterized the entire plan as real estate speculation and charged that a school would "increase the number of Indian drunkards and prostitutes now infesting the town by day and night." Morgan responded by stating that while a school would undoubtedly increase surrounding property values, this was all to the good because it assured business support of the institution. The commissioner brushed aside the charge of immorality by remarking that past experience with Indian schools showed just the reverse. His logic convinced Noble, who authorized renting the hotel on December 30 and promised to seek the needed appropriation from Congress.[28]

Events moved rapidly once the new school was authorized.

On the last day of 1890, Superintendent Rich received instructions to move his headquarters to Phoenix. He and his staff were eager to leave Fort McDowell, where they had been living in primitive conditions for over four months. "We will all be glad to get away from this isolated, dreary place," he wrote on departure, "and will enter upon our work at Phoenix with enthusiasm and confidence." Rich leased the West End Hotel as soon as he reached town. Within a few days he had taken up residence in the structure and was busily ordering goods and supplies. On January 20, 1891, Wellington Rich received his official appointment as superintendent of the Phoenix Indian Industrial Training School.[29] The decision in favor of Phoenix had been made. Fort McDowell would be left to the rattlesnakes.

The most pressing matter remained the selection of a permanent school site. As it developed, the question of using public land was not dead. This became evident when the Indian Office began to prepare its legislative budget request for the 1892–93 fiscal year. The request of $69,600 for the Phoenix school included $30,000 to construct a permanent facility. As much as $4,000 of this sum was to be available to supplement local donations so that a larger tract of land might be purchased. Commissioner Morgan, however, still hoped to use the government plot. On January 26 he wired Rich to see if the squatters might be persuaded to vacate if compensated for their improvements. When Rich and Colonel Christy met the squatters, they found them willing to sell, but only for the "unreasonable" price of $14,000. Such terms were totally unsatisfactory, so Rich recommended the purchase of another location. Because local citizens were finding it difficult to raise the necessary $4,000, he also asked the government to contribute to the purchase price. Morgan agreed, and the final budget request contained an understanding that a 160-acre site would be acquired with government aid.[30]

Meanwhile, the staff acted on the assumption that classes would soon commence. The delays caused by poor planning and the squatters' complaints made them eager to get under way. In January, the school requested permission to enroll fifty

Indian boys from the Pima Reservation. At the same time Hugh Patton, a well-regarded Pima Indian, was hired to teach academic subjects. Patton had attended the Albuquerque Indian School and taught briefly at Sacaton before securing the position. Although Rich did not consider him to be especially well trained, he believed that having an Indian teacher would make it easier to handle the first class of students. By February the school was prepared to begin classes as soon as the necessary furniture and books arrived.[31]

Plans were dramatically altered in early March when the devastating flood of 1891 washed out the railroad bridges between Phoenix and Maricopa, leaving the supplies stranded at Maricopa Station. After several unsuccessful efforts to have the goods forwarded by freight team, Rich decided to postpone the opening of his school until the fall term. In the meantime he continued to make improvements to the hotel. (The floods provided the schoolmaster with some satisfaction, however. Fort McDowell was severely damaged by the Verde River, enabling him to write Commissioner Morgan praising the fortunate decision to move to Phoenix.)[32]

After one final attempt to acquire the desired piece of public land, Morgan selected a permanent school site in April 1891. By that time he had been authorized to spend up to $6,000. On Superintendent Rich's recommendation, the government entered into negotiations for 160 acres of improved land owned by Frank C. Hatch. Located east of Center Street just south of Grand Canal, the site was described as being of the finest quality with a "fine, rich, sandy loam to a depth of twenty feet at least." The sale price was $9,000, of which $6,000 would be provided by the government. Local citizens were quite pleased with the purchase, especially since they saved themselves $1,000. The only drawback was that the school would be located three miles north of town, but a proposed streetcar line promised to quickly end any isolation.[33]

Rich began planning his school as soon as the Hatch purchase was confirmed. He expected the completed facility to contain a number of structures, but since funds were limited, he incorporated all necessary functions into the first building. In May, James M. Creighton, one of the area's best-known architects, was hired to prepare the required drawings. Working closely with Rich, Creighton designed a large multipurpose, two-story, wood frame building, complete with sleeping porches for use in warm weather. Although the building would initially house students, administrative offices, a dining hall, and classrooms, it was intended ultimately to be converted into a girls' dormitory. Commissioner Morgan approved Creighton's plans without objection. The only drawback was that the government could not take possession of the Hatch Ranch until August 1891, making it necessary to start classes in the converted hotel.[34]

In July the school received permission to enroll the fifty Pima boys. Several weeks later Superintendent Rich visited the reservation, and with the help of Agent Cornelius M. Crouse, signed up students and met with village leaders. Although there is no record of the Indian response to sending their children to Phoenix, there was no trouble in selecting the initial class, which consisted of thirty-one Pima and ten Maricopa boys. Despite his hope of obtaining a large group of advanced students, the headmaster was forced to settle for "raw recruits," the majority of whom were "large boys or full-grown young men" who had not attended school previously and did not understand English. The students were forwarded to Phoenix by train, and on September 3, 1891, the Phoenix Indian School officially opened.[35]

As soon as the boys arrived on campus the process of acculturation began. Realizing it would require some time before the students would think and speak like white Americans, the staff contented itself with giving the boys a "civilized" veneer. Using the philosophy that "Soap precedes Godliness," Professor Rich gave each new pupil a bath, a haircut, and a suit of clothes consisting of "a hat, hickory shirt, blue drilling pants, shoes and stockings." Although the converted hotel building was not well adapted to educational purposes, as much of the standard program as possible was implemented. Because there were no girls in the institution the boys were assigned work "that would properly belong to the girls." This meant they kept house and did all domestic chores, including cooking, waiting on tables, washing, and ironing. Half of each day was spent at this kind of work and the other half studying the most rudimentary subjects, mainly English. Of the forty-one pupils, thirty-five were placed in the lowest primary grade (somewhat equivalent to kindergarten) and six rated slightly advanced placement. Hugh Patton taught classes, and after December 1891, two of the more experienced students, Charles Blackwater and Oldham Easchief, were hired to maintain discipline and operate the farm. On Sundays the boys attended the Presbyterian Sabbath School and church services in town, where they were lectured in English by prominent church members.[36]

Phoenicians responded favorably to the opening of the school. During the first few months, newspaper reporters and dignitaries regularly visited the old hotel to observe Indian education in action. Though mildly concerned with what the students were doing, local observers showed more interest in financial and social benefits to themselves. One newspaper article announced that the presence of the schoolboys had inspired some of the immodest Indian girls who frequented city streets to begin "dressing after the manner of their white sisters" in an effort to impress the dapper male pupils. Even though this report exaggerated conditions, it demonstrated what the residents hoped the school would accomplish. Another article remarked that the school promised to "use an element about this valley that heretofore civilization had no use for." Agent Crouse, after touring the school, noted that "the farmers and fruit growers in the vicinity of the school are ready to employ these boys and girls as soon as their labor becomes sufficiently skillful to pay them." The businessmen of Phoenix, he continued, "made a wise investment when they gave, as an inducement, $3,000, which paid one-third of the cost of the school." Indeed, within weeks of opening the school, local agriculturalists were asking Professor Rich for pupils to work the upcoming harvest. Residents pictured Indian youngsters as better adapted than "the

The centerpiece of the Phoenix Indian School for more than three decades was the "girls' building." Constructed in 1892 as the first campus structure, it was designed by local architect J. M. Creighton in conformity with Indian Bureau specifications. Although it originally housed offices and classrooms as well as dormitory facilities, it eventually became the girls' residence hall. The second-floor porch permitted beds to be moved outdoors for more comfortable sleeping during the warm season. Courtesy of Smithsonian Institution.

Mexican" to working in the hot climate and were eager to secure their services.³⁷

Superintendent Rich did nothing to discourage the financial and racial preoccupations of valley residents. He knew the school needed public support and that the community would turn against him if there seemed to be any threat to the status quo. The adept schoolmaster consequently avoided the rhetoric so popular among eastern reformers about integrating Indians into white society. Knowing that immediate assimilation was not favorably regarded in frontier communities, he took a different approach. "I have no sympathy with the scheme of *diffusing* the educated Indian youth among the whites," he stated. "They should as a rule, in my opinion, return to their people and assist in the civilization of the latter."³⁸ From the beginning then, the Phoenix Indian School deviated from eastern expectations. It would not be another Carlisle, and the term "Americanization," as used locally, had a different meaning. It was acceptable for the school to place great emphasis on vocational training, and students might even be encouraged to get work experience in town, but no one believed that large numbers of Indians were destined to live permanently in Phoenix as equals.

For the moment, at least, theoretical concerns seemed less important than getting into the permanent facility. During the winter of 1891–92, Rich spent much of his time planning future improvements, including a separate hospital building and a dormitory. Most of his attention, however, centered on the completion of the first building. In December 1891 contractor Edwin Sunderland received a government award of $18,380 to construct the main unit. Because of the meticulous planning, local wags described it as the "cheapest public building in Arizona," but the Victorian structure with its Italianate influence proved to be one of the most attractive in the valley. As construction progressed, school employees and pupils helped beautify the campus by planting trees and putting in gardens. In late February, Reverend Dorchester visited the new school. The man who once opposed the Phoenix site now described it as an oasis in the desert: "I cannot recall a single building in the Indian School Service, which for excellence of arrangement, quality of lumber, faithful workmanship, and architectural attractiveness, is its equal." Dorchester also praised the scope of Superintendent Rich's planning, predicting that Phoenix would be the home of a great Indian school, "a grand project for the education and civilization of the 35,000 Indians in this Territory, heretofore sadly neglected."[39]

As the school building neared completion in the spring of 1892, the superintendent turned his attention to securing additional students. In particular, he needed Indian girls to relieve the boys of their domestic chores so they might work on the farm. From his perspective, women belonged in the dining room, kitchen, and laundry. When the building was finished in April, the original students were moved in and a number of additional boys and girls were recruited from the reservation. By the time the school closed for the summer, it had one large permanent building, a stable, shed, and outbuildings, some livestock, and sixty-nine students.[40]

At the completion of its first year in operation, the Phoenix Indian School hardly looked like a major component of the assimilation program. Plagued by hasty planning, the use of a temporary building, and haphazard recruiting, first-year students made little progress and returned home for the summer with nothing to show for their experiences. Yet the die had been cast, and residents as well as school administrators anticipated the future with confidence. In an article on Indian education, the *Arizona Republican* proudly proclaimed that history gave ample evidence that civilizing the Indians was practical. And, added the *Herald,* "under the able tutelage of Professor Rich, Maricopa county will soon have a number of educated and intelligent laborers, whose training will be especially appreciated by the fruit growers."[41]

3

Marking Time

BETWEEN 1891 AND 1897 the Phoenix Indian School grew rapidly under the aegis of Thomas Morgan's idealistic program for a national system of Indian education. Superintendents Wellington Rich (1891–1893) and Harwood Hall (1893–1897) fostered this growth, equating it with progress and accomplishment. Both men were dedicated to making the new facility a major component of the federal system and they pressed for visible evidence of success. Their efforts led to the enrollment of a large number of students, the creation of an impressive and attractive campus, and firm links between the school and the community. The school was not as successful as it appeared, however. The preoccupation with superficial development covered up the fact that the educational program, the real reason for the school's existence, was unable to get into meaningful operation. Local circumstances were preventing the full implementation of government policy, and as a result the school failed to make much headway in preparing students for assimilation.

Federal administrators, of course, had no intention of letting this happen. They expected institutions like Phoenix to concentrate on preparing Indian children for life in American society. Each school had an assigned role to play and the Indian Office attempted to keep close control over the schools and their programs. During the reform era, an elaborate administrative structure supervised Indian education. At the highest level of responsibility sat the commissioner of Indian Affairs and the

33

Education Division of the Indian Office. In addition, a corps of field supervisors inspected schools, reported on problems, and encouraged the transfer of students to industrial schools. The superintendent of Indian schools (primarily responsible to the commissioner) and a group of inspectors (reporting to the secretary of the interior) provided supplemental advice and guidance. When the standardized rules for Indian schools, and an occasional law passed by Congress, are added in, it becomes clear that the schools were closely scrutinized and supposed to concentrate on national goals.[1] Yet places like Phoenix somehow fell through the cracks.

Commissioner Morgan had great expectations for the Arizona school. His belief that Indians could be assimilated in one generation, and that the nonreservation institutions would develop into centers of advanced learning, placed great pressure on staff members. School officials, however, were imbued with the same general presumptions and welcomed the challenge. Wellington Rich dreamed of making Phoenix a center of Indian education, expecting his school to provide a brand of training superior to anything available on the reservation. Not long after moving into his permanent quarters, the headmaster elaborated on his hopes for the future. He strongly endorsed Morgan's standardized program, particularly the notion that off-reservation schools must sit atop the educational pyramid. Little doubt entered his mind that reservation schools were limited in their capabilities and had attempted to accomplish too much. He therefore endorsed a policy restricting reservation schools to elementary training and requiring that advanced study take place at elite locations like Phoenix, where the educational atmosphere seemed more favorable.[2]

Like any good administrator, Rich knew exactly what he wanted to achieve. "In order to civilize, to make good citizens of Indian youth," he wrote in 1893, "it is absolutely necessary that they be inspired with a strong desire for better homes, better food, better clothing, etc., than they enjoy in their natural state, and that they be qualified to obtain these things by their own exertions." These goals could only be attained through specialized industrial training: "Hence each one should be taught an industry or trained for a calling which he can utilize, by means of which he can earn a good living and accumulate property after leaving school."[3] The end product would be an assimilated Indian, one whose traditional way of thinking and tribal life-style had been obliterated in favor of the individualism associated with American life.

Although actively favoring vocational training, the schoolmaster's approach to the subject was limited by his opinion of Indians. In common with many professional educators during the 1890s, Superintendent Rich doubted that native peoples possessed the same intellectual capacity as Anglos. His previous work with Indian children had convinced him that assimilation would be a long and hard process. Indians, therefore, needed to be trained for occupations they might logically be expected to fill in the near future. As he stated on several occasions, Indian youngsters could not be expected to "compete successfully with the white youth of the community in any of the mechanic arts, mercantile pursuits, or professions." Operating under these self-imposed constraints, Rich expected his school to concentrate on familiarizing Indian children with white society. Every activity would be a pragmatic lesson in "civilization." Even the school cook had a role: "I have insisted," Rich wrote, "that it is not only the duty of the Cook with the aid of her assistants to provide a sufficient amount of well-cooked food for the school, but to do this in such a way as to make intelligent reliable cooks of the pupils." In short, he expected the kitchen to be a "well conducted cooking school."[4]

Despite his limited view of the Indian's potential, Rich intended to make his school as successful as possible. His first task was to enroll students with prior educational experience. At the time the Phoenix facility moved to its new campus, there was little to distinguish it from the most primitive reservation school. With most pupils unable to speak English, the institution was able to do little more than maintain order. Painfully aware of this condition, the headmaster decided to seek instant improvement by signing up pupils of sufficient caliber to take advanced courses. This decision led Superintendent Rich into a recruiting war, one of the more unfortunate aspects of the federal school system during the Morgan era. The problem was created by the dramatic increase in the number of schools and the desire of competitive administrators to prove the success of their efforts. One of the best ways for new schools to give the impression that they were making progress was to enroll a number of pupils who could speak fluent English and were well along in their studies. In essence, every school wanted a few showpieces that could be paraded before the public on any occasion to prove that government money was being well spent. The only place to get advanced students, of course, was from other schools.[5]

Regarding his current pupils as "quite backward in their studies," Rich began an active recruiting program during the spring of 1892. He found some of the scholars he wanted at the Pima boarding school and the Presbyterian mission school in Tucson. As early as April, the aggressive superintendent made overtures in their direction, suggesting that the Pima children enrolled at Tucson really belonged in Phoenix. He simultaneously asked the district supervisor to furnish him with the entire advanced class of the Pima School at Sacaton. If such transfers were not forthcoming, he argued, "I will be compelled to take them from the camps, and to fill the school mainly with pupils who cannot speak English. This course would render the school one of very low grade."[6]

Pima students who attended school elsewhere were heavily recruited when they returned home for the summer. Shortly after receiving permission to enroll uncommitted students from the reservation, Rich provided the Indian Office with a list of thirteen Tucson students who supposedly desired to attend classes in Phoenix. These youngsters, all Pimas, were exactly what Rich wanted: they had been in school from two to six years, spoke English, and were rather mature. The letter recommending the transfer implied that both parents and students desired the change. In a separate attempt to bolster his student body, Rich also requested permission to retain several advanced pupils who had reached eighteen years of age and were technically ineligible to remain in school.⁷

Before approving the transfers, Commissioner Morgan routinely checked with the Reverend Howard Billman, director of the Tucson mission school. He found the Presbyterian minister agitated. Billman maintained that his students had not taken the initiative in requesting transfers, that two of Rich's Pima employees had visited the students in their homes and pressured them into going to the new school. Pupils were promised superior training, and the older ones were guaranteed employment as student assistants. The missionary teacher was particularly irked that the recruiting drive remained a secret until after many children had signed enrollment papers. "Superintendent Rich has so far as our school work this year is concerned, wrought us incalculable harm," he fumed. "It is easy through promises of material gain to induce large numbers of them to desire a change. He has a large number of our choicest pupils. Their leaving has disheartened and discouraged others who have not returned because their companions will not be here."⁸

When the commissioner asked Rich to explain his actions, he got a straightforward admission that his employees had indeed recruited the Tucson students. The schoolmaster claimed that the pupils were free to move and that he had carefully rejected any child who was under firm obligation to return to the Presbyterians. Despite Billman's protest, Rich defended his actions by stating that he desperately needed to enroll a group of advanced students who could also work as assistant cooks, laundresses, and seamstresses. Unable to use "raw recruits" to help operate the school, he felt justified in turning to the nearest source of trained student labor.⁹

The recruiting controversy presented Morgan with something of a dilemma. In theory he supported the transfer of advanced pupils to the off-reservation industrial schools and believed there should be a continuous upward flow of children from the lower schools. Yet in practice, as demonstrated by the Phoenix case, taking the best students from local schools threatened to disrupt the educational program at those schools. And stealing them away from the mission schools angered religious leaders, many of whom strongly supported the Indian Office. Faced with a potentially explosive situation, Morgan backed down and ordered the Tucson students returned. To ensure that the Phoenix school would have access to a few good students, however, the commissioner permitted the school to continue taking pupils from the government facility at Sacaton. Agent Crouse, who stood to lose all his good students, was simply informed that the nonreservation schools needed to be filled and that places like Sacaton were "recruiting stations for the nonreservation schools."[10]

This decision restricted the school's activities, and only the handful of advanced scholars available at Sacaton could be enrolled. Most of the pupils continued to be fresh from reservation villages, without any prior education. Yet, if Rich was discouraged by this development, he did not let it hinder the growth of his school. The 1892–93 school year began with more than a hundred students in attendance and more waiting to be admitted. The glut of potential students caused Rich to begin expanding the plant: no matter how much he desired advanced pupils, it was embarrassing to have to turn anyone away. The first step was to hire Mrs. M. K. Culbertson as principal teacher to help the overworked Hugh Patton. Unfortunately, the Anglo schoolteacher was given Patton's job and salary, forcing the hard-working Pima to accept a subordinate position. At the same time, Rich launched his building program. During the 1892–93 school year a large two-story addition to the main unit, a brick storeroom, and a bakehouse were completed. These facilities, though significant additions, proved insufficient to meet the growing needs of the school. The superintendent therefore began making plans for the addition of a classroom and hospital, the construction of which would require an increase in federal appropriations.[11]

From an educational viewpoint, Professor Rich was dissatisfied with the progress his students made during the year. He expected pupils to learn English and advance in grade much more rapidly than they did. Many of the children seemed confused, some objected to the strict discipline, and very few appeared to be making any headway. As the term progressed, it also became obvious that plans to have the school specialize in citrus and fruit culture were unrealistic. The potential for student employment in that field might have been reasonable, but the school needed all the supplemental income it could generate, and this necessitated planting the farm with alfalfa, a more stable cash crop.[12]

Frustrated, the Phoenix headmaster made another attempt to recruit advanced students. This time he proposed enrolling Yuma and Mohave children from the Colorado River region and Papagos from the south. These youngsters were attending reservation schools, although the government expected to transfer many of them off-reservation as soon as they completed primary training. Hoping to enroll such children, Rich tried to prevent them from being sent to Albuquerque or the industrial school at Genoa, Nebraska. Pointing out that several Arizona students had died at distant schools, Rich maintained these children should be kept in their native climate. Additionally, he argued, desert Indians needed to be taught to work in their own environment. "Teaching an Indian to farm in Nebraska," he noted, "is of little use to him if he is to return to his people in Arizona when he has completed the course of training assigned him."[13]

When Rich contacted the Colorado River Agency to enlist some of the better Mohave students, he discovered that the Albuquerque Indian School was actively recruiting the same children. The resulting competition upset and confused the Mohave people. The Mohaves, as Agent George W. Allen knew, were a very conservative group. They had never sent their children away from home and were much opposed to off-reservation schools. Allen maintained that taking children from their own school and sending them to distant locations would prejudice parents against the government's education program at the agency; they would stop cooperating if threatened with the eventual transfer of their offspring. As a consequence, the agent estimated that about six pupils might safely be sent to Phoenix, but the Mohaves would never consent to moving their children to Albuquerque. With both schools demanding the Mohave pupils, the Indian Office was forced to mediate. Despite warnings by Allen, government bureaucrats in Washington apparently decided that Albuquerque offered better facilities, and in April 1893 they ordered fifty Mohave children sent to New Mexico. As predicted, the Mohave people protested, the order was voided, and neither school got what it wanted.[14]

The spectacle of schools fighting over students had become a national embarrassment by 1893. As one federal official later remarked, the behavior of superintendents had become "so undignified as to call for drastic measures." In the midst of the controversy, Thomas Morgan resigned as Indian commissioner. A staunch Republican, he refused to work for the Democratic administration of newly elected Grover Cleveland. He was replaced on April 18, 1893, by Daniel M. Browning, an Illinois politician. Although Browning did not have the charisma or leadership ability of his predecessor, he subscribed to the program in place and tended to follow the advice of his staff. Shortly after assuming office, Browning issued an order on recruiting procedure that undoubtedly originated with Morgan. The decree simply stated that henceforth no pupils were to be transferred to nonreservation schools without the full consent of their parents and agent. In defending the order as a means of curtailing unsavory recruiting practices, the commissioner acknowledged that "even ignorant and superstitious parents have rights."[15]

Though the Indian Office recognized that parents should be consulted about sending their children to distant institutions, the order was not viewed as harming the industrial schools or changing educational priorities. Indeed, the office believed that every effort should be made to convince the Indians of the benefits of attending advanced schools. "Transfer from a reservation to a nonreservation school," Browning wrote, "should be looked upon as a promotion and a privilege, and selections for such transfer should be carefully made and based on merit and proficiency. Such a system, fully carried out, will give the higher schools a more earnest class of pupils, better able to use profitably the very excellent advantages which these schools offer." It was thus clear that the Indian Office expected "cheerful cooperation" between schools, and that reservation and religious schools should expect to send their best pupils to advanced institutions. Browning also maintained that granting Indian parents the right to approve the transfer of their children did not abrogate recently passed legislation permitting the government to force school attendance by withholding rations and annuities. Perhaps the best way to end conflicts, suggested the commissioner, was for each industrial school to be assigned a defined area of recruitment.[16]

Wellington Rich did not survive the change in administrations. Perhaps because of his controversial recruiting efforts, or simply because Browning wanted to dispense patronage, Rich was released. The superintendent could not even claim protection under civil service regulations; the Indian Office had been under the system since 1891, but Browning insisted that bonded school superintendents were exempt. The commissioner's choice for a replacement was Harwood Hall, an amiable and ambitious young Missourian who was offered the job in July. Like Rich, Hall was an experienced educator. Only thirty-four years old, he had spent eight years in the Indian Service, the last four supervising boarding schools at the Quapaw and Pine Ridge agencies. Hall's new position carried an annual salary of $1,800. Unfortunately, the depression of 1893 prevented him from raising the required bond, and he was forced to accept a nonbonded position at the Cheyenne boarding school in Oklahoma. The commissioner still wanted Hall in Phoenix, however, and eventually arranged for the necessary bonding. Consequently, Hall finally left Oklahoma for Arizona in early October.[17]

While the confusion over the appointment of a new superintendent sorted itself out, Rich dutifully remained on the job. Although bitter about being fired, he regarded his three years in Arizona as a success. Just before Hall arrived, an inspector for the Interior Department described the campus. He noted that 128 pupils were currently enrolled, that they were "the most *cleanly* & intelligent-looking Indian children that I have yet seen," and that fine progress was being made. In addition to classroom activities, the boys were being instructed in fruit growing and stock raising, while the girls were learning to cook, wash, and serve. Many students were looking forward to being hired in town as soon as they received sufficient training. The inspector noted that the school farm sported 110 acres of alfalfa and that during the year five thousand pounds of seed and over a hundred tons of hay had been sold to the public. The school also owned some livestock and operated a dairy. "Upon the whole," concluded the report, "*the school is in excellent condition,* its buildings are new & suitable for the purpose, & its management has been good." His only suggestion involved expanding the facility to accommodate three-hundred Indian students.[18]

What the report did not say was that the school had made practically no progress in meeting Commissioner Morgan's goals. No academic training of consequence had taken place, and the institution still had only entry-level students. Harwood Hall would make several policy changes as he strove to build the facility into an Indian school rivaling any in the West. He, too, tended to equate growth with successful education and consequently concentrated more on quantity than quality. But Hall broke with his predecessor over recruiting. Though he believed the Indians of central Arizona to be "immoral to the lowest degree," he abandoned attempts to enlist pupils from outside the local area and contented himself with enrolling Pimas, Maricopas, and a few Papagos. He decided to fill the school with as many children as possible and hoped that a few good students would rise from the ranks. Known more as a practical administrator than a teacher, Hall also spent a great deal of time linking the school to community interests and left the teaching to his subordinates.[19]

One of the most persistent concerns during Hall's administration was enlarging the physical plant to care for an ever-increasing student population. By the mid-1890s, Indian parents had begun to accept the necessity of educating their children, and the school was overwhelmed with requests for admission. For a while this did not seem to pose a problem, and school administrators took in every child they could. In August 1893, for example, all the Pima students attending the industrial school at Genoa, Nebraska, were, at the superintendent's request, sent back to Phoenix. Additionally, Hall visited the Pima Agency and, with the help of Agent J. Roe Young, secured every pupil who could be induced to leave home.[20]

The influx of new students necessitated construction. An inspector visiting the school in the spring of 1894 noted that the school needed more space. With most activities confined to the main building, he suggested that a separate schoolroom be erected. Hall accordingly requested an increase of $33,000 in the appropriation for 1894–95, the extra funds to be used for building. But the Cleveland administration was suffering through hard financial times, and Interior Secretary Hoke Smith refused to authorize what he considered "unnecessarily expensive buildings." Eventually a compromise was effected, permitting the construction of a hospital while postponing the completion of a dining hall/kitchen complex and the classroom unit. Hall expressed great disappointment over what he considered false economies. From his perspective the school needed to expand, but additional students could not be enrolled without adequate sleeping space and classrooms. "It seems to me," he wrote, "that with so many Indian children asking for admission from the Pima and Maricopa tribes, that accommodation for them, at a mere nominal increase in facilities and cost, should be provided."[21]

In his search for additional funding, Hall made effective use of the increasing number of children seeking admission. Having to refuse Indian youngsters made good propaganda, and Hall played it to the hilt. When the school opened in September 1894 more than 250 children showed up. Not having sufficient room, Hall immediately sent a dramatic telegram to Browning: "Indians persist in leaving children at this school. More than

Typical of the early campus buildings was the Victorian-style hospital, probably built in the mid-1890s. After the turn of the century, when a new hospital was constructed, this building became the "domestic cottage," where teachers attempted to create a homelike atmosphere so that small groups of Indian girls could live in circumstances similar to those of an average American family. Courtesy of Arizona Historical Foundation.

one hundred sent home already. Present attendance one hundred seventy-five. Are funds available to support excess?" In a follow up letter, the clever schoolmaster remarked that his school was authorized to enroll only 130 students and something needed to be done immediately. Hall also used newspaper articles and inspection reports to support his cause. Stories about turning children away not only made the local press, but were carried by such eastern missionary journals as the *Indian's Friend*. And almost every government inspector who visited the school came away convinced that the facility needed to be significantly enlarged. These tactics proved so successful that by the end of 1894 the Indian Office relented, authorizing a new dormitory building, which, when completed, promised to provide enough room for two hundred students.[22]

Hall continued to push for expansion, pointing out that the rooms in the original building were crowded, poorly lit, and fitted with improper furniture. His persistence paid off, and by September 1895 a boys' dormitory, hospital, employees' quarters, and small office had been finished, enabling the school to accommodate three hundred pupils. Yet even these improvements were not enough for the aggressive headmaster, who continued to flood the Indian Office with demands for greater appropriations. He used every argument possible, including a promise that increased enrollment would reduce the number of Indian youngsters "lying around in idleness."[23]

The efforts of the superintendent had a visible impact on the school. By the end of the 1895–96 term the school boasted almost 350 pupils and was continuing to grow. All of the students were full-blood Pima, Maricopa, and Papago children ranging in age from five to eighteen. One inspector called the school the "Carlisle" of the Southwest and suggested enlarging it to a capacity of eight hundred. "It should be to the Pacific coast what Carlisle is to the east," he said, "and under its present able management can be made so, if it were enlarged." As the growth continued, Superintendent Hall worked tirelessly to make improvements. In 1896 the entire facility was provided with electric lighting. By the following spring there were twelve buildings, an operating farm producing a variety of crops, and 380 students. Moreover, five industrial shops were under construction, enabling teachers to "develop properly the industrial and mechanical side of this institution."[24]

Although the Phoenix Indian School may have reminded some visitors of Carlisle, a review of its educational programs quickly dispelled the illusion. For the most part the school followed standard Indian Office guidelines, and the literary program never amounted to anything extraordinary. Following customary practices, students spent no more than a few hours each day in the classroom, devoting the remainder of their time to vocational training. With nearly all the pupils at entry level, most of the academic work focused on teaching the English language and a few rudimentary subjects such as arithmetic, geography, and American history. These subjects were not intended to answer any particular Indian need, but were similar to those being taught in public schools. Teachers stressed a form of rote learning that required little intellectual exertion. Advanced pupils spent hours writing words on the chalkboard and then learning to pronounce them, while primary students were kept busy drawing the alphabet. Because children of all ages were taken in, it was not uncommon to find a full-grown eighteen-year-old sitting next to a six-year-old. And as in most Indian schools, the emphasis on speaking English was reinforced by regulations prohibiting students from using their own tongue. Standard textbooks, laced with rhetoric promoting patriotism and moral values, came from lists provided by the Indian Office. Although teachers were usually considered qualified, at least one inspector remarked that they had no training in the psychological problems faced by Indian students, thereby reducing their effectiveness.[25] As a result, students advanced through the grades slowly, and none managed to meet the eighth-grade graduation requirement during the first decade.

In line with government priorities, and Hall's own opinion of Indian potential, the school placed much more emphasis on vocational training. Even though there was no guarantee that jobs would materialize, federal officials praised the superintendent for "having had experience enough in the Indian service to know that an Indian boy or girl will have to make their living by the 'sweat of their brow,' and not their brains." Accordingly, young boys were expected to learn a skill that would be of value to themselves and the community. The school operated several vocational departments—carpentry, blacksmithing, tailoring, shoemaking, and harness making—each directed by an experienced tradesman. The farm, which helped the school financially by growing its own fruits and vegetables as well as by producing a cash crop, provided work training for forty boys. Some of the boys' trades did not prove particularly useful, however, and one inspector recommended eliminating the tailor and shoe shops because these occupations were unimportant in Arizona where "people in this climate have less use for an abundance of clothes and shoes than in any country I have been to."[26]

The training of young Indian women received equal attention. School officials viewed the girls as "the uplifter of the Home" and considered their education a vital part of the assimilation program. Womens' activities were supervised by the matron, and in addition to classroom activities, they were put to work in such departments as housekeeping, sewing, kitchen and dining room, or laundry. Like the boys, much of their labor went into keeping the school solvent. They made, washed, and ironed their own clothes; cleaned their rooms; swept, dusted, and scrubbed the buildings; and prepared and served the food. Administrators claimed that all such work had educational benefit. Superintendent Hall stated that by cleaning rooms and dormitories, the girls strove "to excell each other by performing their work and attaining that which makes the true woman. . . . From slouchy, dissatisfied girls, the year produced neat, ladylike, agreeable young ladies, who are proud of exhibiting their achievements, and who I feel have made great strides toward civilization and the higher aim in life."[27]

Another key aspect of the educational program was discipline. Taking their cue from the Carlisle and Hampton schools, the officials believed that strict discipline and a military-type organization was the most effective way to break Indian children of habits considered to be lazy and unproductive. As a result, the school ran like clockwork, and every aspect of student life was regulated. Pupils rose early in the morning, marched everywhere they went, and practiced army drill routines whenever possible. The benefits to be reaped by such discipline were later explained by Superintendent Hall: "Too much praise can not be given to the merits of military organization, drill and routine in connection with the discipline of the school; every good end is obtained thereby. It teaches patriotism, obedience, courage, courtesy, promptness, and constancy; besides, in my opinion, it outranks any other plan or system in producing and developing every good moral, mental, and physical quality of the pupil."[28] In common with most Indian schools, the campus had a jail where uncooperative students could be confined, but it was apparently little used. Most punishment came in the form of paddling, ridicule, or work assignments, and was similar to that used in public schools. Disciplinary measures were most often employed for running away or violation of the rules forbidding the use of native languages. As Hall explained, "Obedience to those in command is respected at all times, and the idea of strict obedience is inculcated from the first entrance of school."[29]

The net effect of the school's educational program was to produce children who only partially met expectations. After the first few years many of them learned to speak English and had become skilled enough that they could perform a particular mechanical task or domestic chore with some success. Dressed in uniforms and calico dresses, they gave the appearance of following the white man's road. Yet these children were far from being assimilated, and a review of their experiences indicates the great gulf existing between government perceptions and what was actually happening.

Ironically, Indian parents seem to have had a positive attitude toward the school during its first years of operation. Once the initial fear about having their children taken away from home faded, parents tended to be extremely cooperative. There seem to have been a number of reasons for this reaction. Tribal leaders generally supported the necessity of education and urged their people to cooperate. The school also offered material advantages in the form of food and clothing, important considerations for parents who had to struggle for the necessities of life. The most significant reason for sending children to Phoenix, however, was that the Pimas and Maricopas quickly developed an attachment to the institution, coming to regard it as "their school." Because it was located just a few miles from their homes and enrolled only Pimas, Maricopas, and Papagos, parents found the school socially acceptable. In 1895 the Pima agent remarked that parents were willing to send their children to Phoenix, but refused to have them go elsewhere. Parents also liked the school because they were able to visit their children. Although such visits often irked the superintendent, he was careful not to offend the Pima people or make them feel unwelcome.[30]

The students themselves were less enthusiastic. There can be little question that the first few days at school were difficult. Pupils, most of whom were unfamiliar with the ways of the outside world, were subjected to the confusing process of "de-Indianization." They were immediately provided with new clothes, a new look, and a new routine. Students lived in dormitories and were required to keep their living area spotless, to use modern bathing and toilet facilities, and to eat food prepared to white tastes. They were also forced to live by a fixed schedule and obey rules which sometimes seemed senseless. Except for other students, most of their contacts were with white teachers and matrons, all of whom stressed the necessity of casting off traditional ways. Every facet of the child's social life was regulated. School officials were preoccupied with morality and went to great lengths to assure that no embarrassing transgressions occurred. Boys and girls were strictly segregated and, with the exception of a few social occasions or in the classroom, were not permitted to speak to each other. The school matron supervised the girls' social activities, and the head disciplinarian did the same for boys.[31]

Pupils were also made to practice Christianity. Those with an established Catholic background were permitted to attend their own church, but all others attended Protestant services. In addition, female pupils were encouraged to do church-related service. Sometime during the mid-1890s a chapter of The King's Daughters, a Christian service organization similar to the YWCA, was established on campus. This program organized girls by age into "circles" to spend spare time producing handcrafted goods for charity. School officials supported such activities because they supposedly instilled a spirit of Christian charity.[32]

The pressure to conform to an alien culture created tensions and pressures that were exacerbated by the unsympathetic attitude of school officials. Some students responded by running away. In most instances, they simply became homesick and headed back to the reservation, where they were quickly apprehended and returned. In other cases, however, there were more serious misunderstandings. One older boy ran away as a result of being denied permission to attend a tribal ceremony; others left as a result of severe discipline and punishment. In one incident Superintendent Rich punished a girl, whom he believed had a reputation for being "unchaste," by cutting off her hair. The unfortunate and confused girl ran away at the first opportunity. Occasionally there were even more drastic consequences. At least one Pima student committed suicide. As was often the case, the school authorities had no clue as to what was bothering the boy.[33]

Such incidents involved a minority of the pupils, yet they indicate the type of pressure that was created by the attempt to "Americanize" Indian children. Another problem involved uncertainty regarding the future. Except for students who were involved with the outing system, few jobs were available. Some of the older pupils were hired by the school to act as assistant farmers, carpenters, cooks, laundresses, and matrons at salaries ranging from three to fifteen dollars a month, but most had no prospect other than returning home. Still, while a majority of students would probably have preferred to be elsewhere, most made the best of the situation, and some were even eager to participate. In one well-publicized story, a Maricopa teenager, named Katie Armstrong, had to escape from her relatives (who wanted her to stay home and do chores) in order to remain in school. She was considered one of the brighter students because she could "answer any ordinary question about the descriptive and physical geography of her country."[34]

While school administrators developed their educational programs, they simultaneously worked to link the school to the community. Being a self-contained entity located away from the downtown area, the institution participated in city affairs only to the extent permitted by white residents. It was therefore necessary to assure that school activities were well supervised, posed no threat of becoming a public nuisance, and visibly contributed to the community. Both superintendents Rich and Hall were eager to win the confidence of Phoenicians, and they accomplished the task in remarkably short order.

The community's relationship with the school was dominated by economic factors. Phoenicians supported the school largely, though not exclusively, because it contributed to their financial well-being. The most obvious monetary contribution to the community came with ever-increasing federal expenditures. Although classroom supplies were usually provided by outside vendors, the school purchased merchandise locally, maintained a sizable payroll, and used Phoenix contractors for construction projects. Even though the Indian Office preferred getting bids from nationwide companies, it inevitably ended up awarding construction contracts to local builders. When the cost of the building projects was added to purchases of material, the hiring of irregular labor, and staff salaries, the school funneled more than $50,000 annually into the local economy.[35]

From a practical perspective, the outing system was the school's most valuable contribution to the community. Although there had always been considerable pressure to provide a pool of cheap labor, school authorities hesitated because most pupils spoke no English. By the spring of 1893, however, Superintendent Rich was ready to give it a try. A few older boys were hired out on agricultural or construction projects, and eleven girls were sent to work for Phoenix families as domestic servants. The use of Indian girls began a Phoenix tradition in which the school provided valley housewives with maids and servants under the auspices of the outing system. Each girl received a salary of ten dollars per month and was expected to attend school part time. Realizing the public relations value of such services, Rich was very careful with his first outing students. "We have," he noted, "been careful to send out only those girls that were sure to do well, as we could not afford to have any failures at the beginning of this 'outing' business."[36]

Harwood Hall was even more enthusiastic about the apprenticeship program, expanding it as rapidly as possible. He envisioned his school serving as "an employment agency, whereby the desiring pupil can secure employment as soon as qualified." The pragmatic schoolmaster knew that Indian labor was in demand in Phoenix, and he entertained no illusions about employers' motivations: "The hiring of Indian youth is not looked upon by the people of this valley from a philanthropic standpoint. It is simply a matter of business." Even though the outings involved the most basic type of menial labor, they were justified as being educational. "Such a system can only be productive of good," Hall wrote, "as the stimulation given educated the Indians to look upon the battle from a business standpoint in which they must expect no quarter."[37]

The school hired out as many students as it could. When Hall became superintendent in 1893, about twenty pupils were working for local employers at wages "not equal to those paid to white people but . . . quite satisfactory to the Indians." To maintain a connection with the school and permit supervision, working students returned to campus on Saturday evening and went back to work on Monday. Hall took every opportunity to expand the system and frequently complained that the demand for students exceeded the supply. The Indian Office supported his efforts. Superintendent of Indian Schools William N. Hailmann was especially enthusiastic, expressing great pleasure that western schools like Phoenix were adopting the old Carlisle program.[38]

With local as well as national encouragement, Superintendent Hall got carried away with the program. Indeed, if the supply of English-speaking pupils had been more abundant, the scope of the program would have been unlimited. Early in 1896, with sixty pupils at work, he attempted to expand the system to southern California. He justified this experiment on grounds that sending students away to work would separate them from the influence of parents, who sometimes disturbed them at their Phoenix workplaces. This particular proposal was too radical for the Indian Office, and Hall had to content himself with increasing the number of local outings. During the summer of 1896, for example, he attempted to keep female students from returning to the reservation by offering them to valley families at "no pay further than board, proper care and instruction." So successful were these efforts that by 1897 Hall could boast that nearly two hundred students had been at work at various times during the past year.[39]

As the outing system became an established part of the Phoenix scene, it developed into something different from what federal officials or town boosters expected. Government bureaucrats expected the outings to operate much like Carlisle's celebrated system, with Indian students living with white families on the basis of some equality, learning a middle-class occupation, and developing a desire to assimilate. But at Phoenix, as at other western schools, the outing students were treated as employees and assigned menial tasks. Furthermore, they were not given much reason to expect advancement. Indian boys never became the permanent source of labor that city businessmen and school administrators desired. The economic depression of 1893, which hit just as the outing system began, curtailed many of the more ambitious local ventures that might have used Indian labor. Low-income white and Hispanic workers also began migrating to the valley, taking potential jobs away from students. As a result, although young Indian men were hired to harvest crops, work on construction projects, and do odd jobs, there were always more boys than jobs. Such was not the case with girls, who made up the valley's major source of domestic labor. During the 1890s the employment of female students skyrocketed. Indeed, the demand for Indian girls was so great that the school could not keep pace. Consequently, the girls' side of the outing program easily outdistanced the boys' in importance.[40]

Meanwhile, the Indian school provided another, if somewhat intangible, asset to the city. Fostered by Harwood Hall, who recognized the value of good public relations, the institution became a center of community social life. It served as a tourist attraction as well as providing a vast amount of free entertainment—a highly valuable commodity that helped relieve the boredom of isolated Phoenix residents. The school's manicured grounds, fountains, and shaded walks presented a stark contrast to the surrounding desert and attracted a large number of visitors.

Using this charm to full advantage, school officials invited the public to attend a variety of functions. The memorial exercises at the end of the school year quickly became an important annual social affair. In 1894 the program reportedly drew a thousand visitors. Guests were treated to decorated buildings, flower arrangements, and grounds lighted with lamps and Chinese lanterns "presenting an appearance rarely if ever seen in Arizona before." After a tour of facilities, the visitors witnessed a program of musical selections provided by a group of "neatly attired" Indian boys and girls. The audience thoroughly appreciated the show and emerged convinced that the school was "accomplishing great and good work." The following year Hall initiated the custom of inviting citizens to the annual Christmas program. From then on, programs designed to maintain community goodwill and illustrate educational achievements became a regular feature of the school. A typical presentation during this era included songs by the chorus, an address by one of the more fluent students, several costumed skits, an

"American Flag" ceremony by recent arrivals, and precision military drills.[41]

The school also capitalized on the promotion of tourism, which was just beginning to assume importance in Arizona. City fathers staged a variety of carnivals, parades, and fairs designed to attract visitors. Indian students proved to be a big asset to these affairs. The annual winter carnival, for example, concluded with a grand parade featuring a frontier theme. Because these affairs tended to invite a large number of "wild Indians" outfitted in war paint and traditional dress, school students were used to contrast the past with the predicted future. School officials happily provided organizers with the school band, marching battalions of boys and girls, a drum corps, and student floats. In this manner, visitors who came to see a representation of frontier history were reminded that the "Indian problem" was being solved. Newspapers often took note of the great contrast between the "uncivilized" reservation Indians and "the native youths and maidens who marched like old soldiers, shoulder to shoulder and heads up." To such observers these scenes were proof that the success of Indian education no longer remained in doubt.[42]

It was with some regret that Phoenicians learned of Hall's transfer in June 1897. Though much attached to the school, the popular schoolmaster had never been able to adjust to the hot weather. After several requests, he was placed in charge of the industrial boarding school at Perris, California.[43]

Hall's departure coincided with the end of Cleveland's administration and the beginning of several changes in the direction of educational policy. In the years before 1897, while the commitment to General Morgan's school system remained intact, the Phoenix Indian School had been transformed from a one-building facility housing 69 students to a large operation employing 50 people and capable of caring for 380 Indian children. From a superficial perspective, the institution seemed to be making great progress. Yet Indian education at Phoenix failed to accomplish what evangelical reformers had expected. Preoccupied with enrollment and construction, superintendents Rich and Hall really made little progress in implementing the assimilation program, as demonstrated by the fact that the institution had only four academic teachers in 1897.[44] To be sure, many children learned to speak some English, and some were at work, but the school made no headway in becoming an elite center of advanced learning, students showed little prospect of assimilating in one generation, and the school seemed to be doing nothing to get them permanently off the reservation.

In essence, the headmasters who guided the school during its early years were faced with a choice between making their institution appear successful by enrolling a large number of children or providing an education for a smaller number of students that might have prepared them for integration into American society. Because they wanted to please their superiors, because they doubted that Arizona Indians could rapidly assimilate, and because they expected little immediate success, they took the former path. As a result, meaningful progress toward assimilation remained as elusive as an Arizona mirage.

4

A School for Many Tribes

FEW MEN IN THE INDIAN SERVICE were more ambitious, aggressive, and outspoken than Samuel M. McCowan. He arrived in Phoenix in the summer of 1897 determined to advance his career by making a success of the Phoenix Indian School. Like his predecessors, he tended to measure progress in terms of enrollment and growth. Yet this young educator was perceptive enough to realize that student performance must improve. To attain this end he decided to change the structure of the institution and improve the way it functioned. In an effort to eliminate the school's provincial atmosphere, he sought to enroll children from a variety of tribes; to demonstrate that education was the answer to the "Indian problem," he concentrated on training and jobs. Although McCowan was the first headmaster to insist on more than merely superficial improvements, he often resorted to questionable methods, running roughshod over anyone—white or Indian—who opposed him. By the time he left Arizona in 1902, he had significantly enhanced the school's reputation, but reform-minded educators of the preceding era would not have applauded his methods or what he called Indian education.

McCowan was able to have a significant impact on the school partly because his stay in Phoenix coincided with the first stirrings of a shift in federal Indian policy. By the time William McKinley took the oath of office in 1897, the religion-dominated policy of immediate assimilation was clearly on the wane. As much of their early optimism faded, Americans began to question the practicality of rapidly integrating the Indian into mainstream society, their doubts reinforced by the reform program's failure to produce more than a handful of assimilated Indians. When the "immediatists" began to lose their influence in the halls of government, they were replaced by a group of federal administrators who wanted to take a more gradual approach to assimilation.[1] McCowan aligned himself with the "gradualists," even though he probably never thought of himself in such terms.

Indian education was significantly affected by the changing focus of national policy. Although the new policy did not mature until the early years of the twentieth century, an early sign of change came with the declining interest in off-reservation education. Opposition to nonreservation schools had been mounting during the 1890s as critics objected to excessive costs and limited results. Federal officials consequently began to rediscover the reservation school. This trend became evident during the administration of Indian Commissioner William A. Jones (1897–1904). Like an increasing number of his contemporaries, Jones doubted that Indians could directly compete with whites in the commercial and mechanical skills. He expected them to remain close to their home localities, working as laborers, farmers, and stockmen, pursuing a life of manual labor. Such ideas had been common among school personnel for some time, but Jones was the first national administrator in decades to express such sentiments. As a consequence, his support of nonreservation schools, backed by reports from the field, grew increasingly lukewarm. This was partly because the schools had failed to become institutions of advanced learning. Instead, school administrators simply filled their rooms with any available pupils, making them almost indistinguishable from reservation schools. Additionally, Commissioner Jones became convinced that reservation schools possessed certain advantages in preparing children for rural life. So, while he proposed no dramatic changes in the number of nonreservation schools, Jones sought more realistic ways to use them.[2]

The declining prestige of off-reservation education was accompanied by changes in turn-of-the-century American society. As the nation became engrossed in the Spanish-American War, colonialism, and the Progressive movement, the public lost much of its interest in Indians. Historian Frederick E. Hoxie has attributed the waning interest in Indian matters to a changing racial perspective. Noting that reformers like Pratt and Morgan had believed the Indian could be fully absorbed into American life, Hoxie contends that the ideas of Anglo-Saxon supremacy that surfaced around 1900 "suggested that total assimilation was an unrealistic goal; perhaps partial accommodation to 'civilized' standards was all that policy makers should hope for." Whether such ideas actually influenced governmental decisions is debatable, but there is no question that expressions of Indian inferiority became more common among the upper bureaucracy. And if Indians seemed less likely to be incorporated into the national mainstream, then the purpose of Indian education, including the role of the nonreservation facilities, needed reevaluation.[3]

The notion that native peoples could function only at the lower levels of society and should not be trained to compete with white workers did not mean that Indian children should not attend school. In fact, Commissioner Jones strongly supported compulsory education and did his best to increase enrollment at all levels. Late in 1897 he began a campaign designed to fill the Indian schools to capacity, and the following year he made an unsuccessful attempt to secure congressional approval for legislation requiring mandatory schooling. From then on Jones pressured superintendents and agents to recruit more students, reminding them that the reservations still contained "ample material to fill your schools." The same campaign led the Indian Office to intensify its efforts to push the better students into off-reservation facilities. Such transfers made more room at the lower levels and promised to use the industrial schools to maximum efficiency. Unfortunately, the pressure for increased enrollment created many problems. As events at the Phoenix school soon demonstrated, competition for students increased, overcrowding became prevalent, the quality of school life declined, and unsavory methods were used to fill classrooms.[4]

Samuel McCowan could see the writing on the wall when he arrived in Phoenix. If he did not make his school a vital part of the federal system, his career could be stalled and he might end up presiding over the institution's demise. As he saw it, the Phoenix school would survive only if it ranked among the best in the country, a status he firmly believed it did not then possess. Unlike his easy-going and congenial predecessor, McCowan had little interest in winning popularity contests. He was an experienced educator who knew exactly what he wanted to accomplish. Only thirty-four years old, the schoolmaster had been in education all his adult life. After serving as the principal of several small midwestern schools, he joined the Indian service in 1889. For six years he had labored as the supervisor of the Fort Mojave Indian School, before a brief stay at Albuquerque paved the way for the Phoenix appointment. An active Republican, he had excellent connections in Washington.[5]

Controversy began to swirl around the superintendent almost as soon as he settled into his office. His initial review of the institution confirmed the impression that students were making little progress. The Pima and Papago pupils were several grades behind children in other government schools and appeared to be especially deficient in knowledge of the English language. McCowan, who expressed a bias against local tribes from the start, attributed the school's failure to the homogeneous makeup of the student body. The similarities in background, language, and interests seemed to impede the "civilization" process. According to his view, the best method of correcting this condition was to import students from other areas. As he noted, "I regard the bringing in of Indian children from many tribes, as the best, surest and speediest method of civilizing the Indians. A school that is filled with representatives of a single tribe finds it exceedingly hard to train the children into talking any language but their own. They are, moreover, very clannish and much harder to discipline."[6]

McCowan thus committed himself to diversifying and expanding the school's tribal makeup by enrolling children from all over the Southwest. He proposed that all Arizona reservations, plus the southern half of California and portions of New Mexico, be subject to his drafts. This plan appeared to have two immediate benefits: the children he wanted to recruit were already attending "lesser" institutions, so their experience would improve the overall quality of the school; and their diversity promised to break down Pima and Papago provincialism. Such a program would be costly, however. School officials would be required to make recruitment trips as well as pay the cost of transporting children to and from Phoenix.[7]

The Indian Office supported the superintendent because his views complemented the government desire to improve the quality of selected nonreservation schools. In an attempt to buttress the better schools, Commissioner Jones had divided the government's off-reservation campuses into two categories. Those institutions possessing limited facilities were placed in Class I, while Class II schools, which included Phoenix, offered a full program and provided special instruction in such vocations as agriculture, stock breeding, and mechanical and domestic arts. Class I schools were designated "feeder" institutions, which meant that they were expected to send advanced students to Class II institutions much the same way that reservation schools were supposed to operate. Although administrators were still required to obtain parental consent to any off-reservation transfer, this policy promised to enhance the advanced schools by eliminating their need to draw upon "raw material from the camps." The Indian Office may have seen an additional benefit from the classification scheme by permitting it to set the stage for eliminating ineffective nonreservation schools. To prevent Class II schools from competing with each other, each was assigned a recruiting district.[8]

Armed with permission to proceed, Superintendent McCowan expanded his school. During the 1897–98 school year, approximately fifty outside students were brought to Phoenix. They represented tribes as far away as Oregon and New Mexico, although the majority came from within territorial boundaries. McCowan was perhaps most pleased with his success in enrolling pupils from two extremely "conservative" tribes—the Mojaves and Hopis. Although both peoples were known for their opposition to sending children away from home, several students from these tribes were persuaded to attend the central-Arizona facility.[9]

Despite apparent success, the recruitment effort was soon embroiled in controversy. From the beginning, the Pimas did not like mixing with "foreign" students. Having come to regard the school as their own, they resented the infusion of new students and refused to welcome them. Some pupils, forced to associate with old enemies, could not accept the situation and ran away. In fact, the number of desertions, which had been relatively low, jumped dramatically once outside students appeared on campus. Superintendent McCowan branded the Pima reaction unreasonable, maintaining that after a short time new friendships would be formed, misunderstandings would disappear, and harmony would return.[10] In his optimism he ignored the fact that the Pimas remained sullen and unfriendly, a condition which eventually erupted into protest.

Momentarily, however, a greater problem involved agents and superintendents who were reluctant to give up their best pupils. Adding fuel to the fire, McCowan did not hesitate to inform the commissioner when he encountered opposition. His troubles began during the summer of 1897, when he sought permission to enroll two Pueblo teenagers who were attending the Albuquerque school. The mother of these children wanted to remove them from the influence of an abusive father, but Albuquerque superintendent George Allen did not agree with this solution and refused to sanction the transfer. Thereupon, the Phoenix headmaster appealed directly to Commissioner Jones, stating that "if they remain there the father will take them home where they will go to the devil." This emotional entreaty succeeded, enabling the students to come to Arizona, but it created some bitter resentments. In another controversial case, McCowan requested the transfer of the entire fifth and sixth grades from the Fort Mojave Boarding School. The school's director was decidedly opposed to losing his best students, but received orders to comply after McCowan appealed to Supervisor of Indian Schools Frank Conser. In this instance, the government failed to secure parental consent and only a few students could be persuaded to transfer. Even so, the incident proved harmful to the Fort Mojave facility. Parents quickly expressed a reluctance to send their children to school if it meant they might be pressured to transfer.[11]

Despite mounting complaints, McCowan persisted in his attempts to secure new students. He openly criticized any superintendent who seemed to be less than enthusiastic about securing parental consent. In one letter to the commissioner, he accused several educators of "doing all in their power to thwart the desires of the Office in this matter." Schoolmasters were charged with blocking transfers because it would break up a football team or prevent a "junketing" trip to take a student to Carlisle. McCowan wanted all the advanced students in Arizona, Nevada, and southern California sent to Phoenix, a demand that became more emphatic after Congress authorized him to increase his enrollment to six hundred pupils. "Until this matter is fully impressed upon the heads of schools and they are made to feel that the Office regards more highly their efforts to transfer advanced pupils than the foolish policy of keeping pupils merely for show," he reminded his superiors, "the Indian school system will not be doing the work it should be doing."[12]

A particularly bitter dispute developed between McCowan and Harwood Hall, the former Phoenix superintendent who directed the school at Perris, California. Hall objected to sending his advanced pupils to Phoenix, preferring instead that they attend Carlisle. McCowan claimed that Hall was so prejudiced against Phoenix that he threatened to send troublesome students to the "untold horrors" of Arizona if they did not behave. Although Hall readily admitted he did not want his students sent to Phoenix, his motives illustrate the stiff competition between schools during this period. An ambitious man, Hall had great plans for his small school and refused to have it become a feeder institution. Responding to McCowan's complaint with an angry letter of his own, the embittered schoolmaster demanded that the commissioner ban all transfers from Perris to Phoenix. Hall's argument reveals some of the biases existing in the Indian service. He maintained that California Indians were morally and intellectually superior to Arizona Indians, and placing them in contact with Pimas and Papagos would lead them to ruin. The commissioner's office was unimpressed by such logic, however, and he ordered Hall to cooperate with the Phoenix school clerk when he made a recruiting trip to California in September 1898.[13]

Because of the aggressive recruiting campaign of the late 1890s, the Phoenix Indian School became the second largest institution in the federal system, surpassed in enrollment only by Carlisle. By June 1899 more than seven hundred Indian students were attending the school. Almost all of the increased enrollment came from students representing tribes outside central Arizona.* Phoenicians actively supported the school's expansion, and some citizens predicted the school would soon house two thousand Indian youngsters. This evidence of community support spurred the superintendent to even more ambitious plans. When he heard that the Indian normal school at Santa Fe would be relocated, McCowan, in characteristic fashion, recommended placing it on his campus. "We are," he stated, "in the midst of a vast Indian population, among whom many schools will be established in the near future, and these schools will require teachers."[14] Although nothing came of this suggestion, it demonstrates how aggressive school officials had become.

The dramatic increase in enrollment created a number of

---

* Between 1898 and 1900 the school enrolled or attempted to enroll students from Keams Canyon, San Carlos, Fort Apache, Fort Mojave, Fort Yuma, Fort Defiance, and the Colorado River Agency in Arizona; Hoppa Valley, Perris, Round Valley, and Mission Agency in California; Carson City and Nevada Agency in Nevada; Klamath Agency in Oregon; and Albuquerque and Santa Fe in New Mexico.

problems. In the rush to secure more students, the question of how to provide for them was overlooked. As a result, too many children were packed onto the campus, creating severe overcrowding and endangering health. When the Indian Office ruled that every child must be provided with at least forty square feet of dormitory space, school authorities responded by making some of the older boys sleep in sheds or hastily constructed tent houses. Faced with intolerable conditions, McCowan was able to obtain permission to erect additional buildings, and during the years between 1897 and 1900 new dormitories, a dining hall, additional shops, and employee residences were completed. Despite this construction and an expanded budget, which reached $131,200 for the 1898–99 fiscal year, there never seemed to be enough room, and students continued to live in cramped conditions.[15]

An even more vexing problem involved the attitude of local students. Although Superintendent McCowan tried to deemphasize the disruptive impact of outside students, the situation reached a state of "passive mutiny" in April 1899. At that point a group of Pima, Maricopa, and Papago students sent a letter of complaint to the Indian commissioner. Their petition, which was not signed for fear of reprisal, presented a devastating list of charges against McCowan and gave some idea of their mounting hostility. The students accused the superintendent of discriminating against them, being tyrannical and overbearing, and forcing them to violate moral principles. Specifically, the students objected to the policy of indiscriminate enrollment of "foreign" students because it hindered their own education. They even suggested that, if given his way, the headmaster would totally exclude local children. Additionally, they believed there was a general atmosphere of hostility toward them. To make their point, the pupils recounted an incident in which a newly arrived Papago boy was severely beaten by McCowan because he had misunderstood instructions. The superintendent was reported to have become so enraged with the youth's inability to understand English that he threatened to kill him. The students were also upset by the introduction of a social dance class where the girls were pressured to dance with strangers. This insensitive breach of tribal customs left some female students weeping "at the outrage imposed on their maidenly modesty." As a result of these and other transgressions, the students called for McCowan's removal, but the Indian Office failed to respond to their concerns.[16]

McCowan tended to blame others for school problems. When a supervisor's report in the spring of 1900 noted that the kindergarten class was not very successful, the superintendent replied that such classes had no place in a Class II institution. He reminded the Indian Office of his attempt to fill his school with advanced students and claimed his efforts had been frustrated. He had pursued excellence, "but owing to lack of transportation funds and to the fact that the best children, from the coast, are sent past the Phoenix school to the far distant Carlisle institution, I have been unable to secure as many of the desirable class as I need. In consequence of this failure, I have, of necessity, filled the school with small and less desirable children."[17]

Throughout the remainder of his stay in Arizona, the headmaster continued to recruit outside students and defend his policy. Descriptive statements of children sent to Phoenix show that active recruiting went on throughout the Southwest. One of the drawbacks, as McCowan saw it, centered on the necessity of securing parental consent to send an Indian child off the reservation. Thus, when Commissioner Jones decided to consider several policy changes in the fall of 1901, McCowan was quick to offer his advice. The Phoenix administrator favored the adoption of a compulsory policy that would eliminate any need for parental consent. Like many schoolmasters, he believed that Indian parents should have no say in their children's education. He preferred a rigid system where all Indian children, on reaching the age of six, would attend a day school for two years, then be sent to a reservation boarding facility for three more. At that point, he believed that they should be transferred to an off-reservation institution, where, once enrolled, the youngsters should be kept until they graduated. The current practice of signing children up for a three-year term created problems because parents wanted their children returned as soon as the stipulated time expired. With no escape possible, McCowan predicted that the schools would be filled and a uniform education could be imposed.[18]

McCowan also believed that agents and school directors must be forced to comply with this policy. In maintaining that these people objected to transfers for reasons other than educational advancement, he pointed out one of the glaring contradictions in the program. "The Agent," he said, "objects to sending Indian youth under his charge away because he wants to get along with his old Indians with as little trouble as possible and because by keeping them at home, he thinks he can increase his Agency appropriations, add new buildings and gain much glory by making many so-called improvements." He suggested that reservation schoolmasters objected to transfers because they wanted to please the agent and avoid antagonizing elderly Indians who wanted children kept at home. However accurate his assessment, McCowan's solution was a system of punishments for uncooperative employees that ranged from demotion to dismissal.[19] His suggestions were too drastic to be practical, but were in line with what Commissioner Jones hoped to accomplish through mandatory schooling.

All of these factors had their impact on the educational atmosphere at Phoenix. Yet, some four years after the arrival of the first "foreign" students, the main purpose for their coming had not been realized. Instead of inspiring Pima and Papago children to greater achievements, the outsiders had caused bitter resentments, leaving the local pupils to cling to one another as never before. Being singled out for scorn did not inspire them to work harder or do better, and the educational environment for them clearly worsened. Students from local tribes tended to remain in the lower grades, were not encouraged to excel, and were generally neglected while the new students received most of the attention. Those few children from central Arizona who eventually did rise above the norm did so on their own. There is no doubt that the presence of outside students increased attendance in advanced classes, but not to the extent anticipated. McCowan was often unsuccessful in recruiting pupils above the fourth-grade level and had to settle for second and third graders. As a result, no Indian children were qualified to graduate before 1901. Despite such problems, Commissioner Jones was pleased with the increases in school enrollments and remained convinced that transferring students to nonreservation schools was beneficial.[20]

Aside from increasing enrollments and diversifying the student body, McCowan's main priority was strengthening the school's vocational program. During his administration, as had been the case earlier, emphasis was placed on work-related activities. The superintendent summed up his philosophy in 1898 by boasting that "we pride ourselves on being a working school. No child is permitted to work as he pleases. 'Putting in time' is not sufficient. The child is taught how to do a thing, when to do it, and to do it whether he wants to or not." Indeed, teaching Indian students to work became the supreme goal of the institution, its motto being "Indolence is the cankerworm of progress, so our pupils are taught to kill the worm."[21]

Work-related activities proliferated in such an atmosphere. By 1898 a large variety of industrial arts were being taught. In addition to standard trades such as blacksmithing and carpentry, students were involved in harness making, wholesale laundry operations, farm and garden crafts, commercial sewing, and bee culture. After the completion of new shop buildings in 1900, the facility bragged of its capability to teach eighteen different trades ranging from agriculture to wagonmaking. Children were generally assigned to one of the vocational departments, where they were expected to become proficient in that particular skill. Under ordinary circumstances they had no choice in the matter and were simply told they were going to become a carpenter, laundress, or whatever. This type of industrial training coincided with the government's expectation that most pupils would either return to their reservations or find menial employment in white society. Under these circumstances intensive academic training was deemed unnecessary, a position confirmed by Commissioner Jones in 1900, when he stated that government schools would stress industrial over academic training. "Higher education in the sense ordinarily used has no place in the curriculum of Indian schools," the commissioner proclaimed. Using the training of Indian girls to make his point, he remarked that students should not expect to compete with white workers. Instead, they should learn the "dignity of work" and come to understand that the government owed them nothing "beyond a qualification for the actual duties of real life."[22] McCowan shared this sentiment and operated his school accordingly.

As a consequence, the academic program became even more subordinated to the vocational program. School officials, of course, insisted that the academic and vocational departments were of equal importance. Yet a number of practices countered such statements: students interested in academic programs could not graduate unless they had become proficient in a vocational skill; the school had up-to-date machinery but no library; and the quality of the academic faculty was rated adequate, while the vocational staff was praised for its excellence and recommended for pay increases. When the new superintendent of Indian schools, Estelle Reel, visited the institution in 1899, she praised its vocational programs while hardly giving the literary department a second glance. Quick to realize what had been going on at the local level for years, Reel had become one of the government's leading advocates of work training. During her stay in Phoenix she recommended the establishment of a "commercial department" capable of teaching stenography, typing, and general business principles. McCowan eagerly supported the concept, and by 1900 a commercial program had been introduced. Training in this field was to follow completion of eight years of regular schoolwork. The Phoenix schoolmaster was proud of this small program, yet made it clear that he did not expect dramatic results. A few boys and girls might secure employment in stores and offices, but the primary value was in teaching Indians to care for their personal affairs.[23]

A variety of other events illustrate the strong emphasis on vocational programs. In 1901, a full decade after the school opened its doors, the first graduation ceremonies were conducted. At the commencement exercises in April, four students were recognized as having completed the eighth grade. The honored students were all from tribes outside the local area (Apache, Pueblo, and California Mission) and represented the type of students McCowan had so actively recruited. Surprisingly, the headmaster was not particularly impressed with the graduates. His tendency to stereotype Indian abilities led him to conclude that only one had "ambition enough to become more than an ordinary breadwinner." Another of the pupils was described as being quite bright but tending to the "indolence peculiar to his tribe." McCowan predicted this student would soon become "a degenerate blanket Indian." During the same ceremonies eleven girls were awarded certificates in domestic science. In contrast to his assessment of the "scholars," McCowan described these girls as bright and enthusiastic. He clearly had more hope for such students, who possessed a "general liking for cooking and humble household work." They were the ones who seemed to hold the key to the future.[24]

Another indication of the strong vocational emphasis was the increasing use of the outing system. McCowan favored the system because of its many benefits: it found employment for students, made dormitory space available, and created community goodwill. As a consequence, the school devoted considerable energy to expanding the outings. But the quality of the program suffered. By the summer of 1898 some 150 children, mostly female teenagers, were working for local employers. Although the employment of so many young girls was gratifying, finding jobs for young men had become a problem. Local tradesmen objected when the school attempted to place Indian boys in positions where they might compete with white workers; and in one case white bricklayers walked off the job when schoolboys were hired.[25] This situation forced McCowan to search for jobs that whites were unwilling to take, even if it meant twisting the aims of the outing system.

An example of the questionable use of the outings is the school's relationship with Phoenix businessman Ben Heyman. This entrepreneur owned a local onyx mine and proposed locating a factory at the school where Indian boys might be used to cut and polish the gemstones. McCowan linked the scheme to the outing program and encouraged the Indian Office to approve it, although the student employees would remain on campus instead of mingling with white citizens. Indeed, the headmaster became so enthusiastic about the idea he suggested the school open a program in mining technology. Proclaiming that the Indian was a natural prospector, he predicted that they could earn a livelihood in mining while keeping out of "direct competition with thousands of equally deserving but less fortunate white people." The Indian Office did not share McCowan's enthusiasm, but the onyx manufacturer's proposal was approved and became a part of the vocational program.[26]

The expansion of the girls' outings in the late 1890s raised additional questions. Soon after arriving at Phoenix, McCowan began to realize that wholesale employment of Indian girls by local families tended to diminish the amount of supervision. The situation, as he described it, had gotten out of hand: "Sending unformed, undisciplined girls out to serve in families that care nothing for them except the work they can get from them, *without careful supervision,* is often more of a curse to the girl than a blessing." As a result, on August 3, 1897, he asked the Indian Office for permission to appoint a matron to oversee the girls' outing program. The superintendent suggested that this individual take responsibility for placing the girls, working with employers to assure proper supervision and making frequent visits to make sure that all was going well. The hiring of an outing matron was considered of enough importance by the Indian Office to merit quick approval.[27]

Unfortunately, the school's desire to place as many girls as possible worked against the new matron. Within a short time she was overwhelmed. When an inspector reviewed the program in early 1900 he noted that, despite efforts to the contrary, the outings had become impersonal and simply a means of providing menial labor to the community. He was particularly critical of local families who regarded the school as an employment bureau and sought "Indian help because it is somewhat cheaper and can be controlled to better advantage." Interestingly, McCowan, who had noted the same problems a few years earlier, now chose to mute the criticism by remarking that while the inspector's comments were correct in a few cases, a majority of employers "think as much of their Indian help as any family on earth." The superintendent's sudden tendency to see only the positive side was prompted by his awareness of how fashionable it had become for Phoenicians to have an Indian servant. He was also influenced by Estelle Reel, who reviewed the Phoenix outings in May 1900. Meeting with prominent families, she was impressed by how much they valued their Indian help. She applauded when told that the wives of leading local citizens traveled about the country taking schoolgirls with them to serve as maids and nurses. To Reel this type of paternalism was the essence of Indian education. It gave the girls a chance to travel, "and they acquire in one year as much cultivation and civilization as could be engrafted upon them in four or five years of ordinary intercourse in the school."[28] Since the federal superintendent offered no criticism of such procedures, it is not surprising that McCowan continued operations as usual.

Despite official statements to the contrary, the outing system as practiced at Phoenix and other western schools was no longer what it was designed to be. Devised originally as an educational technique to promote rapid assimilation, it evolved into a method of supplying cheap labor to white employers. The emphasis was now on giving students experience with the menial jobs they might be expected to find in cities or on the reservation. Intimate contact with white families had lost most of its original meaning. Superintendent Reel reiterated this position in 1901 when she prepared a course of study for all Indian schools, based partly on retaining the outing system. As she saw it, great advantages remained in placing the Indian "in the midst of the stir of civilized life," but this experience could no longer be used as a tool to assimilate Indians into the dominant society. After a few years in the outing program the boy was expected to return home, start a farm, and "arrange a home and live in it as the people do at the home he has just left." It was the same for girls. They were to become efficient housekeepers when they returned to the reservation and got married. With the money they earned in the outings the young man would build a home and the young woman would furnish it. Nothing was said of living in middle-class white society.[29]

In certain other respects, the outing system at Phoenix fared well. By 1902 as many as two hundred boys and girls were earning wages ranging from five to twenty-five dollars a month, much of which was deposited in a savings bank "to teach them proper business methods as well as permitting their savings to earn money." To set an example, Superintendent McCowan took two boys and a girl into his own home, paying them monthly wages as high as thirty dollars. He also took a public stand against abuse of the outing system. A 1901 newspaper story detailed some of the things that would not be tolerated. They included making students do all the household dirty work, keeping them segregated from the family, paying them in cast-off clothing, and generally working them under "slavish" conditions. When such abuses were discovered, the superintendent promised to return the children to school. He let it be known that if exploitation proliferated, he had the authority to abolish the system completely. But he also admitted that "a howl would go up from the residents of this valley" if he ever took such an action, and obviously it would take a major scandal for him to resort to such drastic action.[30]

The participation of Phoenix faculty and staff in summer educational institutes provides another example of the strong emphasis on vocational training. Annual gatherings of teachers had taken place since 1884, but using such gatherings to improve the quality of instruction gained significance in the mid-1890s. In 1894 the Indian Office began offering week-long institutes designed to develop enthusiasm, share experiences, "turn them out of ruts into new lines of thought and method, and bring those outside and inside the Indian service into contact." The emphasis on vocational education was especially pronounced after Estelle Reel became superintendent of Indian schools in 1898. Reel's belief that Indian children could not be treated like white children led her to demand that teachers be prepared to deal with a different type of pupil. In the summer of 1898 she organized a three-week institute. Agents, superintendents, teachers, disciplinarians, cooks, field matrons, and nurses met in Colorado Springs to discuss methods for educating Indian children. Not surprisingly, the meeting stressed work-related activities.[31]

The following summer another institute was held, this time in conjunction with the annual meeting of the National Education Association in Los Angeles. This enabled Indian service teachers to associate with other professionals, and the government pulled out all stops to impress the educational world with its sophistication. Talks by Assistant Commissioner A. C. Tonner, Merrill E. Gates of the Board of Indian Commissioners, and Captain Pratt of Carlisle drew big audiences, but the significant activity was handled by Reel, who hoped to get the NEA to put its stamp of approval on the Indian education program. Arguing that Indian service teachers should be considered a part of the profession, the head of the nation's Indian schools asked the NEA to make the summer institutes a permanent part of the national organization. The NEA Board of Directors agreed to the union, and, beginning with the Charleston convention in 1900, Indian school institutes were held at the NEA annual gathering. To celebrate this victory and impress the teaching fraternity with its methods, the Indian Office exhibited a collection of student work that reinforced prevailing stereotypes by concentrating almost solely on manual skills.[32]

Phoenix personnel played a prominent role in the annual institutes. Superintendent McCowan was particularly visible. He attended nearly every meeting, was one of the leading forces in uniting with the NEA, and led discussion groups. A number of his vocational teachers attended sessions, and in 1899, Mrs. Bertha Canfield, honored as one of the best seamstresses in the nation, conducted a class in how to teach sewing and needlework. As could be seen from Mrs. Canfield's presentation, the institute tended to emphasize the vocational side of Indian education. A lecture by Josephine Richards of Hampton Institute, entitled "The Training of the Indian Girl as the Uplifter of the Home," was fairly typical of the general atmosphere. In discussing the future of Indian women, the entire emphasis was on "civilizing" the traditional home. Nothing was mentioned about assimilation, only that girls should keep a pleasant reservation home where they might inspire others with the ideals of white society.[33] It is little wonder that after returning from these institutes, schoolteachers and their superiors were more than ever convinced that the schools were headed in the right direction.

Regrettably, the strong emphasis on vocational training did not produce the expected short-term results. Although a good number of students spent three or more years learning a skill and were undoubtedly qualified for a variety of jobs, there appears to have been a notable lack of success in finding employment for these pupils. Aside from the outing program, which accounted for almost all student employment in the Phoenix area, Indians were unable to get jobs in the urban area. Beyond domestic servants and seasonal field hands, who could be secured from the outing program or directly from the reservations, Phoenicians had little need for Indian workers. Consequently, when students finished their term at school they were left with no option but to return to the reservation. Once home the former students generally did not practice what they had learned at school. As McCowan remarked, the returned "child is made so welcome and life so easy that he forgets the strenuous school life that had begun to make its impression and succumbs to the ease and abandon of reservation existence." With the exception of a few who were able to secure agency jobs, most had no opportunity to use their skills and "returned to the blanket."[34] Despite concern for this situation, neither

McCowan nor his superiors were willing to admit that the vocational program was not working.

Vocational programs, of course, were not the only important matter during the McCowan years. Student welfare and community relations consumed a considerable amount of time. One concern that became increasingly significant was student health. Contagious diseases had always been associated with Indian schools, and student deaths were not uncommon. Yet with the tremendous increase in school population during the 1890s, children were packed into facilities so rapidly that health became severely endangered. Overcrowded conditions produced epidemics of smallpox, influenza, measles, and whooping cough at most western boarding schools. In some instances schoolmasters were so anxious to fill their classrooms that they knowingly enrolled sick children, thus spreading disease even more rapidly. To compound the problem, many government institutions were beginning to show their age and lack of maintenance. In the period between 1897 and 1901 inspectors reported such unhealthy conditions as inadequate sewage systems, defective plumbing, contaminated drinking water, dilapidated buildings, foul air, and tainted food. As a result, the years after 1898 saw hundreds of lives lost as epidemics hit dozens of schools.[35]

Many of the same conditions existed at Phoenix, although school administrators had somehow convinced themselves that they were immune from danger. Located in what was regarded as a particularly healthful environment, the school had never been bothered by illness, a fact proudly repeated by the staff. The 1898 superintendent's annual report remarked that student health, as usual, was excellent. McCowan based his opinion on the fact that the school was relatively new and had the capacity to provide the children with fresh vegetables and dairy products. Unfortunately, he overlooked other factors. The school had grown enormously during his administration and overcrowding had become a significant problem. An Indian service inspector noticed the danger when he visited the school in April 1898. He remarked that the water quality was poor and the sewage system inadequate. The sewage from all the buildings emptied into a large cesspool only two hundred feet from the main building. "This cesspool," he noted, "they are obliged to constantly pump out by hand, in order to keep the 'system' in service. This matter is pumped out on the ground, and the odors arising often make it very unpleasant at the school." The washrooms were listed as being substandard, and the outside toilet facilities used by the boys needed cleaning. A small, poorly ventilated frame building, which "would be of little use in case of an epidemic," served as the hospital.[36]

Catastrophe was avoided until December 1899, when measles broke out among the pupils. The disease spread slowly at first, but reached epidemic proportions about the first of January. During the first two weeks of the new year more than two hundred pupils were stricken. To care for so many patients, McCowan was forced to dismiss classes and use the staff to nurse the sick. When pneumonia developed, two trained nurses were hired. Before the scourge ended, 325 cases of measles and 60 cases of pneumonia were reported. Nine children died within a ten day period. Several cases of consumption also developed. Because all but one of the fatalities were local children, the school purchased caskets and sent the bodies home for burial. The school was clearly unprepared to handle such an emergency, and when the epidemic erupted, the alarmed citizens of Phoenix spread rumors that the campus was infected with scarlet fever, chicken pox, diphtheria, and even smallpox. Indian parents, too, became alarmed and many visited the school during the crisis. McCowan provided them with food and forage and was quite relieved when the "ignorant old people" agreed to leave their children in "the care of the white man." By March the epidemic had run its course. School authorities were confident they had done all they could to save lives and concluded that conditions at the school were not to blame.[37] Such an attitude hardly boded well for the future.

Questions regarding the spiritual welfare of pupils tended to receive more attention than health. On one occasion McCowan found himself accused of failing to protect the morality of the students and being lax on religious instruction. Although the complaint came from a disgruntled teacher, the charges were taken seriously by government authorities who were extremely sensitive to any accusation of student misconduct. The Indian Office was therefore relieved when other staff members sent a letter to the commissioner repudiating the teacher and defending McCowan and his policies. The letter reveals that the children's social life was quite closely regulated, with the staff on guard against any questionable behavior. Not only were classrooms supervised, but safeguards such as escorting pupils everywhere they went, not permitting boys and girls to see each other without a chaperone, and keeping boys away from the girls' areas were used to ensure strict morality.[38]

Religious instruction was just as regulated. Indeed, all standard religious policies were employed. Pupils were required to attend Sunday school as well as a YMCA or YWCA meeting each Sunday afternoon, and clergymen from the churches of Phoenix continued to offer lectures and sermons. In keeping with government rules, all religious activities were officially nondenominational. In December 1900, for instance, W. H. Gill, a missionary at the Salt River Reservation, approached McCowan with the suggestion that he be allowed to train missionaries on campus. He wanted to enlist pupils from each tribe represented at the school, train them in Bible studies and the doctrines of Christianity, and then send them back to their people to lead the Christian effort. The missionary was convinced that this method provided the best solution to the "betterment of these people," and he secured the backing of several prominent Phoenicians. Although McCowan believed that an Indian youth could never receive too much moral training, he feared that Gill's proposal "would subject the Service to considerable criticism from those who would persist in seeing sectarianism in any move of this kind." Consequently, the schoolmaster recommended that Gill "exercise his zeal" on the reservation and enlist former students who "are usually ripe for any effort along the lines of moral or educational instruction."[39]

In addition to his involvement with student affairs, the superintendent and his staff invested considerable effort in working with the community and getting as much public recognition as possible. The Phoenix Indian School carried on an intensive and successful public relations program that rivaled any in the country. The main goal was to publicize the cause of Indian education and build political support for the institution. Like modern colleges and universities, much of this was accomplished through the school's extracurricular activities. The public relations value of such programs was clearly recognized and well exploited. By all accounts, the most popular feature of the school was the band, a trademark of many Indian schools. Organized about 1894 to encourage musical training, it became the school's greatest asset. The young musicians performed at all principal school functions in addition to traveling extensively throughout the Southwest. Every major event in Phoenix gave the Indian band prominent billing. Its forty musicians regularly spent their summers and holidays playing for audiences at fairs and celebrations; whatever fees they commanded went into the school's general fund. Officials were particularly proud of the band and lost no opportunity to emphasize its great benefits. McCowan frequently quoted statements of community appreciation, specifically pointing out to his superiors how pleased citizens were to see this visible sign of "improvement" in the Indian race. He also selected favorable comments from the band members to support his contention that the Indians themselves recognized the value they were receiving from their educational experience.[40]

In addition to the band, the school supported a thirty-member choir, an orchestra, and a debating club, all of which entertained the public. On one occasion some Apache students were permitted to present "a real Apache war dance." Although retention of traditional cultural practices was discouraged, it was permitted on this occasion because members of the territorial legislature were in attendance. It appears that school administrators wanted to impress their guests with the great changes in Indian behavior and used the traditional dance as a point of contrast. In a similar vein, the school continued to provide its

The Phoenix Indian School Band was formed in the mid-1890s and performed for the student body, civic groups, carnivals, and fairs, and went on extended tours. From the perspective of the general public, the band represented a sure sign that Indian education was a "civilizing" endeavor. Courtesy of Arizona Historical Foundation.

drill team and band for any public event. In many instances, the students brought up the rear of processions featuring "wild" Indians. The Phoenix Winter Carnival in December 1900, for instance, promoted such events as a simulated battle between the Pimas and Apaches, foot races between Pimas and Maricopas, and an Indian tug-of-war on horseback. As usual, students were present to demonstrate that the old ways, so vividly presented to the audience, were really a part of the past.[41]

The athletic program provided additional community involvement. By the mid-1890s boys' football and baseball clubs were well established. The teams followed in the mold set by Captain Pratt at Carlisle, who believed that competition built character and physical well-being. The Phoenix boys played a variety of local clubs, including Phoenix High School and Tempe Normal. They also made several road trips, going as far as Prescott and Bisbee, and the football team visited schools in southern California. Although the caliber of competition was perhaps not too high, there was considerable local interest. Fans liked to wish the athletes well by recalling their Indian heritage. "It is hoped the Indian school footballists will return with a number of scalps dangling from their belts," wrote one newspaper. School officials, while encouraging the athletic program, strictly regulated the boys' conduct. In this way, they could be pleased when the team "won universal commendation for strict adherence to rules and gentlemanly behavior," even at the expense of being mauled by some of their less "gentlemanly" opposition. Such a philosophy was needed on New Year's Day 1900, when the Carlisle team played Phoenix in the first football game between two Indian schools. Phoenix was thoroughly trounced.[42] Women's sports, later an important activity, did not begin until after the turn of the century.

Another public-relations tactic involved exhibits at expositions and fairs. This activity was encouraged by the Indian Office, which hoped to acquaint the American public with its educational program. The government set the stage for such displays during Chicago's Columbian Exposition of 1893 by constructing a model boarding school and filling it with Indian students. In this setting children from various institutions spent from two to four weeks demonstrating school life. All this was intended to point out to exposition visitors that the Indian people were progressing toward civilization. In fact, the model school was placed directly next to the anthropology building in order to maximize the contrast.[43]

Although Phoenix did not send any students to the Chicago Exposition, it became involved with succeeding events. In 1897 the school prepared a large collection of handcrafted items for the Nashville Exposition. All items were designed to show the pupils' expertise in vocational skills and included samples of fancy sewing, needlework, and embroidery, a redwood cabinet, and jars of fruit and farm products. Two years later organizers of Omaha's Greater American Exposition asked the school to send it a representative of each Arizona tribe. McCowan accepted the invitation, offering to take the desired students as well as the band, and personally heading the delegation. Besides providing him an opportunity to leave Phoenix during the heat of summer, the tour permitted the headmaster to "show the differences between the undeveloped and educated Indians." The band was such a great hit that the Exposition's management contracted to have it stay through the summer. In another bit of strategy, the school played host to the Commercial Club of Chicago when it visited Phoenix on a trade mission in March 1901.[44]

The first issue of the *Native American* was published in January 1901. Officially regarded as a newspaper, the journal was published once a week and followed a format established by the Carlisle, Hampton, and other Indian school newspapers. The journal was written and printed by students and contained information on school activities, other schools, returned students, and Indian affairs in general. Local merchants provided economic support through advertising. The paper was touted as providing educational benefit, but its real purpose was to publicize the school within the local community. For that reason, its contents were closely regulated and nothing unfavorable to the school or the assimilation program was tolerated.

Nevertheless, the *Native American* proved a success. It was avidly read by Phoenicians and it enhanced the impression that Indian students were making real progress. On the whole, the school paper, which was published for some thirty years, did much to promote the institution.[45] As time passed the paper also became an important vehicle for providing the Indian community with information about current and former students.

By 1901, Superintendent McCowan had accomplished most of his objectives. The Phoenix Indian School had blossomed into one of the largest centers of Indian education in the country and had acquired a national reputation. Its outing system was large and impressive, and the vocational departments were the envy of many school administrators. The student population was well mixed, with Indian children attending classes ranging from the most basic instruction to advanced work. Phoenix, moreover, was regarded as one of the best run and most firmly established off-reservation schools in the federal system and its future seemed assured, all because of the efforts of Sam McCowan. A final tribute to the headmaster came in May 1901 when President McKinley visited the campus. The visit came as part of a western tour and was greeted with great enthusiasm by students and administrators. McCowan pulled out all the stops to impress his guest. All seven hundred students, including the outing pupils, were on hand, and the presidential party was treated to a spectacular celebration of the assimilation program. The band played "Patriotic Airs"; McCowan, mounted on a black horse, led a massive procession of marching students, and the students shouted "we give our head, our hands and our hearts to our country." McKinley uttered a few words, shook a few hands, and left for his next destination, leaving everyone convinced that Indian education had made great strides in Phoenix.[46]

Soon after Mckinley's visit, McCowan began to look for a new challenge. He succeeded in late 1901 when he accepted the position of headmaster at the Chilocco Indian School in Oklahoma. When he left Phoenix in January 1902, there could be no doubt that McCowan had done much in his five-year stay, and the lists of accomplishments were long. Yet many of his achievements were more cosmetic than substantial. The school had indeed grown rapidly, but there was trouble below the surface. Some of the programs were hastily conceived and poorly implemented. In addition, progress was still being measured in terms of growth, and a careful observer might have noted that after a decade of operation the school had succeeded neither in promoting assimilation nor in improving reservation life.

5

Stability in an Era of Change

ALTHOUGH PHOENIX INDIAN SCHOOL possessed a considerable degree of stability and maturity by 1902, it had not really done much to move its students into American society or train them to improve reservation life. During the next thirteen years, under the leadership of Charles Goodman, the school began to make some headway in graduating students, finding them jobs, and producing a small cadre of trained workers. These advances were made despite a series of distracting events that drew attention away from routine activities. In particular, the national controversy over the usefulness of off-reservation education intensified. Not only did outside observers demand a revamping of the entire educational system, but a new generation of federal administrators began to consider significant changes in the program. To Phoenix and other western schools, this meant increased interference and more centralized control. Yet, as the years before World War I proved, changes at the top did not always filter down to the school level in the expected way.

Charles W. Goodman became superintendent on January 8, 1902. Somewhat older than previous headmasters, he came to the institution as the result of an exchange that saw McCowan transferred to the Chilocco Indian School in Oklahoma where Goodman had worked for several years. Like other school administrators during this era, the new superintendent was a professional educator, having begun his career as a field supervisor, advancing to top educational positions at Keam's Canyon, Arizona, and Pawnee, Oklahoma, and finally establishing himself at Chilocco. The handsome, distinguished-looking Goodman was pleased to be in Arizona, although somewhat concerned that his new school lacked some of Chilocco's refinements. On the other hand, he considered Phoenix a "real" Indian school because of the high percentage of full-blood students. Goodman was determined to run his institution efficiently and to raise the "standards of right thinking and right living among our pupils."[1]

The superintendent inherited a large and active facility. The main part of the campus occupied about ten city blocks, with the major buildings located on either side of a landscaped parade ground. With the girls' building at its center, the other major structures—mostly two-story brick or large Victorian frame buildings—gave the school the look of a large college campus. Everywhere lawns, hedges, mature trees, gardens, and fountains softened the harsh desert landscape. In addition to the twenty frame and fourteen brick buildings, the surrounding farm had 240 acres under cultivation and produced large quantities of hay, cabbages, turnips, melons, and tomatoes. The stockyard housed cattle, horses, mules, pigs, and chickens. Figures compiled in 1902 and 1903 showed an institution with an official capacity of 700 students. On the average, 701 pupils were in attendance, with boys slightly outnumbering girls. The typical student was thirteen years old; 95 percent of the pupils were between six and eighteen. More than three-quarters of the youngsters were full bloods, a proportion that increased during Goodman's term. The school employed twelve teachers (eleven of them female) and a total staff of fifty-six (eleven of them Native Americans). Salaries and other expenses for the 1902–1903 fiscal year totaled $93,211.50.[2]

Goodman expected his years at Phoenix to be routine, and for a time he devoted his energies to ordinary administrative tasks. In the spring of 1902, for example, he negotiated the purchase of an eighty-acre plot of land located a mile east of campus, in an effort to provide a better source of well water.[3] During the same period Estelle Reel, the superintendent of Indian schools, spent six weeks in residence introducing teachers to the new *Course of Study for Indian Schools* that she had prepared for the Indian service. This guide focused on providing students with a "practical" education. Teachers were reminded that Indian pupils were not likely to make any great intellectual advances and that classes should emphasize developing the work ethic. The staff warmly received the new course of study and expressed the sentiment that it would improve the effectiveness of their teaching.[4]

In December 1902 the school hosted a three-day institute. Educators from all over the West converged on Phoenix to visit the school, listen to such personalities as Miss Reel, and attend receptions hosted by local dignitaries. Territorial residents were extremely proud of the honor bestowed on their school. Governor Alexander O. Brodie delivered the opening address, and University of Arizona President F. Yale Adams speculated on "Educating the Indian for Citizenship."[5]

These matters were soon interrupted by a disturbing controversy involving the outing system. The problem surfaced as the result of the inherent weakness of the outing program and the fact that reservation Indians had begun to find jobs in town. Indian Office administrators had long been nervous about charges that the outing system was not functioning properly, and in February 1902, Goodman was ordered to provide a full report on the Phoenix situation. This gave him an opportunity to review thoroughly the eight-year-old apprenticeship system. In the first significant internal review of the program, the headmaster reported that most Indian boys were placed on nearby ranches while the girls were working as domestics in residences. Most students were sent out for the summer, but many remained out year-round. During the preceding six months eighty boys had been employed for various lengths of times at wages ranging from eight to ten dollars per month. At the same time seventy-nine girls were working for Phoenix families. An additional thirty-five students, mostly female, were permitted to work in town on weekends. The boys were supervised by the head disciplinarian, who collected their wages and turned them over to school officials. The girls continued to be managed by the outing matron, who also handled student earnings. The amounts collected were credited to the pupil's account; half was placed in a local bank, and the remainder could be used to purchase personal items.[6]

Goodman summarized the positive features of the program by remarking that pupils were compelled to speak English, to learn to work "as it should be done in their own homes and on their own farms," and to earn a wage and learn the value of money. He then presented a list of disadvantages. He noted that the disciplinarian and the matron could not adequately supervise the pupils; local citizens cared little about their wards and offered them practically no instruction; and outing pupils did not attend public schools. The most significant problem involved interaction with the town's undesirable element. It proved almost impossible to keep outing students indoors in such a warm climate, and employers often turned them loose in the evening. Without supervision, many youngsters gathered with groups of reservation Indians who worked near Phoenix. Boys and girls met each other on the streets or at special gathering places, causing "much trouble and a great amount of worry." Some of the nonschool youth persuaded outing girls to stay out late and carouse around town. If this were not enough, teachers with long experience believed that the program hindered rather than aided education. "By my own observation," wrote one instructor, "I believe that the pupils whose school work is constantly broken into soon lose all interest in their studies, must be degraded from class to class, are by far more difficult to manage, and that they do not speak or understand the English language as readily as the pupils who for the school term have been unmolested in their school work." Despite such harsh statements, the headmaster believed that the outing system's advantages continued to outweigh the disadvantages.[7]

While Goodman's report was making its way to Washington, the Indian Office received a report from one of its inspectors confirming the headmaster's conclusions. Indeed, the inspector was even more critical, calling the girls' program a total failure from "a moral point of view." Acting Commissioner A. C. Tonner, therefore, ordered the school "to avoid future trouble and scandal" by discontinuing the "practice of putting the girls out from the school in what is known as the outing system." This step was justified on grounds that students could not be satisfactorily supervised. "The moral conduct of pupils and employees," he reminded the schoolmaster, "is of paramount importance at Indian schools." Goodman's report was received just as this order was issued, and it reinforced the Indian Office opinion, although Tonner did concede that a few girls might still be placed with "selected families." The school thus began to notify families that their outing students would no longer be available, and by September 1902 all the monthly girls were returned to school, leaving only the weekend help employed.[8]

Goodman no doubt hoped that the curtailment of the outing program would put an end to the controversy, but his expectations were dashed by a scandal that erupted during the summer of 1902. It started when a visitor to Phoenix wrote the commissioner that there was a strong probability that schoolchildren were engaged in "immoral" (sexual) activities at Sunday evening band concerts. The Indian Office, although not accepting the veracity of the report, quickly warned the headmaster to be more vigilant, remarking that "such reports if given circulation injure the integrity not only of yourself and school force but of the service itself." Goodman conferred with the school's matron, Mrs. Schach, who maintained that no misbehavior occurred at campus concerts. Female students were always segregated from the boys and employees prevented any contact. Moreover, girls were returned to their dormitory before dark, "after which the gates are locked and every precaution is taken to prevent any association on the part of the boys and girls." She did admit, however, that she had little control when concerts were held in town. Such performances tended to attract reservation youth who were not living "respectable lives" and were free "from all restraint of parents, agent or superintendent." The matron thus maintained that although reservation children might be guilty of carousing, students under her supervision were not. "It is my greatest desire that every girl in my care should become a self-respecting, pure minded woman, and to that end I give my best thought and effort," she said.⁹

In line with this reasoning, Mrs. Schach asked that the school stop sending girls to town altogether. She maintained that girls who worked on weekends often did not return directly to school and let their "moral weakness" lead them astray. Additionally, she disliked the people who hired Indian girls because they "simply pile up all the hard and dirty work till Saturday, and then complain if the work is not perfectly done." Goodman recognized the truth of these assertions, but he decided not to abolish the weekend outings. He argued that the girls needed the experience and money. Yet his main concern seems to have been the great hardship it would work on the people of Phoenix, "who for years have had much help from this school. Other help is almost unobtainable in this country, and especially the mothers with little children, most of whom have been very kind to the girls, find it a great trial to have to do without assistance even one day in the week." When the schoolmaster refused to modify his position, the matron submitted her resignation, because, she said, "I can not permit myself to be made instrumental in the moral downfall of the girls whom I am here to guide and uplift."¹⁰

The matron's resignation prompted the Indian Office to order the school to call in all remaining girls and let no more go out. The superintendent expected the fuss to blow over rapidly and to be able to resume the outings in short order, but his expectations were frustrated by the continuing concern of local citizens. Led by the Reverend Lapsley A. McAfee, a number of residents began a campaign to regulate reservation youngsters who were working in town without supervision. McAfee complained that during evenings and in their free time these juveniles were falling "into distressing ways" and suggested they needed some form of supervision. Although the children referred to were not associated with the school, many Phoenicians assumed the contrary, further damaging the institution's reputation. The Indian Office consequently ordered Goodman to exert every effort to regulate such activities.[11]

The headmaster could do nothing about nonstudents. He reported that whites who employed such youngsters concealed them from the authorities, and the Indians themselves refused to cooperate, knowing that school officials had no jurisdiction over them. All this proved frustrating, especially because the school was "blamed for the conduct of these boys and girls by outsiders who cannot distinguish them from pupils." The only solution Goodman could offer was for the government to hire a "competent, middle-aged Christian woman" to serve as a field matron in Phoenix. With duties similar to a modern social worker, she would work with both children and employers to improve the situation.[12]

Community concern about the conduct of Indian children assured that there would be no quick resumption of the outing system. In May 1903 the school reported that seven boys, and no girls, were working away from the campus. This development left something of a vacuum in the school's domestic science program. In searching for another method of giving girls some practical experience as homemakers, the school decided to open an "Industrial Cottage." The idea of operating a model home on school campuses had been popular in the Indian service for some time and seemed the best substitute for outings. When the Industrial Cottage opened at Phoenix in late 1903, it used the old hospital building, which had been remodeled into a six-room house similar to an average middle-class residence. One of the teachers took charge of the cottage, which housed nine girls at a time. The teacher acted "in the capacity of the mother of the family and conducts the home according to the methods used in a well regulated household where mothers and daughters 'do their own work,' practicising strict economy and at the same time living well." Although it was unrealistic to expect that female students would ever have such a home of their own, the cottage was touted as a place where all the routine chores of an American housewife could be practiced. To prevent any hint of immorality, males were permitted in the building only on special, closely regulated occasions.[13]

Concern over the collapse of the outing program at Phoenix prompted the Indian Office to investigate the program at other institutions operating such programs, requesting a full report on student apprentices and requiring the submission of quarterly "Outing Pupil Reports" providing the name, age, specific job, and wage of all pupils. A tabulation of these reports showed that similar problems existed at many locations.[14] This information led the government to intensify its demand for more supervision and lent ammunition to critics of the system.

Meanwhile, the issue of religious instruction surfaced. For more than a decade the Indian Office had been attempting to diminish the influence of the Catholic church, and in the early 1900s the question of the "Browning Rule" became controversial. This rule dated back to 1896, when Commissioner Browning mandated that Indian parents had "no right to designate which school their children shall attend" when the question involved mission versus government schools located on reservations. This regulation so embittered Catholic missionaries that they began a campaign to have the decision rescinded. Their efforts succeeded early in 1902, when the secretary of the interior again permitted parents to select a religious institution.[15]

The Phoenix school had generally maintained good relations with the Catholic church, although some runaways took refuge in Catholic mission schools on the Pima reservation. Before the abrogation of the Browning Rule they had been routinely returned, but no sooner had the secretary issued his order than Father Justin Deutch, the priest at Gila Crossing Catholic day school, refused to give up a youngster that Goodman wanted returned. Deutch argued that during the past summer the student's parents decided to send him to the Catholic school. The police had arrested the boy and returned him to Phoenix only to have him flee to the Catholic school again. The abrogation of the Browning Rule, said the priest, gave parents the right to choose schools, and the student in question must be permitted to remain at Gila Crossing. Goodman did not want to make an issue of the incident, but he knew that if Deutch's interpretation was upheld it could set a precedent that would encourage church and government schools to raid each other whenever parents changed their minds.[16]

The prospect of a new round of recruiting wars led the Indian Office to deal with the situation very delicately. Goodman was ordered to permit the student to remain at the Catholic day school. To prevent complications, however, the schoolmaster was informed that future departmental policy would deny parents the right to change schools during the course of the academic year; all transfers must take place during the summer recess. To ensure that religious schools gained no advantage from this arrangement, Goodman was reminded that he had the right to make similar rules. Even though this decision quieted the specific controversy, the government had so many problems with the repeal of the Browning Rule that it finally issued a circular reminding superintendents that although Indian parents had more latitude in selecting schools, they would not be permitted to use that right to defeat the basic purpose of Indian education. Therefore, before parents could transfer their children from one school to another, they were required to make a personal appeal to the superintendent. Once enrolled at a mission school, a child must faithfully attend that school or be placed back in a government institution.[17] In effect, this requirement made it difficult to transfer students to religious schools, while giving the impression that Indian parents had freedom of choice.

In another flap involving the Catholics, the school was forced to make concessions on the nature of religious instruction offered its students. Flushed with success in defeating the Browning order, local church leaders decided to demand that Catholic pupils be given full religious freedom. In the spring of 1902 the Reverend Casimir Vogt, superior of the Franciscan Missionary Home in Phoenix, requested permission to provide additional on-campus religious instruction to Catholic pupils. School authorities had traditionally sent the hundred or so Catholic children to church in Phoenix on an alternating basis, boys one week and girls the next. As soon as services ended, the students were returned to school. This limited exposure to Catholicism was not sufficient to please Vogt, who noted that children were not permitted to worship regularly and were unable to obtain the instruction necessary to help with the mass.[18]

After several unsuccessful attempts to get a commitment from Goodman, Vogt wrote directly to the Indian Office. He backed his request with a letter to William H. Ketcham, director of the Bureau of Catholic Missions in Washington, asking that Ketcham remind the Indian Office that similar privileges had been granted priests at Carlisle, Haskell, and other government schools. When the Indian Office queried Goodman about the matter, he responded that he desired to make all religious services at the school nonsectarian, but, if necessary, Catholic students would be granted an hour on Sunday afternoons. Goodman believed that this concession favored the Catholics because other denominations were not permitted the same privilege. The acting commissioner told him to cooperate anyway. Six months later, when several Protestant churches asked to conduct evening Bible classes on campus, the headmaster cooperated fully.[19]

While Goodman was occupied with problems of religion and student employment, educational policy on the national level shifted again in 1905, when Francis E. Leupp replaced William Jones in the commissioner's office. Leupp would act to move Indian education even further away from the nonreservation schools, and in a sense he represented a full swing away from the humanitarian reformers. During his four-year tenure a number of subtle policy changes were instituted which affected the future of Indian education.

The new commissioner was one of the best-prepared men to head the Indian service. For the previous decade he had been deeply involved with Indian affairs, serving as a member of the Board of Indian Commissioners and as a representative of the Indian Rights Association. His involvement with issues of reform in Indian affairs had produced a hearty disagreement with the educational philosophy espoused by conservatives like Captain Pratt. By the time he assumed leadership of the Indian Office, Leupp was convinced that Indians could not easily fit into American society. He believed that significant differences existed between the races and that educational policy must take this into account. As a consequence, his school program reflected a bias that regarded Indians as unlikely candidates for immediate assimilation.[20]

This outlook affected the Indian schools in several ways. Building on a viewpoint that had already manifested itself among school superintendents, Leupp wanted to place additional emphasis on vocational training. Under the presumption that Indians would remain in remote frontier locations and either become farmers or work in "the general labor market as lumbermen, ditchers, miners, railroad hands or what not," academic education seemed useless. Only a few fundamentals were deemed necessary. "Now," he sarcastically remarked in 1905, "if anyone can show me what advantage will come to this large body of manual workers from being able to read off the names of the mountains of Asia, or extract the cube root of 123456789, I shall be deeply grateful." The Indian schools consequently were pressured to intensify their vocational programs. In a corollary move, Leupp made an effort to bring more Indians, including students, into the national workforce.[21]

Even more significant from the standpoint of the Phoenix school was the commissioner's determination to place more emphasis on day schools. He accepted the necessity of continuing all types of schools for the present, but even more than Jones he hoped that boarding schools, including the nonreservation instititutons, could ultimately be phased out. In contrast to day schools, which he called "the outposts of Indian civilization," Leupp maintained that boarding facilities did not meet modern Indian needs and were unlikely to produce significant results. He called boarding schools an "anomaly in our American scheme of popular institutions" and "educational almshouses." In his opinion, civilization should be carried to the Indians rather than the reverse; distant schools produced an unhealthy situation by separating child from parent, and youngsters in such institutions failed to appreciate the value of work.[22]

Leupp was not alone in holding these sentiments. His ideas on Indian education echoed those of an increasing number of public figures who wanted to abolish some of the inhumane practices of the Indian service. Western publisher Charles F. Lummis, for example, had taken up a crusade against the boarding schools in general and Carlisle in particular. His articles, published in *Land of Sunshine* and *Out West*, favored an education that kept Indian children at home and trained for a "practical occupation instead of trying to force them into an unworkable version of a white man." Lummis objected to the assimilationist approach to Indian education championed by the likes of Captain Pratt and implied that such human relics of an earlier age were "professional" fools.[23] The same general sentiment was expressed by the former superintendent of Indian schools William N. Hailmann. Writing in 1904, Hailmann remarked that among the shortcomings of the current educational program was "the unintelligent warfare waged against the Indian idiom; the introduction of certain brutalities of military discipline. . . . ; an equally unintelligent effort on the part of some schools to wean Indian association by stimulating a feeling akin to hatred of Indian family ties."[24] Considering the strength of such sentiment, in and out of government, it was no coincidence that Pratt was forced to retire from Carlisle in 1904. His departure, along with Leupp's appointment, marked a changing of the guard.

Francis Leupp brought several other modifications to federal school policy. One of his favorite ideas was to encourage Indian children to enter public schools. By the turn of the century many authorities, including Commissioner Jones, had come to believe that the ultimate goal of federal policy should be the elimination of Indian schools. Leupp adopted this concept because it promised to reduce the cost of Indian administration. He hoped that arrangements could be worked out whereby public schools would eventually assume the responsibility for Indian education, and he began working toward that end.[25] In another important matter, Leupp became the first commissioner to tackle the problem of improving Indian health. By 1907 he had become convinced that diseases such as tuberculosis were a great threat to the Indians' survival. Although much of his attention focused on the reservations, he began a program aimed at improving sanitary conditions at the schools and providing health services to deal with what had become an alarming condition.[26]

Some of the new ideas quickly showed up in Phoenix, but they did not all have much of an impact. During this period there were no serious attempts to close the school or alter its basic assimilationist curriculum. The changes that were introduced were more subtle and usually complimented existing conditions. In several cases, the proposed changes simply did not work when put to a practical test.

For example, one of the commissioner's first concerns was that no child be forced to leave home against a parent's will. Noting that he disliked forced attendance, Leupp reminded all superintendents that regulations requiring parental consent to enroll children in nonreservation schools would be strictly enforced. When complaints from parents and pupils continued, an even stronger reminder came forth. Addditionally, he attempted to end the recruiting wars that plagued the school system. Leupp commanded that "there must be no 'pulling and hauling' of either parents or children to get them to patronize any particular school." He vigorously sought to stop the practice of bribing or pressuring parents to obtain their consent and tried to give them more control over the education of their youngsters. As a result of his concern (and continuing recruiting violations), an order was issued in June 1908 which abolished the assignment of a recruiting territory to each nonreservation school. Off-reservation facilities were instructed to stop sending out recruiting agents. In the future institutions would be restricted to writing reservation officials about the merits of their school and sending out advertising brochures. These changes in recruiting practices had little immediate effect on Phoenix, which continued to attract maximum enrollment.[27]

The plan to enroll students in public schools was raised in an unusual way. For some time the headmaster's office at Phoenix had been entrusted with the supervision of several hundred Indians living outside Phoenix. Most of these people were Apaches and Yavapis living in the Verde valley on the north or at the Camp McDowell Reservation east of Phoenix. As soon as Leupp settled into office he attempted to have Superintendent Goodman place the children of these people in public schools. When Goodman investigated the situation, he concluded that public schools were impractical. He noted that no white children resided at McDowell to support a public school and the Verde valley communities exhibited a strong prejudice against enrolling Indian children in their schools, especially since the Indians were poor and paid no taxes. Goodman thus recommended that the commissioner's policy be discarded and that the government day school at McDowell be retained and a new one be opened at Camp Verde. He went one step further, in fact, suggesting that he had no business supervising these Indians. If the Indian service wanted to be effective, it should appoint a superintendent for the McDowell reservation instead of trying to save a few cents.[28]

Goodman was a bit more successful in getting Phoenix schools to admit Indian pupils. A few outing students had attended public institutions in the past, and this trend was encouraged whenever possible. The main difficulty was that no Indian families resided in town. To remedy this situation, former pupils were encouraged to establish homes and seek jobs locally. It required some time before that effort produced any visible results. By 1910, however, the school reported that ten young married couples, mostly former students, were maintaining households in the city. The presence of these families caused the public schools to open their doors to the Indian children. Four were enrolled at Phoenix Union High School, and four more were in local grammar schools. Although these figures were too small to have an impact on the enrollment at the Indian school, they did mark the beginning of a trend. Phoenicians seemed to accept these youngsters and did not demand segregation. "They are now welcomed into these schools in small numbers," noted one official, "and keep up in their grades and are respected and kindly treated by their white associates." Accordingly, those children eligible to attend public schools were encouraged to do so, although the numbers were never very large.[29]

Leupp's interest in vocational training had little impact at institutions like Phoenix. These schools, after all, had been stressing a work program for years, and short of completely abolishing the academic curriculum, little more could be done. Changes, therefore, were largely cosmetic and directed at attaining greater public visibility. For example, in December 1905, Estelle Reel sent letters to schoolmasters requesting that commencement exercises place more emphasis on vocational skills. It was suggested that a graduating student perform "a piece of mechanical work in the presence of the audience" and that commencement essays devote themselves to the skills pupils were learning, the demand for those trades back home, or how they expected to profit from their training. Reel closed her letter by reminding superintendents of the obvious fact that "the Office deems it essential to the best interests of the Indian School Service that the annual commencement exercises shall be of a practical rather than a mere rhetorical character." Several months later the Indian Office issued a circular that confirmed the commitment to a more visible work-related program. In essence, this document required all schools to ensure that academic work "be of a useful character." Only the most basic courses should be taught. The Indian child needed to "learn to find employment for himself, to be an independent worker and to know that success or failure in life lies within himself alone." No more coddling would be permitted. In words that echoed Leupp's belief that Indian students were being spoiled, the directive proclaimed that the day was rapidly approaching when the United States would no longer provide for the Indians' welfare, and they had better learn to make it in the real world.[30]

The most significant effect of Leupp's commitment to vocational training was the resurrection of the outing system. Of all the old educational programs, the commissioner considered this one most worthy of preservation. Indeed, the greatest compliment he ever paid to Pratt involved the outings, which, he said, "brought the young Indian into contact with the big white world outside of the walls of a seminary of learning." Leupp supported the system precisely because it forced the student to enter "the real world." His enthusiasm for the outings was motivated in part by the desire to get away from what he called the artificial environment of the boarding schools. Getting students into the workplace seemed eminently more desirable. He told an education panel in 1907 that he hoped all nonreservation schools could develop such a program "instead of shutting them up in a hot house and trying to train them artificially by furnishing them with special implements and teachers and everything else." He even praised the outings as the "best feature of our schools."[31]

Superintendent Goodman was eager to reactivate the Phoenix system. In the years following 1902, while the system was virtually shut down, community demands created considerable pressure to revive the program. Although federal administrators were still sensitive to charges of abuse and lack of supervision, they loosened restrictions soon after Leupp entered office. Boys were once more encouraged to work in town on weekends and a few selected girls were allowed to work for Phoenix families. By early 1907 about a dozen girls were employed by the month.[32] Although these figures were small compared with the size of the program before 1902, the outing student once more became a part of the Phoenix scene.

The system returned to normal in the decade between 1905 and 1915. The number of students sent out rose yearly; in 1908, 32 pupils were working away from the school, by 1911, 87 girls were employed as domestics, and in 1914 the figure increased to 169. During this period the demand for Indian students continually outstripped the supply.³³ Much of the increase in employment could be attributed to Amanda Chingren, who was hired as outing/field matron in 1906. Chingren, a social worker from Illinois who had been with the Indian service since 1903, served as teacher and matron. Zealous in her commitment to supervise the outing program and safeguard the moral welfare of her wards, the middle-aged matron worked long and hard to see that the system operated properly. During an ordinary month she wrote letters to prospective employers, visited homes where girls worked, and offered advice and counsel to her students. On Saturdays she patrolled the streets, mingling with the large number of reservation Indians and school pupils who congregated on city sidewalks. She believed it important to become "aware of friendships and affiliations that help me to understand and be able to advise in their affairs." In addition, "the telephone work done is beyond computation, all sorts of matters for and with them being arranged through that medium daily." Chingren enthusiastically supported vocational education and encouraged her girls to make a living as domestic servants rather than "going back to the blanket."³⁴ The crusty matron became a fixture at Phoenix, dominating the lives of her girls.

Despite the commissioner's active support of the outing system and vocational education, his greatest impact on the Phoenix school was clearly in the area of health care. Government worry about the spread of communicable diseases and the poor state of Indian health generally affected the institution and led to the opening of the East Farm Sanatorium. Although Leupp was slow to comprehend the magnitude of the problem, concern for health-related issues received a considerable boost during his administration. In 1905, for example, a circular went to superintendents emphasizing that more attention should be paid to the "hygienic condition" of buildings and grounds. In particular, the government instructed schoolmasters to avoid enrolling unhealthy children, even if it meant accepting fewer students. Reminding them that "Indian children should be *educated,* not *destroyed* in the process," school superintendents were "positively forbidden to receive pupils without the proper medical certificate as to physical soundness." Much of the concern centered on tuberculosis. School physicians were warned to handle carefully any case that developed and to return afflicted pupils to their homes before the disease could spread. Administrators, moreover, were admonished not to overcrowd their facilities. Violation of rules could result in dismissal.[35]

Phoenix managed to avoid a major epidemic in the years following 1900, but health conditions still were far from good and many small outbreaks occurred. In the spring of 1907 measles broke out at the school, and almost half the students were stricken before the disease could be checked. No reliable figures are available on the number of deaths, but a number of students were hospitalized in critical condition. In the following years students were stricken by outbreaks of infantile paralysis, smallpox, and spinal meningitis. These diseases, however, tended to run their course and disappear. The illnesses that really worried school officials were tuberculosis and trachoma. In November 1907, for example, twenty eight Papago children were brought to the school, all in good health. Seven months later five of these children had been sent home because they were seriously ill with tuberculosis. Two of the returned pupils eventually died, and two more probably did not survive.[36] Such incidents were not uncommon; deadly disease was being spread at the school.

Outbreaks of tuberculosis were so serious and widespread that the Indian Office joined with the Smithsonian Institution in 1908 to investigate the problem. During the summer of that year Dr. Aleš Hrdlička visited the Phoenix Indian School as part of a western tour. He found several disturbing conditions. Of particular concern was the fact that the school was surrounded by private lands being used as tuberculosis camps. Because of its dry climate, Phoenix had become a haven for health seekers, especially those afflicted with respiratory ills. Many of these invalids flocked to squalid tent colonies, some of which were adjacent to the school. "In fact," Hrdlička remarked, "the district in which the school is situated is, as a whole, a Mecca for consumptives, particularly in winter, when the number of sick patients in the valley reaches into the thousands." The school itself had a number of sanitation problems. One of the worst involved the swimming tank, which had its water changed weekly. Custom provided that employees use the tank to bathe in on the day it was filled; the girls used it the next day, and the boys swam in it the remainder of the week. The water quite naturally became polluted and easily spread disease. Hrdlička's report was highly critical of such conditions, remarking that much could be done to prevent the spread of disease.[37]

The tuberculosis survey of 1908 spurred Leupp into action. Acknowledging that "in general the tuberculosis scourge is the greatest single menace to the future of the red race," he committed the Indian Office to "doing more than had ever been done before in the way of protecting the Indians against the ravages of this disease." Leupp believed that the off-reservation schools were a major source of trouble. In the 1908 annual report, he castigated such schools for their unsanitary habits, noting that strict routine, crowded quarters, overheated buildings, and close confinement "furnish ideal conditions for the development of germ disease among the race put through the forcing process there." Admitting it would be impractical to close the nonreservation schools, the commissioner nevertheless insisted that much could be done to provide sanitary conditions. In addition, to treat victims of the disease, he promised to open a series of "sanitarium camps where the inmates can fairly live in the open air, be constantly under the eye of the physician, have their diet, clothing, etc., carefully regulated, and be subject to the most stringent regulations as to those matters which make for cleanliness of the person and surroundings and affect the spread of infection."[38]

Most of Leupp's program was implemented at Phoenix. Indeed, the school became something of a test site for the improvement of Indian health. One of the first concerns was to correct sanitation problems. The use of swimming pools and tubs was ended and "shower baths" substituted. All lavatories were provided with running water, individual towels were issued to each student, hospital laundry was separated from the general wash, and a large sterilizer was installed to disinfect hospital linen. In addition, attention was given to such things as the careless use of musical instruments and the proper method of disinfecting mouthpieces. At one point, the school band was even prohibited from using wind instruments until hygienic precautions could be taken. As soon as practical, the school entered into negotiations with the city to have the municipal sewer system extended to the campus so that septic tanks might be eliminated. Although this project took some time to complete, by 1915 a major source of trouble had been removed.[39]

Even more significant, a special eye clinic was opened on the Phoenix campus. This was made possible by a congressional appropriation of $12,000 to fight trachoma, a highly contagious eye disease afflicting many Indians. Noted oculist Ancil Martin was hired in June 1909 to run the clinic, survey the extent of the infection, and treat patients. Dr. Martin examined the entire school population, finding evidence that 75 percent of the schoolchildren had some form of trachoma. Many cases were severe enough to require operations or other radical treatment. At the same time, the eye hospital was opened to reservation Indians willing to come in for treatment. During its first year of operation, the clinic treated more than a hundred reservation patients, keeping most of them for as long as a month. Dr. Martin reported considerable success in his endeavors. Many Indians suffering from the disease had their vision improved and were able to get relief from pain. Some seven hundred cases were treated during the first year, and the results were so encouraging that Martin was retained for another year. In 1912 the problem had eased enough that the workload could be transferred to the regular school physician. By that time the incidence of trachoma among schoolchildren had been significantly reduced. All students received a quarterly examination, and new arrivals found to be diseased were operated on immediately. Adults from the reservation continued to come in for treatment, keeping the eye clinic busy.[40]

Another major step involved opening the East Farm Sanatorium. Although Leupp initially suggested the idea of using the school farm (purchased by Goodman in 1902) as an Indian health center and the first patients were placed there during his last days in office, the sanatorium was developed by Leupp's close associate and successor Robert G. Valentine, who became commissioner on June 19, 1909. Valentine was vitally concerned with health matters. With the incidence of tuberculosis increasing, it seemed logical to find some location away from the main campus where ill pupils could be cared for. For this reason, in May 1909, three girls were sent to East Farm to be housed in small tent houses. These patients were cared for by a matron. This program seemed to work so well that in early 1910, without any special financial aid, a tuberculosis camp was established, more tent houses constructed, and a kitchen and dining room opened. In all, thirty-nine patients were admitted that year, with much noticeable improvement. The camp format was favored over hospital buildings because children did not seem to do well when confined. Superintendent Goodman listed the advantages of the camp in terms of providing early diagnosis, relief from heavy work, life in the open air, a dry climate, and segregation from healthy pupils. Seriously ill pupils were not admitted, but plans quickly developed to increase the camp's capacity to fifty and make it permanent.[41]

From this simple beginning, the East Farm Sanatorium grew rapidly. In 1911, when a total of eighty-four tuberculosis patients were treated, a large two-story girls' building, furnished with modern facilities and "upstairs two large open air screened sleeping rooms," was completed. Male patients were assigned to "neat and attractive tent houses." About the same time, an open-air school was established, enabling confined students to keep up with their studies. More improvements came the following year. Because of the increasing administrative burden, the school physician, who had been in charge of the facility,

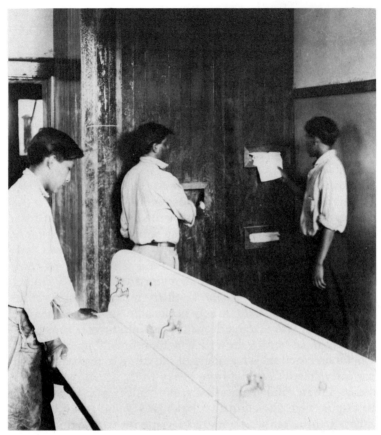

Washroom at Phoenix Indian School, 1914. This publicity photo shows boys using running water and individual towels as a way of preventing the spread of disease. During the period around World War I the school was under heavy pressure to eliminate such diseases as tuberculosis. Improved sanitation promised significant benefits. Courtesy of Smithsonian Institution.

was replaced by a doctor specifically assigned to operate the sanatorium. With a continuing influx of patients, more cottages and bungalows were added, the dining room enlarged, and modern kitchen and fire prevention equipment installed. As facilities improved, the hospital began to admit patients from distant reservations and other Indian schools. In the succeeding years, adult Indians made up an increasing percentage of the sanatorium's case load.[42]

The improved quality of care and expanded facilities did not eliminate tuberculosis. As late as 1913, 5 percent of the school's students contracted the disease and were placed in the sanatorium. Depending on the severity of their condition, students were kept at East Farm for periods ranging from six to eighteen months. Most pupils were treated successfully, primarily because the disease had not reached advanced stages, and were either returned to school or sent home. Those who came from other schools or from a reservation environment tended to have more advanced symptoms and were treated less successfully. The physician complained that many such patients refused to submit to an extended stay at the hospital and drifted away without notice. As a result, the mortality rate was fairly high; of nearly three hundred patients treated between 1909 and 1915, thirty-nine (mostly adults) died. Demands placed on the sanatorium were so heavy that as many as seventy-three patients were confined at one time in 1914, and the institution had to be enlarged to one hundred beds.[43]

By 1915 the Indian service had opened three other tuberculosis sanatoriums (Fort Lapwai, Sac and Fox, and Laguna). Because of its location and general reputation, however, the Phoenix sanatorium was besieged with applications for admission. In many instances, persons suffering from severe cases asked to be admitted, often as a last resort. Letters from across the country poured into Goodman's office. In one typical case, an eighteen-year-old returned student from Carlisle offered to enroll herself at the school if her little sister might be permitted to come to the sanatorium: "This is the third year she has had tuberculosis of the lungs. We would like to know if you will

The East Farm Sanatorium, circa 1918. In 1909 the campaign to eliminate tuberculosis prompted the Phoenix School to open the East Farm Sanatorium. The facility eventually became a major tuberculosis hospital, available to reservation residents as well as school students. The sanatorium featured large, spacious rooms and bungalows with sleeping porches, in addition to medical and dining facilities. Courtesy of Smithsonian Institution.

take her at the Sanatarium or not?" Many similar requests were made. Though sympathetic, the schoolmaster was forced to turn away most of the prospective patients. He preferred to admit those cases reasonably sure to recover. Even then, there was not enough room for all who wanted help.[44] By the time

Goodman retired in 1915 the East Farm Sanatorium had become a well-established unit, functioning more and more as a separate health-care facility. Overall administration remained under the school superintendent, and a good portion of the patients continued to come from the school, but the independence of the sanatorium became more apparent with each passing year.

Aside from major concerns like health care, the years between 1907 and 1915 were routine. Only a few matters attracted more than passing notice. One involved a trend toward loosening restrictions regarding cultural and religious activities. Coinciding with the new concern for parental input, the Indian Office reviewed the whole question of religious instruction in 1907. Schoolmasters reported on the religious activities of their students, discussing in particular whether they were permitted to attend the church of their choice and what penalties were imposed on those who refused to attend Christian services. This survey and subsequent directives were apparently intended to ensure that students and their families were permitted more latitude in making such personal decisions as what denomination they preferred. In a similar vein, Leupp issued an order permitting students to incorporate some of their native traditions into classroom activities. Although none of this was viewed as inhibiting the assimilation goals of education, the commissioner saw no reason why Indian music, arts, and crafts could not be made a part of the educational process. He even made concessions on the language restrictions, remarking that "I do not consider that their little songs in their native tongue does anybody any harm, and it helps to make easier the perilous and difficult bridge which they are crossing at this stage of their race development." As a consequence, the classroom setting was made more familiar for children as they were permitted to make some reference to their cultural heritage. The impact of this decision was soon evidenced at Phoenix, where pupils began winning recognition for their skills at the state fair. Indeed, school students were so successful in winning prizes for basketry, pottery, and silverwork that it became a matter of school pride.⁴⁵

Although Superintendent Goodman appreciated these achievements, he was more concerned with filling his school. After the practice of recruiting students was abolished, it became increasingly difficult to enroll "healthy, bright, and somewhat advanced pupils from the reservation schools." The headmaster felt his heavy investment in teachers and equipment was not being used to maximum advantage, especially now that the Indian service seemed to favor reservation schools. Believing that his institution offered the best kind of education, he worried that the quality of students might be downgraded. In particular, he was fearful that good students might be retained on the reservation and only the problem child sent off reservation. As early as 1910 he expressed concern that "those who are a burden to their people and properly subjects for asylums, hospitals, or reform schools" would be sent in his direction.⁴⁶

Such fears were not entirely unfounded, but the general performance of pupils improved somewhat during Goodman's administration. Almost unnoticed among the press of other business was a renewed emphasis on academics. Although this trend had no official backing, the school staff after 1910 began to exert more effort to get students through the eighth-grade curriculum. Part of the motivation may have been to demonstrate that the school was on a par with public schools and that Indian education was not inferior. It also made the school look good when graduates could successfully transfer to local high schools (as they did occasionally after 1911). The act of graduating also gained more prestige. The number of graduates varied from year to year, but on the average fifteen students completed their academic training annually. Although more pupils regularly finished the domestic science program and were awarded certificates of achievement, they clearly took a back seat to graduates. Slowly but surely academic accomplishment began to receive recognition.⁴⁷

Most students, of course, neither graduated nor completed the domestic science program. At the end of the required term they returned home or sought work locally. Still, this was not considered a failure. Indeed, the school began to report success in accomplishing its goals. Starting in 1905, the campus hosted an annual gathering of returned and graduated students. Through this well-publicized meeting, and the school's formal tracking of former students, it became more and more obvious that the number of educated Indians was increasing. Even more had found jobs and were raising families in an urban environment or were emerging as reservation leaders.[48]

By the time he retired in 1915, Charles Goodman could boast that a total of 175 pupils had graduated from the Phoenix Indian School, almost all of them under his stewardship.[49] Although this figure represented less than 5 percent of the children who had attended the school since it opened in 1891, it signified that some progress had been made toward educating the Indian population of Arizona. However, this "progress" came from the administrative perspective. It is now appropriate to consider the students and their reaction to this educational situation.

6

Student Life

"BE A PHOENIX STUDENT not a reservation bum" was a well-known student slogan symbolizing the committment to assimilation. Indian children, of course, were expected to benefit from their education, and an analysis of the school's success or failure must include the student perspective. The day-to-day life of the pupils—their expectations, trials, tribulations, and personal concerns—were all part of the educational adventure. For Indian youngsters the long years away from home could be either pleasant or emotionally disturbing. For some it was a meaningless waste of time; others regarded it as one of the most important and rewarding periods of their lives. Certain aspects of school life were similar to those found in most public schools. In other ways the institutional confinement bore no relation to white schooling. In general the student experience proved to be more positive than it is usually given credit for. Despite this qualification, school years were filled with uncertainty, stress, and occasional bitterness.

Any survey of former students must proceed with caution, primarily because little or no information exists about the majority of them. Their names were recorded, but feelings, ambitions, fears, and resentments have largely fallen into historical obscurity. Despite this, it is possible to obtain a glimpse of student life. After the turn of the century, general information on the pupils became more plentiful. The school paper and yearbooks reported on social and academic activities, the institution began to keep track of its former students, and a number of students eventually memorialized their experiences in print. In addition, some of the youngsters who were at Phoenix Indian School between 1900 and 1930 have been willing to share their experiences through oral interviews. It should be kept in mind, however, that while these and other sources provide information on campus life, the records are far from complete. Moreover, those who left their reminiscences tended to have a positive educational experience, and the material derived from school sources seldom included unfavorable comments. Extracting the feelings of those who had a negative reaction is therefore more difficult.

The students' initial reactions to the school varied considerably, ranging from a trying emotional crisis to a curious excursion into the "white man's world." For most Indian children, the trip to Phoenix did not represent the first encounter with the government's educational program. By and large, they had previously attended a reservation day or boarding school (although a few continued to be enrolled without prior schooling until the 1920s). Pupils from the Papago reservation, for example, had ordinarily been trained at a government day school or the Catholic boarding school at Saint John's. Hopi children had attended day schools near their villages and perhaps the Keams Canyon boarding school, while most Pimas went to Sacaton before advancing. As a consequence, a majority of the new students had passed their tenth birthday, and many were well into their teens. Despite this physical maturity, they were not by any definition acculturated or prepared for the indoctrination into white society they were about to receive.[1]

Some came willingly, others did not. Parents or guardians generally made the decision to transfer their children off reservation, although pressure from federal officials could be so intense that it was not really a matter of choice. Older children wishing to enroll without parental consent could obtain special admission for three years. In the long run, many factors entered into a commitment to off-reservation education. Although in most instances the initiative came from an agent or superintendent, some parents felt that conditions on the reservation were not promising and believed their children stood a better chance of earning a living if they were enrolled in an industrial school. Occasionally youngsters were packed off to school because parents could not provide support, knowing they would be taken care of by the government. A 1917 comment of Superintendent John Brown that "we have today an Indian father who has brought a motherless girl of nine years from a community where she has worse than no protection, and whom he wishes to enroll here until she has reached her majority" was not unique. Parents also chose Phoenix because they feared educational decisions ultimately might be taken out of their hands, leaving their children to be sent to some remote location like Haskell or Carlisle. Phoenix seemed preferable under such circumstances. In a few exceptional cases, the children themselves felt a need to reach beyond what could be provided at reservation schools.[2]

The trip to Phoenix was often frightening. Few children had been separated from home and family for any length of time. Among the Hopi, where there was considerable opposition to the transfers, heartbreaking departures were common. Because they might run away if they knew what was in store for them, children were not told of the move in advance. Tony Youhongva (Dukepoo)* remembered that his mother packed him a lunch one September morning and sent him off to Polacca Day School. When he arrived, the superintendent told him he was to go to Phoenix. Along with several other youngsters, he was loaded into the back of a Dodge truck equipped with a wire cage and driven to Winslow to catch the train. The children were frightened by their first contact with the white world, clinging to comrades for dear life and afraid they might never see home again. To ease fears, the school occasionally enlisted the aid of prominent tribal leaders to act as escorts. This seemed to work fairly well with the Navajo, giving the govern-

* Students often attended school under different names than they now use. In cases of oral interviews, I have used their school name with the modern name in parenthesis when first referenced.

ment an opportunity to calm pupils as well as to impress influential tribesmen with the "palatial splendor" of the campus.[3]

The first few days at school provided an experience seldom forgotten. Upon arrival, whether by train, bus, or wagon, children were met by a matron and perhaps an older student from their own tribe. Despite efforts to ease the transition, the strange surroundings and unfamiliar mix of people produced a feeling of gloom and homesickness. "I got up there in that strange dorm, with a whole bunch of tribes and everything," recalled a Papago girl of her first night, "and I laid down and, boy, the tears came out. It seemed like every time I waked up my tears would come—all night long." Others experienced similar reactions during their first days at school. For those like the Hopi who came from cooler climates, the Phoenix heat was even more uncomfortable.[4]

One of the most difficult adjustments involved what one historian has termed "de-Indianization." The school, of course, operated on the assumption that Indian children needed strict discipline. The introduction of military-style routine—"the forming of regular habit, that mother of self-control, which distinguishes civilization from savagery"—therefore came immediately. Permitted to retain their traditional clothing only long enough to have a photograph taken (which might later be used to contrast with their "civilized" look), new pupils were issued a uniform, school clothes, and work outfits, and were assigned a dormitory. Almost as rapidly, they were separated from friends and fellow tribesmen to make it more difficult to speak their native tongue. Indeed, the first thing new arrivals learned was to avoid using their own language, although, admitted one, "sometimes we forget and talk Pima."[5]

Organizing boys and girls into military companies was the most visible feature of the indoctrination program. Children found it difficult to understand the logic of getting up at five o'clock in the morning, marching everywhere they went, and following the orders of student officers. Anna Moore noted the demanding adjustment, remarking that "when we went to the bean hall, or dining room, we marched to a military tune. . . .

The school drill corps reflected the military emphasis so common at government Indian schools. These young men wore uniforms, learned military drill routines, and followed a strict regimen. Although the drill corps was trained to perform for the public, all students were expected to follow the same general regimentation. Discipline was one sign of "civilized" behavior. Courtesy of Arizona Historical Foundation.

At first the marching seemed so hard to learn, but once we mastered the knack, we couldn't break the habit." In fact, once accustomed to the routine, students took great pride in their marching skill. Being elected a student officer or becoming a member of the band or drill team was a matter of considerable importance. A company of boys drilled with the Arizona National Guard and eventually were attached to the 158th Infantry. Calling themselves "Bush-misters," this company, trained by a former military officer, formed an elite campus group.

STUDENT LIFE 117

During training sessions and military ceremonies they took special satisfaction in outperforming non-Indian detachments.[6]

The militaristic atmosphere extended far beyond uniforms and drills. Everything operated on a schedule, and the campus resembled an army boot camp. In contrast to the leisurely pace of reservation life, children were required to study, clean their rooms, sleep, and eat at specific times. Sundays were devoted to discipline. All pupils (described by the school paper as "former denizens of some 'Land of Poco Tiempo'") had to stand inspection at 7:30 A.M. Once lined up on the parade ground, companies were reviewed by school dignitaries. Young men dressed in army uniforms, while the women were "uniformed

Women students also wore uniforms and participated in military parades. These young women are student officers, who were responsible for enforcing rules and assuring conformity to regulations. Courtesy of Arizona Historical Foundation.

in white shirt waists and blue jumpers, well tailored suits, but unmistakenly feminine." Hopi schoolgirl Helen Dowawisnima (Sekaquaptewa) described Sunday inspection: "The boys gave a military salute as the officers passed, and the girls held out their hands to be inspected. The officers noted every detail and would say, 'Your shoe string is not tied right,' 'Your hands are dirty,' or 'Your shoes do not shine.' " Inspection was followed by church services and an afternoon dress parade. The evening meal followed prescribed routine. Students marched into the dining hall, waited in complete silence until grace was said, ate in twenty minutes, and marched out to musical accompaniment.[7]

Pupils did their own housekeeping. They cleaned their sleeping space and served on squads responsible for sweeping, mopping, and oiling dormitory floors. After health became a concern, considerable emphasis was placed on cleanliness and sanitation. Frequent inspections and constant reminders to keep the school clean went hand in hand with domestic chores. In addition, students were assigned to work details. Groups of youngsters worked in the kitchen preparing daily meals, in the sewing room mending clothes, and in the wash room doing the laundry. The older girls made "nearly all the articles of wearing apparel used by the 325 girls, also some of the garments that find their way into the boys' home." Papago schoolboy Theodore Rios remembered his chores in the following terms: "If you're in poultry, you got to work with chickens. And there's always a boss looking after you, taking care. And you got to gather the eggs. They use the eggs. You got to gather 'em and they take 'em to where they cook 'em." These assignments, of course, saved the school money and were justified on the grounds that they kept pupils alert and their hands, if not minds, occupied. Schoolchildren had little choice of assignments and frequently disliked work details.[8]

Punishment played a big part in the routine. Students were chastised for infractions of the rules, not doing their work properly, or running away. Corporal punishment was meted out, though not excessively. Penalties more often consisted of a stay in the guardhouse, several days on bread and water, and various forms of ridicule. Treatment of this sort was alien to most Indian children. Anna Moore remembered that "we did not understand this punishment at the time; we just assumed that [the matron] was mean like a witch." The rigorous routine and harsh punishment could be baffling. "I worked in the dining room, washing dishes and scrubbing floors," Moore continued. "My little helpers and I hadn't even reached our teen-aged years yet and this work seemed so hard! If we were not finished when the 8:00 a.m. whistle sounded, the dining room matron would go around strapping us while we were still on our hands and knees.... We just dreaded the sore bottoms." Students whose chores were not completed by the weekend would have to scrub or wash while classmates enjoyed a Saturday picnic or trip to town.[9]

In spite of the hardship and frustration, most students made the best of their situation. A camaraderie developed in the face of shared experience. Although not representing the attitude of every student, a surprising number remembered their ordeal in a positive way. One girl explained that "we were one big happy family." Another said, "The school was just like home.... Once you got there, you're just in the whole family. Everybody knows you and they miss you and it's just like coming home." Indeed, some found relief from the pressure by joking about the discipline and mimicking the matron. One particularly stern matron was given the name of a legendary Pima witch, bringing on a round of giggles whenever the girls would imitate her. As usual among schoolchildren everywhere, the boys had a good laugh whenever they saw girls receive a strapping.[10] But not everyone could make light of their situation, and some never adapted.

Most pupils took their classroom work in stride. Having already attended school, they found the academic routine relatively familiar. By 1916 the curriculum, officially at least, paralleled the public schools except for special emphasis on learning English. Lack of proficiency in an alien language slowed some students, but statistics showed that 80 percent advanced in grade each year. This regularity permitted the school to all but eliminate the practice of mixing children of all ages in the same class, though in a few instances it proved impossible to prevent such occurrences. The classroom environment was similar to any well-equipped school of the era. Rooms were furnished with desks and blackboards, walls hung with "inspiring pictures," and shelves stocked with books and periodicals. Boys and girls sat next to one another in a classroom setting that placed considerable emphasis on oratory. Students were required to memorize selected classics and compete in recitation. Given the government's expectations, youngsters were probably asked to do more than might reasonably be expected. Fourth-graders were supposed "to read current events and magazines and to pass judgement on what they read with regard to the beauty of thought expressed, its truth, and its rhythm." One official noted with some truth that most adults could not meet the same requirement.[11]

The academic curriculum varied over the years, increasing in variety as time went on. By 1915 advanced students took classes in writing and penmanship, history, geography, mathematics, science, and literature. Teachers used standardized textbooks that made no concession to a pupil's cultural heritage. Indeed, many instructors did their best to ignore or ridicule tribal heritage by emphasizing the achievements of the white race and stressing theories of Anglo-Saxon superiority. A particularly interesting device that perhaps unconsciously supported this attitude was the general use of "educational" motion pictures. Many of the early films were typical of the strong racism prevalent in American society. Nevertheless, some concessions to Indian tradition were tolerated. Female students, for example, were allowed to make traditional baskets and blankets to decorate their reception room.[12] Such activities, however, were not sufficient to make many students feel at home. As a consequence, although most students learned to behave in an approved manner, they never learned to think like whites.

The relationship between student and teacher was one of re-

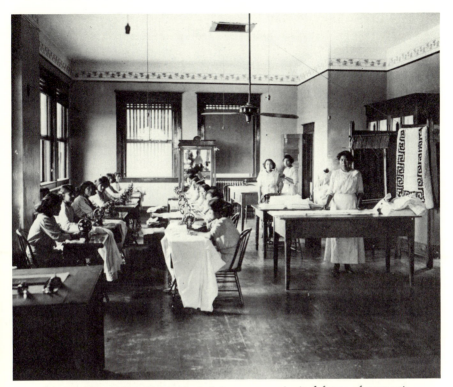

Sewing class, 1914. Domestic training was a principal focus of women's education. These students are learning to be seamstresses in a typical classroom setting. Using sewing machines may have prepared the students to become domestic servants, but they were virtually useless for the reservation life, where no such machines were available. Courtesy of Smithsonian Institution.

spect sprinkled with fear. Former students generally remembered instructors as being very strict. Few apparently formed bonds of friendship with their teachers. This was partly the result of Indian service policy, which frowned on employees getting too close to the pupils (a responsibility assigned, if at all, to matrons and disciplinarians). Instructors who seemed too "soft" were likely to receive poor performance reports, a

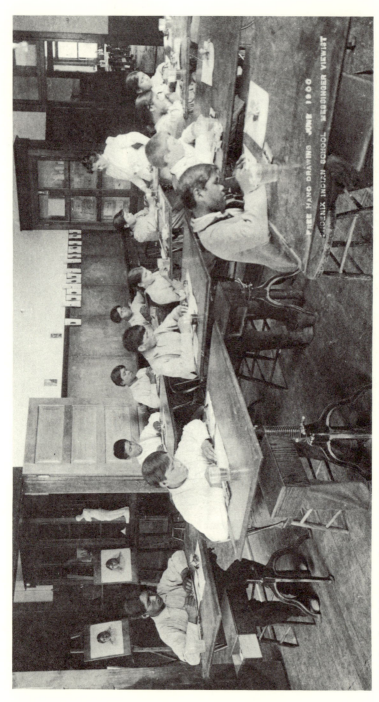

A free-hand drawing class, 1900. This was a typical classroom situation for male and female students, who were expected to acquire some of society's refinements as well as learn to read and write. Courtesy of National Archives.

circumstance that could lead to dismissal or transfer. Thus, as more than one student recalled, there was "real, honest-to-goodness teaching, and no funny business." Another reason few students were close to their teachers involved the natural Indian suspicion of strangers. Youngsters sometimes viewed white instructors as the enemy, were ill at ease in their presence, and were afraid to act natural in the classroom. Perhaps the warmest relationship developed among the students and advisers who took part in literary, musical, religious, and other extracurricular activities. Teachers tended to pay more attention to the more promising pupils.[13]

With such great emphasis on vocational education, it is not surprising that pupils were largely preoccupied with occupational training. Practical learning was the reason they came to Phoenix, a fact continually reiterated by teachers. Work programs operated on the assumption that a youngster would learn a variety of mechanical skills while becoming particularly adept at a specific trade. Once school days were over, Indian boys were expected to be able to return home, reclaim the family allotment, farm it, build houses and sheds, mend harnesses, and repair just about anything. The same skills promised to be useful if they chose to remain in an urban environment. Girls were supposed to emerge from the institution as skilled homemakers or productive domestic workers. Under ordinary circumstances, pupils were shifted from one vocational department to another until they seemed to find a niche. Young men commonly spent time in the carpenter, blacksmith, print, and paint shops, and did some additional work in the bakery, dairy, and garden. Young women generally devoted a term to the kitchen, dining room, hospital, laundry, and sewing room. Students had little choice of assignment. In a few cases, instructors took a liking to a particular child, keeping him or her under their wing. Papago schoolboy Peter Blaine remembered expressing a desire to become a blacksmith, but the principal responded by saying, "Pete, I think we got a better trade for you to learn than blacksmithing. You are too smart to be a blacksmith." As a result, he went to the print shop. Another boy remarked: "If you want a choice you have a choice, but if you're doing what you're supposed to do, well, they keep you at it, or else if you're not smart enough, they might change you."[14]

Native youngsters tended to learn mechanical skills rapidly and were proud of their accomplishments. Tony Youhongva expressed an interest in almost everything requiring manual dexterity, but was especially pleased with the finely crafted cabinets he made in the carpenter shop. Indeed, the boys of the carpenter shop produced a wide variety of items crafted in the tradition of meticulous detail, consistently winning prizes at the state fair. In 1906 a hand-carved desk was presented to Commissioner Luepp, who praised the boys on the quality of their craftsmanship. Not only did such accomplishments generate considerable pride, they created a lifelong commitment to quality workmanship in such pupils as Youhongva. Much the same happened to pupils in other trades. The young men of the print shop, who published the *Native American*, worked extra hours and proved themselves accomplished printers. Because of the dominance of male-oriented programs and the subordinate role women were expected to fill, the same sense of accomplishment failed to develop among girls working in the laundry or sewing rooms, although they too became quite skilled.[15]

Some of the student attitude can be gleaned from home letters. School authorities encouraged frequent communication with relatives on the reservation, although they also censored mail and made every effort to suppress negative comments. Even so, the letters are revealing. "Father," wrote one boy, "I am so thankful to God for the beautiful school I am in and the good chance we are having to learn, for we will sometime go out into the wide world and find something to do which God intended us to do." Another child told his parents, "I am quite proud to say that almost all of my classmates were promoted, including myself. I thank you very much for sending me here. I can still remember that several years ago when I first entered school I was wild and ignorant; but I am glad to say that now I am neither."[16] These comments naturally reflected what school officials wanted students to say and may not represent their true feelings at the time. Yet decades later many former pupils still expressed the same sentiments and would not have materially disagreed with their classmates.

Not every Indian child, of course, had a positive school experience. Despite a lack of accurate statistics and official cover-ups, there appears to have been a significant amount of hostility and resentment. Runaways provided the most obvious sign of discontent. After the turn of the century the school was plagued with a rash of desertions. Schoolmasters, insisting that runaways be caught and returned for punishment, exhibited little sympathy for circumstances, worrying primarily about the impact on discipline. A Phoenix newspaper pointed out that escapes could not be permitted to pass unnoticed: "Not that Indian boys are so scarce as to be particularly valuable to Uncle Sam at this time, but because strict discipline must be observed if the pupils of the school are to be educated and civilization, happiness and prosperity thrust upon them regardless." The headmaster commonly expressed concern that successful escapes would give pupils the idea they could do as they pleased. As a result, considerable sums were spent apprehending recalcitrants. Trusted students, the disciplinarian, reservation police, and civil law enforcement officers all participated. Because of the time, money, and aggravation involved, punishment for running away tended to be severe.[17]

School authorities ignored individual reasons for leaving, branding them "trivial or wholly discreditable to the deserter." In actuality, children left school for a variety of reasons, some more justifiable than others. Most of the runaways were prompted by homesickness. Being lonely, away from home and family, and living in an alien environment was more than some could handle. Runaways were generally Pima and Papago males who lived relatively close to Phoenix, although girls and members of other tribes escaped on occasion. Other reasons for leaving included a desire to find employment, to return home to participate in religious ceremonies, or to help the family during times of crisis. Occasionally a boy and girl deserted together to get married or to carry on a love affair. Then, too, there were chronic runaways. For the most part these youngsters hated school, refused to cooperate, were belligerent, and used every opportunity to flee. A few of the escapees frequented Phoenix gambling halls and houses of prostitution where they could obtain money and liquor. Many more were simply unwilling to remain in school. In 1928 the superintendent remarked of one boy that "I have no hope of keeping him in this or any other school . . . unless he was provided with a personal bodyguard at all hours, day and night." The desire to escape and return home led to some incredible feats. In 1902, for example, a group of Yavapai boys bolted the school and headed for the Verde valley, a hundred miles away. Despite freezing temperatures, rain, snow, and no provisions, they made it home before the school disciplinarian tracked them down.[18]

Returned runaways were subjected to great humiliation. School authorities deliberately created an atmosphere of fear among the students, hoping to prevent recurrences. Unfavorable comments by relatives and students regularly appeared in the school paper, as did letters from former pupils saying, "Don't be thinking about running away." Public disgrace in front of peers provided an even more effective deterrent. The punishment for girls could range from a stint cutting grass with scissors while wearing a sign saying "I ran away" to being prohibited from going to the movies, sports events, or social gatherings. Boys were usually put in jail. Boys who repeatedly ran away had their hair cut off and were forced to wear dresses. Despite such treatment, some never conformed and were eventually transferred to reformatories.[19]

That students were forced to mix with representatives of other tribes occasionally added to the sense of depression and isolation. Tribal animosities did not die easily and manifested themselves in a variety of ways. Students tended to stereotype members of other tribes in ways not always flattering. Some groups were regarded as clannish and unfriendly; others acquired reputations for being too aggressive, even bullies. Certain tribes were reputed to have a number of "bad apples" who ran away or constantly violated the rules. Most of these images appear to have been based on tribal characteristics and stories heard from parents or relatives. As a result, pupils from different tribes did not mix well and remained isolated. In a few instances roommates refused to speak to each other. Generally speaking, an attitude of suspicion persisted that could be overcome only by considerable interaction among a variety of tribal groups. In most instances, students mastered their inherent shyness and eventually accepted youngsters from other tribes as friends. Still, some maintained an unfriendly attitude toward their classmates. This inability to get along with fellow students created emotional problems which added to the general unhappiness and hostility.[20]

School administrators relied heavily on extracurricular social and recreational activities to counter the sense of isolation. As one student remarked, there were so many activities that every spare moment was occupied. Students were encouraged to investigate their interests and use their time wisely. The school band provided one outlet for youthful energy. Band members formed an elite campus group, taking great pride in their musical ability. It required good grades to become a band member and hours of practice to stay with it. A number of bandmasters were employed over the years, all of them demanding. The musical selections played by the boys ranged from Sousa marches and tunes of their own composition to extremely difficult classical works. There were frequent performances, and many of the musicians practiced on their own to improve the music. Eventually many of the band members became accomplished musicians, and a few, like Russell ("Big Chief") Moore, pursued musical careers.[21]

Band members enjoyed considerable status and many fringe benefits. Despite all the hard work, they found plenty of opportunities to show off. Anna Moore recalled how proud she was of her brother Bill, "one of the outstanding members of the marching band," when he performed in front of the entire school and during President Taft's visit in 1909. The bandmaster might arrange to have a boy with ability relieved of his ordinary chores to practice. One of the major benefits associated with the organization was travel. The band regularly took trips to different cities, performed at parades and fairs, and on occasion spent the entire summer on the road. In 1904, for example, the school's forty musicians spent eleven weeks touring California and various western reservations. They became such an attraction that on one occasion, while they were spending a day at Canyon Diablo, Santa Fe Railway officials, "knowing that the novel sight of an Indian band would please the passengers," stopped a transcontinental train while the boys played and "the tourists snapped their kodaks." In 1926 the band made history by broadcasting live over one of Phoenix's first radio stations. The public-relations value of such performances was enormous, and the boys were treated royally. Their activities earned them money, adding to their prestige and sense of accomplishment.[22]

Sports offered a similar outlet. After the turn of the century, athletics became an important part of school life. All healthy students were required to take part in physical training, and those with athletic talents were encouraged to join competitive squads. No one was permitted on a team who did not maintain a good academic record, nor were pupils enrolled solely because of their athletic ability. Physical activities directly related to the emphasis on discipline, with games and schedules organized to "cover most of what would otherwise be spare time." Initially limited to baseball and football, the number of activities increased to such an extent that by 1930 an all-Indian coaching staff was working with teams in such sports as basketball, track and field, swimming, and tennis. There were also several girls' basketball teams. Several championship long-distance runners attended the school during the 1920s.[23]

Some teams were outstanding, generating the kind of spirit commonly associated with athletic victory. The football team regularly engaged teams from Mesa High School, Phoenix Junior College, and Tempe Normal School. The big game each year

Girls' Basketball Team, 1903. After the turn of the century sports played an increasingly important role in Indian education. Not only did the boys engage in competitive football and baseball, but girls were encouraged to become involved in the "genteel" sports of basketball and tennis. Sports represented a commitment to both discipline and physical conditioning. Courtesy of Arizona Historical Foundation.

Chicken yard, 1903. Domestic training went far beyond the classroom. The Phoenix school was able to raise much of its own food supply, thanks to student labor. The campus operated a dairy and a farm as well as this chicken yard. Students assigned to these areas supposedly received educational benefit from their labor. Courtesy of Arizona Historical Foundation.

was with Phoenix Union High School. The night before the game there would be a big bonfire and a pep rally, and if the Indian boys won, "everything went wild. Even the big city went wild." Athletes became campus heroes and were held up as examples to follow. They were encouraged to train hard and lead an exemplary life: "The athlete can best fit himself for manly sports if he leads a clean, wholesome good life." Some of the boys became good enough to receive offers to turn professional. During the early years of the twentieth century several all-Indian baseball teams recruited on campus. Skilled players were promised a long season with good wages and an opportunity to play with the best athletes from Carlisle, Haskell, and Genoa. The pressure on athletes to leave school was strong enough that administrators briefly considered eliminating football and baseball.[24] There was no question, however, that pupils enjoyed sporting activities and became proficient in the nontraditional competitions that were promoted at Phoenix.

Religious and social organizations offered another means of keeping students occupied. Most such activities provided a strong moral element as well. In addition to regular church services, which were held by Baptists, Presbyterians, Mormons, and Catholics, voluntary religious activities proliferated as the program of religious conversion intensified. School officials, most of them religiously inclined, came to realize that long hours of tedious religious teaching encountered "the law of diminishing returns," and began to encourage pupils to join such organizations as the YMCA, YWCA, Salvation Army, and the Catholic Holy Name Society. Sunday evenings were given over to these groups, and participation was usually substantial. Ambitious and aggressive students were especially active in these groups because they provided a vehicle for special recognition. Class presidents and members of the student cabinet were generally associated with the YMCA or YWCA. Although administrators actively supported the societies, students had room to exercise their own initiative—provided, of course, they stayed within prescribed limits. Most activities centered around charitable causes or the discussion of moral issues.

Representatives of religious and fraternal organizations paid visits to the campus, regularly lecturing young scholars on proper behavior. One issue, for example, that received considerable attention was whether social dancing should be permitted. Superintendent John Brown, a highly religious man, opposed the practice, but when students came out in favor of it, he compromised by permitting square dances.[25]

In a similar vein, Indian youngsters were encouraged to participate in groups connected with issues of public interest, with the exception of activist organizations such as the Society of American Indians (a vocal pan-Indian group opposed to Bureau of Indian Affairs policies), which was not welcome on campus. Before 1915, Women's Christian Temperance Union representatives made frequent visits to enlist the support of Indians. Students were told of the fight against "King Alcohol" and encouraged to take a pledge not to drink. They were also asked to attend WCTU conventions and observe "World Temperance Sunday." Just how effective such activities were is debatable, but some Indian youngsters adopted a strong aversion to liquor during their school years.

In the 1920s other activities seem to have replaced the temperance crusade. In particular, a chapter of the American Red Cross was organized, as were troops of Camp Fire Girls and Boy Scouts.[26] Literary and debating clubs were equally popular. Over the years different groups came and went, but they were all pretty much the same. Divided by sex, the literary societies held meetings emphasizing reading, discussion, and debate with the object of cultivating "the correct mode of speaking, and the managing of business meetings." At the end of the year the girls' groups joined with the boys' to present a joint program in honor of graduating comrades.[27] As in any junior or senior high school, social activities were popular, particularly with those maintaining a positive attitude toward their education.

Another event enjoyed by students in good standing was an occasional visit to Phoenix, called a "town day." On selected Saturday afternoons groups of thirty or so students were es-

STUDENT LIFE   133

corted downtown, often taking the streetcar line that ran by the school. There was always plenty to do and plenty of fun. Those with money spent it on ice cream, candy, a movie, or some personal item from a department store; the rest did considerable window shopping. Some wandered a few blocks west of downtown to where the reservation Pimas set up a colorful camp on weekends. Local merchants welcomed the students and treated them well. Korrick's was one of the most popular stores, selling the girls material for their embroidery work and displaying their handicrafts. Boys were occasionally able to earn a dish of ice cream by taking a stint pulling one of the hand-fans in the confectionery parlor. Anna Moore remembers that she and her friends broke into a march step every time they passed a shop with a phonograph "blasting band music." About the only restriction came in the motion picture theaters, where Indians and other minorities were segregated from the white audience. In general, town days were enjoyable experiences, eagerly anticipated.[28]

Although many of the social activities at Phoenix were similar to those in the average public school, dating and courtship were distinctly different. Most students were teenagers or young adults, and their thoughts frequently turned to members of the opposite sex. Indeed, they were of the age to be married had they remained at home. Yet school officials did all they could to repress natural instincts, prohibiting contact between the sexes as much as possible. A major reason for closely supervising the students' activities was to ensure that the school's reputation remained spotless and free from community criticism. The ethnocentric attitude of Indian service personnel, who assumed that Indians were "immoral" by nature, added to the desire to scrutinize. An example of such feeling was expressed by Commissioner Cato Sells, who told Superintendent Brown in 1916 to be particularly vigilant because he must deal "with the sexes who are only a short way removed from the wild freedom of the forest and of the plains." Brown felt the same, maintaining that pupils came from homes where "the most deplorable promiscuity exists, young girls being among the worst offenders and taking the initiative." Matrons used a similar line of reasoning, often assuming the worst of their wards.[29]

As a consequence, student freedom was severely restricted, and they were constantly badgered about proper behavior. All opportunities for the sexes to mix came under close supervision. The matrons kept tabs on the girls' menstrual cycles and dealt severely with anyone who lapsed into "moral delinquency." Disciplinarians guarded against "certain unnatural sexual practices" and the possible spread of venereal disease among adolescent boys. One student reported that "we had to be on our toes all the time." A Papago youth remembered how hard it was for boys and girls to get together: "You could not even talk to your sister without going to the principal and making special arrangements. You even had to prove she was your sister!" In the years after World War I restrictions were eased somewhat. Social events, picnics, debates, and religious meetings (all chaperoned) made social contact between boys and girls a bit more comfortable. Even so, there was no liberty. One boy remarked that while visiting a girl in the dormitory sitting room, "you were forced to sit around in the open and the matron was always spying."[30]

Despite formidable obstacles, romance flourished and students found numerous ways to avoid the system. Anna Moore aptly remarked that "although boys and girls were strictly separated at Phoenix Indian School, we could not help notice each other." As the adolescents took an interest in one another, they found ways to communicate. Occasionally a few minutes might be found to talk during a chance campus meeting or at a social event. Returning athletes and band members were sometimes able to socialize with classmates who met them at the train station. Secret meetings were arranged, and much went on that school officials never knew about. Note passing, which was against the rules, seems to have been a common pastime. Girls passed notes to their beaus over the dormitory fence or found a courier who was in the same class as a sweetheart. Laundry workers did an extra-good job on the clothes of boyfriends. Some of the more adventurous boys entered the girls' side of campus. For a few it simply involved playing croquet until shooed away by the matron. Others proved more daring. On more than one occasion during warm weather, young men climbed up to the dormitory sleeping porches and girls' rooms. Town days provided another opportunity for liaisons as teenagers broke away from the escort to spend an afternoon together at the movies. In all, there was considerable courtship and student ingenuity, as school officials reluctantly admitted.[31]

Most romances did not exceed the bounds of propriety, but there were exceptions. A few young women would become pregnant every year, producing emotional tension and occasional disaster. Having been taught the evils of sexual activity, girls became quite distraught after an indiscretion. Many times they felt a need to confess and be punished. One girl wrote a matron that "I am ashamed that I did the very thing which brings sorrow to women who misuse the gift that God has given us. . . . Do anything to me you like Dear Miss . . . I am ready to suffer the consequences." In another instance, a girl who had a love affair felt so guilty that she immediately came forward to say that "I am so sorry that I have disgraced Phoenix Indian School. . . . I kneel in prayer again and again and pray to God for the sin I have committed." Occasionally there were more serious consequences. Estelle Brown, who worked briefly at the school, tells a story in her book *Stubborn Fool* about a young Navajo woman who became pregnant while home for the summer. Being a bit on the heavy side, she was able to hide her pregnancy upon returning to school. Eventually she gave birth, then smothered the child. The matron soon discovered the deed. It came out that the Indian mother had been married in a Navajo ceremony, but the matron's insistent preaching that Indian marriages were a sacrilege prompted her to kill the child because "God will burn me forever if He finds out."[32]

The school handled the sensitive problem of love affairs and pregnancies by arranging for Christian marriages and removing those involved from the education system. Some of the most difficult problems centered on the outing pupils, who worked in town and were consequently under less supervision. With outing pupils able to meet young Indians of the opposite sex with some regularity, the outing matron kept close watch on their activities. Whenever romance blossomed, the young couple could expect to be called before the matron to hear a lecture on moral responsibility and the necessity of obtaining a license and having a "proper legal marriage." Staff members frowned on traditional Indian ceremonies. Should a couple insist on pleasing "their people by conforming to the ancient customs," they were urged to have a Christian wedding as well. Most went along with these suggestions, and there might be as many as ten arranged marriages yearly in Phoenix or back home (but never at the school). Those refusing to cooperate with the matron in these matters quickly found themselves out of work and sent home. In actuality, the number of forced marriages remained relatively small, and most students who became romantically involved had little trouble waiting until after they left the school to get married.[33]

A large percentage of the students participated in the outing activities. Although the young Indians were expected to "learn how white folks do things," they viewed it primarily as a way to earn spending money and put something away for the future. Monthly wages ranging from ten to forty dollars enabled some youngsters to accumulate a tidy bankroll over the years. It was not unusual for pupils to be the only family member earning a wage, a portion of which could be sent home to build a house or make some important purchase. Even so, student savings accounts became sizable. Tony Youhongva, for example, left the school with $600 in his pocket to help begin a career.[34]

Patrons and students frequently developed a deep sense of attachment and trust. Some virtually became family members. Young Helen Dowawisnima worked for a while in the home of Superintendent Brown. She participated in family affairs, went on picnics and camping trips, and enjoyed outings in the Browns' Ford touring car. The bond of friendship was so strong that after Brown retired in 1931, he and his wife visited Helen at her reservation home. Other students had similar experiences. One employer wrote that "the boys who have come to me from the school have been very good boys. They do not shirk and are honest. I am careful about not leaving valuables around to tempt them, still there has been times when they could have taken both money and jewelry, if they had been so inclined."[35]

By 1920 most of the Indians working full time in Phoenix were nonstudents. Outing pupils were still urged to secure community employment, but it was generally limited to working on weekends or during the summer. Nevertheless, school boys were encouraged to spend their summer vacations away from home, working on a local farm or in a shop. Girls felt considerable pressure to take jobs as domestics and make money from the heavy demand for household servants. Some of the young women managed to escape the uncomfortable Phoenix summers by traveling with wealthy families, who regularly vacationed on the beaches of southern California or in the tall-pine country of northern Arizona. It was not unusual in such summer resort communities as Iron Springs, near Prescott, to find schoolgirls tending young children and keeping house.[36]

The weekend program operated year-round, usually with more jobs than students. During the mid-twenties well over one hundred boys went out each weekend. Considering that only pupils with good records were permitted to take advantage of the system, the level of participation was remarkable. A resident desiring a schoolboy needed only to call the school, detail the duties involved, and agree to pay a minimum of twenty-five cents per hour. Each Saturday morning eligible boys reported to the outing office to secure a card listing the name and address of an employer. A Papago schoolboy recalled that "on Saturday morning you go out to that place, and then you'd work, yard work or whatever, and get paid. When I got old enough to get around, I'd go out every Saturday to a certain place to clean their yard, cut their grass, whatever they wanted to be done, for so many hours, and I'd get paid for it." When the job ended, the card was returned with a notation as to the amount paid and the behavior of the student. Most youngsters liked the weekend jobs because they were treated as responsible persons and given a fair amount of freedom.[37]

Despite a relatively good record, not everyone had a pleasant outing experience. Without doubt some students were exploited by greedy and insensitive employers interested only in cheap labor. Some patrons felt that the payment of wages absolved them of any responsibility for supervision or training, and cases of abuse surfaced with disturbing regularity. Youngsters were admonished for not doing their work properly or failing to understand what was desired. One girl reported, "I never had any Lady that say things like that to me," after she disagreed with a Phoenix housewife. Many were simply overworked. A girl placed in a Williams, Arizona, home became exhausted within a few weeks. She wrote the matron that she could not celebrate the Fourth of July because "I had been working so hard ever since I came here cleaning house and lots of ironing. I just got through ironing now[,] I'm very tired[,] my feet get so tired standing all morning." Relations with the outing matron also caused distress. Many of the outing girls lived in dread of making some mistake that might be reported to the matron. As one inspector reported, "With the exception of perhaps some few, they fear her and her punishment of them, which is in the nature of privation of holidays and days out, and in extreme cases a return to their reservation or school." Frequent tongue lashings proved traumatic, whether they came from a housewife or the matron.[38]

Most pupils dropped out of school before completing the entire program. The reasons for early departure varied considerably, though they were seldom grounded in animosity toward the school. Students enrolled for a specific term (usually three or five years) and could leave once they put in the required time. More often than not, a personal matter caused them to leave school. Home visits during the summer months were particularly unsettling. Family crises occurred frequently, and many youngsters, as well as their relatives, felt it more important to remain at home than return to Phoenix. Many cases were similar to that of Ella Antone, whose father died while she was in the eighth grade. Ella felt compelled to remain with her grief-stricken mother and help the family. Peter Blaine could not continue because his elderly uncle needed him to tend the family farm at San Xavier. Young Hazel Pehihonema (Dukepoo) left school following the death of her mother and several other personal disruptions. Others departed because the time seemed right to get a job. Having received vocational training, they were eager to begin making a living. In such instances, students generally planned to return to school at a later date, but they seldom did. Tony Youhongva took a temporary job, which led to another, and so on. Returning home for any period of time made it increasingly difficult to return.[39]

Spring commencement exercises were staged for the handful of students completing the full course of study. Until 1920 graduation came at the end of the eighth grade, but in the following decade the four high school levels were added. Graduating seniors were expected to set a good example for their schoolmates. Each year the *Native American* published a commencement issue, featuring pictures of the graduates, a list of their accomplishments, and commencement essays. The graduates, as a group, were high achievers. All were active in social, religious, sports, and military societies. A rather large portion were Pimas, Maricopas, Papagos, and Hopis, reflecting the heavy representation of these tribes at the school. Not surprisingly, they seemed eager to get out and make a living. Expectations, however, were limited by the nature of their vocational training and are indicative of the level at which they expected to fit into society. Students listed their ambitions in terms of manual labor: "to become a first class housekeeper," "to become a nurse," "to become a seamstress," and "to render help to my people." Senior essays were also revealing, most being directed at demonstrating mechanical know-how. Topics included advice on how to start a blacksmith shop, develop farm business methods, operate a steam boiler, and take advantage of one's education. Despite the industrial nature of the essays, they showed that pupils had indeed learned a great deal and expected to benefit from their schooling.[40]

A few graduates continued their education at institutions of higher learning. The motivation seems to have been to acquire additional training in hopes of securing a better job. Before 1920 the most common form of postgraduation schooling involved attending high school, frequently in Phoenix. This option became available in 1903, when John Wolfchief entered Phoenix Union High School, becoming the first Indian to attend a Phoenix public school. Thereafter a small number of Indian students regularly enrolled in the Phoenix high school. They did exceptionally well. One student, Annie Hayes, received highest marks in her English class, despite the fact "those white children have talked English all their lives and Annie has not." Another student became the leader of the school orchestra and graduated with honorable mention. Not all Indian students found it easy, however. George Webb, who was graduated from the Indian school in 1912, got along well with his classmates but had difficulty with his English. Perhaps the most famous Indian student to graduate from Phoenix Union High was Anna Moore. After completing the eighth grade, Anna spent two more years at the Indian school in an experimental program that provided the first two years of high school. In 1918 she entered Phoenix Union, graduating two years later as the first full-blood Pima girl to accomplish that task. While attending high school in Phoenix, she continued to live at the Indian school. Anna made friends among the white students and never noticed much prejudice.[41]

Other graduates continued their education at more advanced government Indian schools. This was particularly the choice for those who hoped to become teachers among their people. Students with such ambitions were usually sent to Hampton Institute. One Apache girl, a 1903 graduate, reported from Hampton that "it is my aim to be a teacher so that I may go out into the world and try to help other people toward a better life and I think that most of the Indian students here feel that they must go among their people and help them to be better citizens." Such students were usually hired by the government once their training was completed. Similarly motivated girls took training as nurses, usually in Albuquerque. They found employment with the Indian service but not in white society, which continued to maintain racial barriers.[42] A few students entered professional schools or colleges. One early graduate of the school went to Park College in Missouri, his tuition being paid by a white benefactor. Always a pacesetter, Anna Moore wanted to attend the State Normal School in Tempe after high school. She quickly discovered that the school maintained a policy of excluding Indians. With the help of Superintendent Brown and the Indian Office, Anna carried her case directly to school officials and finally secured an agreement that the Normal School would lower its racial barriers. By the time of this victory, however, Anna and Ross Shaw had married and it was no longer practical for her to continue her education.[43]

Confirmation of the school system's success, as far as federal officials were concerned, was demonstrated by the ability of students to find jobs and become self-sufficient. As Arizona Governor Alexander O. Brodie stated in 1903, Indian schools should prepare the young generation to become self-supporting "by finding for them proper employment, thus aiding them and preventing their return to former modes of life."[44] Students seemed to feel the same way. Indeed, what happened after leaving school provided the key to evaluating the worth of what amounted in many cases to considerable personal sacrifice. Because Indian youngsters had been groomed to find employment at the lower echelons of white society or on the reservation, that is where they entered the work force, seldom attempting to enter other professions. However, students possessed the training, ability, and determination to find employment in the areas they prepared for, and a surprising number took advantage of the opportunity. Three types of employment were open to former students: (1) working for the Indian service, (2) domestic service and manual labor, and (3) individual enterprise.

Because the school had so much invested in the success of its pupils, it functioned as an employment bureau. Administrators actively sought positions for former students, utilizing the outing matron and assistant superintendent to coordinate job activity. By far the largest employer of educated Indians during this era was the Indian service. Nearly everyone who chose to work could do so, and many former students were able to secure positions at Indian agencies and schools. Of course, most jobs were menial or manual; only a few Indians became teachers or supervisors. None worked as administrators. They were hired as laundresses, cooks, assistant matrons, policemen, caretakers, carpenters, disciplinarians, interpreters, and painters. Sometimes these employees received little more than room and board. Even those who managed to be hired as teachers and nurses received less pay than their white counterparts. While it can be said with some truth that the entire system was artificial and paternalistic, Indian students did not see that. They were happy to find a use for their skills and proud of their work. Indeed, most of the maintenance work in the Indian service was performed by former pupils. One Hopi recalled that he found work throughout the Depression because of the skills he acquired at Phoenix Indian School. Everyone he knew worked for the government.[45]

The Indian Office lamented the tendency of students to seek government jobs, encouraging them to find employment in private industry instead. Despite such concern, few industries besides agriculture were available in the Southwest, and school authorities hesitated to encourage students to move to larger urban areas. As a consequence, most employment outside government was limited to domestic work and manual labor. With an exceptionally large market for domestic servants, many former pupils chose that line of work. Positions with private families were common in the Phoenix area, although some former students could be found working as far away as California and

Oklahoma. Although some Indian women believed that their work provided benefits for later life, others found the work inherently hard and demeaning. At least one Apache woman remembered her years of work in a Phoenix household with great bitterness and resentment. Still, they worked because it seemed the best way to make a living at the time. Young Indian men tended to work primarily at farming and stock raising, although a greater variety of jobs opened to them. In the Salt River valley young men from the school could be found laboring as printers, plumbers, firemen, and clerks for the Railway Express Agency. Some positions proved transient, others turned into lifelong jobs.[46]

A few former students entered business for themselves. One of the school's most notable success stories involved Juan Patton, who, after leaving school, returned to the Gila River reservation and opened a mercantile store at Sacaton. By 1904 he had installed a gasoline pump and gone into the cattle business, reportedly owning six hundred head. A Phoenix newspaper remarked that "the story of Mr. Patton's enterprise shows what education can do for an Indian, or at least some Indians." Other students became involved with private enterprise in more marginal ways. One former pupil reported working as a traveling salesman for a jewelry firm, while another set up a gardening operation in Hemet, California. Many hired out on specific projects as they became available. The construction of Roosevelt Dam near Phoenix employed some Indians, some of whom were returned students. Utility companies also used former students as repairmen.[47] In general, students from the school were able to find a wide variety of jobs, and many of them made at least some attempt to utilize their education.

In 1920, Superintendent Brown informed a congressional committee that between 25 and 30 percent of his students eventually found a job and earned a livelihood away from their home locality. The remainder returned to the reservation. But, he added emphatically, even a year or two at school gave the returned pupil a new life, and only a small percentage went "back to the blanket." According to Brown, as many as 90 percent refused to fall back into the same kind of living conditions they had left. Imbued with modern ideas and technology, they built new homes "with doors and windows... Most of them when they go back, especially if they stay through a period of years, amount to something," he stated.[48]

The superintendent's remarks contained an element of truth, but he exaggerated the situation considerably. Former students indeed returned home in great numbers, but relatively few were emotionally prepared to resist the temptation to slip back into old ways. Lack of an outlet for their vocational training, pressure from conservative tribesmen to conform to traditional practices, and reservation poverty worked against significant change. The inability of returned students to continue their Anglo ways or to change the reservation environment was, from the government's perspective, a great failure.[49]

The Indian Office frequently expressed concern about the tendency of former students to revert to traditional life-styles after returning home. Such backsliding seemed to prove that the effort, money, and time invested in Indian education was wasted; that Indian school children never really changed or lost their ethnic identification. A 1916 survey conducted by the Board of Indian Commissioners revealed how easy it was to revert to traditionalism:

> Then they return to the reservation,—but in many cases, find that they cannot apply their trades because their country is not sufficiently developed to demand the labor they are able to perform. The enjoyments, pastimes, and the society connected with their recent school life are gone, in many cases forever, they naturally become discouraged, and the backward drift immediately sets in and carries them back to the ways and customs of their old people and brings to them a feeling of satisfaction which overcomes their disappointments and enables them to forget the better conditions of life they encountered during their school days.[50]

Though this statement accurately described the way de-acculturation occurred, it failed to note the intense pressures involved.

It required considerable courage to retain the "civilized" ways acquired at school. Young Indians went back to conditions that, said one superintendent, "would stagger the strongest intellect and the most determined character." Those who clung to the new life-style risked alienating relatives, friends, and fellow tribesmen. Reservation residents were suspicious of and often hostile to anyone who had attended school. Parents and elders frequently put great pressure on children to resume the old ways. Hopi agent Leo Crane remarked that "the old people, in strict patriarchal fashion, have set aside and maintained all this time for him, a few horses, cattle and sheep. Gradually he accepts what he has.... The old life is before him." Even retention of "civilized" or "citizens'" clothing sparked opposition. "We know it must be hard to live in a way that makes one unpopular among his or her own people," noted the school paper in reporting that a Phoenix girl insisted on wearing her school garb after she returned to Fort Mohave. Hopi schoolgirl Elizabeth White, who attended Sherman Institute, related an event that many Phoenix girls undoubtedly experienced. She returned home an accomplished cook only to find that her family shunned the cakes and pies she made in place of traditional food, called her "as foolish as a white woman," and treated her as an outcast. As she later lamented, her school-taught domestic skills were inappropriate for the Hopis. Helen Sekaquaptewa remarked that everything she did— bathing, cooking, reading—irritated her sister, who took over a house Helen should have inherited.[51] Indeed, some families were irrevocably split by the educational experience.

Part of the difficulty stemmed from the attitude of the students. Pupils frequently returned home convinced that their parents were backward, degraded people, and treated them as such. Some actually felt ashamed of their relatives and the way they lived. One girl had difficulty fitting back into her family because there was no money to buy dresses and other things she wanted. Her uncle offered to make her an Indian dress, "but I told him I didn't care for anything like that," she said, just before running away to find a job in Phoenix. The school realized that such attitudes intensified the opposition to boarding schools. Yet as long as returned students insisted on doing what they were taught and turned to whites rather than relatives for guidance, the sense of alienation continued and in many cases became so intolerable that the young people left home rather than stay in what they regarded as a repressive environment.[52]

Community attitudes made it even more difficult for students to retain nontraditional ways. A recent study of returned Pueblo students showed that many came home with grand plans and a willingness to earn a livelihood by modern means only to be thwarted at every turn by conservative community members. Schoolboys had been taught to farm efficiently and cultivate nontraditional crops. Girls understood the advantages of stoves, glass windows, electricity, sewing machines, and store-bought groceries. Yet, on some reservations, when they persisted in using modern devices and growing crops with the aid of machinery, they were ostracized. Use of tribal farmlands was denied; they were banned from ceremonies and excluded from tribal councils.[53] Even Christian marriages encountered opposition. Although some four hundred Hopis reportedly turned out in 1905 to witness the "first Christian marriage at the second mesa," involving Vivian Kachina, a Phoenix schoolgirl, there was little sense of approval. In reporting a second Hopi marriage the following year, the *Native American* remarked that the couple, both returned pupils, found it impossible to have a "legal marriage" because "the influence of the old people preponderates to such a degree."[54] Incidents of this nature were not isolated, especially in the more traditional societies.

A final impediment, which existed in varying degrees on all reservations, was unemployment. Hopi agent Leo Crane succinctly summed up the problem in 1916 when he wrote that the returned student usually looks "about for a market for his ability. Likely he makes several trips to the Agency, and is kindly told by the Agent that unfortunately there is no work at which he may be employed. He has found himself in a land where there are Indian blacksmiths without forges, carpenters who seldom see a board, tailors where flour-sacks will do for clothes, shoe-makers and every man his own moccasin-maker, painters with nothing to paint, harness-makers where baling-wire serves all needs." Without doubt such conditions existed, serving to hinder former pupils from putting their training to practical use. Jobs were available, both inside and outside the Indian service, of course, but usually far from home. The young man or woman who wanted to remain among his or her own people yet preserve the ways taught at school had a difficult time. Parents and tribesmen were not generally impressed with the "new Indians." They were even less willing to let anyone change their lives.[55]

Despite the negative aspects of the reservation environment, returned students did have an impact, and not all of them let tribal opposition deter them. In some Indian communities they did very well. Agent Frank Thackery noted that returned students among the Pimas proved relatively successful, especially in those villages where government personnel were supportive. Thus chances of success were good, despite having to return to poorly equipped homes and farms. Leo Crane was even more insightful regarding the Hopis. First he noted that "making good" in the sense of looking, acting, and feeling like a white man was too much to expect, but students really did not return "to the blanket." They might be "a trifle unkempt," but they spoke English, did not become beggars, were aware of sanitation concerns, and were more inclined to send their children to school. "He wants," Crane observed, "vehicles to shorten the desert distance, lumber and furniture for the Household, labor saving devices for the women, implements for the field, and above all—Water in abundance. He wants to be clean, and once the old people are off his neck, will be sanitary." Crane concluded that returned students may not be *"what the tax-payer expected him to be,"* but considering the circumstances, neither were they failures.[56]

The veracity of such statements became increasingly evident

in the 1920s and 1930s. By then enough educated Indians resided on reservations to become meaningful. In some cases they united to oppose the ostracism of traditionalists and began to fight for their rights. Supported by the Indian Office in such efforts, they frequently found themselves deeply involved in the bitter struggle between traditional and progressive elements. Moreover, because many of the returned students were familiar with the outside world and spoke English, they tended to gravitate to positions of influence and power as tribal governments became more complex and traditional leaders fell by the wayside. Former Phoenix pupil Peter Blaine is a case in point. During the late 1920s and early 1930s he was drawn increasingly into Papago politics. Partly because of his education, he was sent to Washington to represent the tribe on important questions, worked on the first tribal constitution, and eventually became tribal chairman. His story is not unique. By the 1930s many tribal leaders and representatives were the product of Phoenix and other Indian schools. With few exceptions they supported the progressive viewpoint and the way of the future.[57]

The lives, emotional reactions, and successes or failures of students who attended Phoenix between 1900 and 1930 are not easy to sort out. No one individual could be called a typical student. They came from varied Indian cultural backgrounds and reacted in substantially varying ways to the experiences of forced acculturation. For every youngster who became embittered and determined more than ever to resist the ways of the outside world, another could be cited as accepting the circumstances and struggling to make the best of the situation. In this sense, students at Phoenix Indian School were no different than students anywhere. They reacted individually, and it is a misrepresentation to assume that Indian education meant the same to everyone. Perhaps Hopi agent Crane stated it best when he said that neither extreme—"the Indian who has reverted to the blanket literally, and the Indian who has, as some of us proudly assert, 'made good,'"—was typical. "There are many Indians who stand on middle ground."[58] Unfortunately, the government assumed that its program would have a uniform, predictable impact and every student would turn out virtually the same. When they did not, demands for change arose with surprising swiftness.

7

Education Under Duress

IN THE YEARS between the outbreak of World War I and the publication of the Meriam Report in 1928, Indian education in America bogged down. For the first time in decades too little money was available, and with more Indian children than ever attending school, problems related to money—overcrowding, health, and maintenance—began to assume major proportions. National participation in World War I also disrupted the educational routine, putting even greater pressure on the schools. If this was not enough, criticism of Indian policy, which had been simmering for years, broke out in earnest as the failures of the assimilation program began to attract nationwide attention. Eventually a new breed of reformers appeared on the scene. Led by such individuals as John Collier, these critics attacked the existing system for its inefficiency, its failure to achieve results, and its clear intent to obliterate native culture. They wanted forced assimilation ended. As the 1920s dawned, this reform movement grew in intensity, eventually focusing significant attention on the problems of Indian education. All these events affected the Phoenix Indian School, making it more difficult than ever to achieve satisfactory results.

The man destined to guide the Phoenix school through these troubled years was John B. Brown, another career Indian service educator. Brown became superintendent at Phoenix in March 1915 after some twenty-two years' experience working in federal Indian schools. During his long career he had served as the principal of several day schools, principal teacher at Haskell, superintendent of two boarding schools, and most recently special supervisor in charge of reorganizing the school system of the Five Civilized Tribes in Oklahoma.[1] Brown probably knew as much about the workings of the federal education system as any government employee. Despite his bureaucratic knowledge, the new superintendent was a member of the "old guard," temperamentally ill suited to deal with twentieth-century Indian problems. He was overbearing, lacked a sense of humor, and held a Victorian view of human relations. Deeply religious, he disapproved of current social fads, considering it a point of honor to protect the good name of his school. Whatever else, he insisted his students live in a wholesome, moral environment. Anyone violating his rules would be subject to harsh and immediate punishment. Like most Indian service professionals, Brown saw little value in traditional Indian cultures, fervently desiring that his students adopt white life-styles. During his stay at Phoenix from 1915 to 1931 these beliefs came under severe attack.

Regarded as one of the leading Indian educators in the country, Brown was frequently called upon to advise Indian Commissioner Cato Sells. Sells had come to office in 1913 with the Democratic administration of Woodrow Wilson. Though he knew little about Indian affairs and apparently nothing about Indian schools, the progressive Democrat believed that government should operate efficiently. In general, he supported the policies of his immediate predecessors, Francis Leupp and Robert Valentine, favoring the use of public schools wherever practical, a strong vocational orientation, and useful employment for former students. Though Sells maintained a conventional attitude that the Indian population must eventually merge into American society, he stressed a financially conservative approach based on organization and effectiveness. He did not adhere as fervently as his predecessors to the notion that off-reservation education ought to be eliminated, but inefficient, unproductive, or useless operations had no place in his scheme of things. The commissioner's enthusiasm for streamlining the school system produced a few changes but very little in the way

The mature campus, sometime after 1900. With the girls' building at its center, the well-landscaped campus included dormitories, a dining hall, employees' quarters, offices, and shop buildings. The green lawns, shaded walks, and fountains drew hundreds of Phoenicians to the school, which seemed like an oasis in the desert. Courtesy of Arizona Historical Foundation.

of concrete results. This was perhaps inevitable given the financial and political limitations placed on the Indian Office by a preoccupied and indifferent Congress.[2]

John Brown well understood what was expected of him as he moved into the superintendent's office at Phoenix. With enrollment hovering around seven hundred, he was in charge of one of the largest and most respected nonreservation institutions in the country (only Carlisle and Haskell had a greater number of students). An initial inspection of the campus revealed that the twenty-three-year-old facility was showing its age. Many of the older buildings needed repair and modernization. Important structures such as the heating plant, the superintendent's office, and baths were in particularly poor condition. Maintenance in general seemed neglected, primarily because of insufficient funding. On the other hand, the students, "largely fullbloods and from tribes unspoiled by too much government aid," appeared industrious and hardworking. Believing fully in the assimilationist approach to education, Brown expected to spend the bulk of his time rebuilding the physical plant, making the vocational program more effective, and securing better teachers. Beyond these improvements, he saw no great changes on the horizon. From his vantage point the federal school system already was headed in the right direction. As one colleague wrote at the time of his appointment, the Phoenix superintendency was "the most comfortable berth" available to a schoolman.[3]

During Brown's first year at Phoenix he devoted a considerable portion of his energy to maintaining good community relations and sorting out several administrative problems left over from previous years. Such matters were not especially significant in themselves, but taken as a whole they demonstrate that public relations and favorable publicity remained an important factor in assuring the continuation of nonreservation education. Because the school was the only visible representative of national Indian policy in Phoenix, local citizens turned to the institution to resolve any Indian-related problem that developed. School administrators naturally did everything in their power to placate and please community leaders, whose goodwill and support they heavily depended upon.

One example of the school's role in community affairs involved a long-running concern about the sale of postcards depicting half-nude Indian girls and women. Just after Brown arrived in Phoenix, some of the more respectable residents launched a campaign to ban the display and sale of the tasteless pictures, popular items at newsstands and drugstores throughout the city. Local citizens, believing the illustrations gave visitors the wrong impression of their community, turned to the school to help, pointing out that modern Indian women were "as modest, well-behaved, and properly dressed as are any white girls." Although the Indian Office could not legally halt sales, Superintendent Brown, as unofficial protector of Indian morality, launched a crusade of his own to remove the cards. By writing letters of protest to newspaper editors and drugstore operators, encouraging his students to speak out against the unsavory images, and generally raising a fuss, he finally drove the cards from public view, much to the relief of proper Phoenicians.[4]

Brown took other steps to firm up his relationship with the community. When residents accused schoolchildren of trespassing on private property, he knew full well that the offending parties were not associated with his institution. Nevertheless, he promised to punish the guilty, to be more vigilant in the future, and to remain personally available to resolve any such problems. In another public relations effort, Brown joined with Governor George W. P. Hunt to establish "Indian Day" at the state fair. Not only did this add a special attraction to the fair, it provided an opportunity to enhance the school's image through exhibits related to student skills in the arts of civilization. The *Native American* (personally edited by Brown) provided free advertising, not an inconsiderable asset considering the paper's circulation of 2,400 copies per week. The new headmaster also placated the religious community by agreeing to take in six young Indian men for training as missionaries. Under this unique agreement, the students spent half a day in industrial training and the rest of their time at nearby Cook Bible School. Typically, Brown expressed few qualms over the lack of academic instruction given these men (each sponsored by a local minister), arguing that moral rewards were sufficient.[5]

The school also took a few minor steps in the direction of improving relations with the local Indian community. When leaders at nearby Fort McDowell reservation suggested that elderly Indians attending the annual commencement ceremonies be permitted to camp on school property and prepare their own food in lieu of eating in the dining hall, Brown readily agreed, recognizing that many older Indians had never eaten in a formal situation and had gone hungry in the past rather than participate in a strange repast. Brown also worked to retain the practice of paying students who were retained during the summer to perform routine maintenace. Despite tightened budgetary restrictions, complaints of exploitation from Indian leaders, students, and reformers made it necessary to pay a minimal wage. Especially disturbing was the growing resentment of older boys who would ordinarily be able to find more lucrative summer employment elsewhere. Brown eventually convinced his superiors to provide the young workers with a salary averaging about fourteen cents per day, nowhere near what could be earned on the open market but enough, he hoped, to quiet discontent. In another direction, the school assumed a leading role in a well-publicized "Save the Babies" campaign, which was intended to lower infant mortality among Indians by promoting hygiene, sanitation, and proper child care.[6]

Within a short time Brown's attention was directed to the realm of policy matters. Recognizing the commissioner's penchant for efficiency, he became actively involved in various reorganization plans, most concerned with saving money or making the schools more productive. Perhaps the superintendent's most significant recommendation involved revising the system of assigning territory to the nonreservation institutions. Even though general districts had been recognized for some time, so many loopholes existed that students could enroll almost any place they desired, placing a severe strain on the system. School superintendents had to spend considerable time, energy, and money bidding "for the personal good will of reservation employees and Indians" in order to fill their schools. In addition to increasing transportation costs, such recruiting measures could (and did) easily become unethical. Brown therefore suggested that each nonreservation school be assigned a definite group of reservations. This promised to assure consistency in education, eliminate costly transfers of "tramp students," and encourage school pride and loyalty. Noting that his own institution currently enrolled almost sixty pupils from Oklahoma and an equal number from California while some two hundred Papagos went out of state, Brown stated that "the Phoenix school would be satisfied with pupils from the reservations and public domain of Arizona alone and might even sacrifice the Ft. Defiance and San Juan Navajos within the state if given exclusive jurisdiction over the remainder of the state." This suggestion ran directly counter to the way the school had been operating since the days of Sam McCowan and promised to be a major organizational advantage. Probably because of the opposition of some superintendents, Brown's suggestion was not fully implemented. Still, his idea was followed in ordinary practice, as he discovered when the school tried to recruit some California students in 1916 and was refused. Thus, while the Phoenix school did not completely eliminate "foreign" students, after this time for all intents and purposes it became an Arizona school, with only a handful of outsiders remaining on the rolls.[7]

Early in 1916 the Indian Office established a new course of study for its Indian schools. With the current system obviously less productive or economical than desired, Sells convened an internal panel of experts to produce the new scheme, introduced with great fanfare in February. The stated aim of the change was to standardize school curriculum in order to "provide a safe and substantial passage from school life to success in real life." It was, in other words, intended to produce more visible results. Much emphasis was on linking Indian schools to public schools. Because public schools seldom offered the kind of vocational training Indian students were thought to require, considerable stress was placed on the new ideas in vocational education, particularly eliminating the old apprentice style of industrial training and replacing it with a more modern "scholarly" format. The new course of study was consequently divided into three segments. The first two sections—primary and prevocational—required six years, paralleled "public school courses in the essential academic work," and were to be handled largely in the reservation setting. During the last four years—the vocational period—efforts were to be "directed toward training boys and girls for efficient and useful lives under the conditions which they must meet after leaving school." This task, from grades seven through ten, would be left largely to nonreservation institutions. In a corollary move, the Indian Office planned to phase out the lower grades at off-reservation institutions and limit such facilities to students older than thirteen years. In this manner the industrial schools would be forced to restrict their work to advanced education and preparing students to enter public high schools. The age limitation, grade consistency, and standard course of study thus seemed to provide real advantages in uniformity and cost effectiveness. In many respects, the proposed reforms revived the 1890 concepts of Thomas Morgan (which had never been fully implemented). Just as Morgan had promised a new era in Indian life, so did Cato Sells.[8]

It quickly became apparent that, although the new policy might be logical in theory, it would be difficult to implement at locations like Phoenix. Superintendent Brown could neither eliminate the lower grades nor confine enrollment to students older than thirteen. This was because reservation schools in Arizona remained few in number and overcrowded. To accommodate as many children as possible from such tribes as the Hopi, Pima, Papago, and Navajo, it was necessary to send the overflow to Phoenix. There was no other place for them. As a result, the lower grades needed to be retained and sometimes filled with students older than thirteen. As Brown explained, "Pupils who have reached the age of 14 can usually be induced to remain in school only where they have interesting industrial work." While the schoolmaster agreed to make every effort to fill his school with older children, he saw no immediate hope of eliminating the lower grades. To do so would deny an education to many Indian children. Not until the government built more reservation schools could Phoenix possibly confine itself to the upper grades.[9]

The school fared little better with the new course of study. The program was obviously intended to do more than standardize curriculum; its goal was to produce more graduates. Sells wanted students to pass a uniform final exam each year, advance regularly in grade, and complete the program, thereby demonstrating a competency to manage their own affairs. As he stated in 1917, "I believe that graduation as the gateway to citizenship should become in some real sense a gathering call for pupils, inspiring many more to complete their education, as well as a maxim for the schools arousing them to the fullest efficiency."[10] Large numbers of graduates, moreover, promised to quiet critics and make the schools appear more productive.

Phoenix put the new course of study into effect on February 1, 1916, by adding two years' work. Superintendent Brown soon found practical limitations to the plan's effectiveness. The passing of tests had little effect on the academic department, which had been utilizing examinations for years. But the vocational department had to be substantially changed. Blackboards were installed in shops, facilities for pupils to take notes and exams added, and vocational instructors ordered to become teachers. Although student objections were relatively few, many vocational instructors protested that they were skilled mechanics, not teachers. Moreover, a few tradesmen objected that full-time vocational work did not begin until the seventh grade, thus negating the apprenticeship system they favored. It was more significant that students did not perform as well as expected on end-of-year examinations. This led to suggestions that unqualified students might be promoted by teachers eager to please the administration and receive a good efficiency rating. Although Brown promised that no pupil would be promoted without meeting all requirements, he remained skeptical about the entire program. Pupils would be able to complete the new course of study, he predicted, but would not necessarily be in a position to enter high school or compete with white pupils.[11]

Although Brown did not admit that his school was under the gun to produce results, such was the case. Adding to the pressure was the issue of returned students, which continued to attract unfavorable publicity. The Board of Indian Commissioners, after an investigation in 1917, succinctly summarized the problem: "For some years we have been painfully impressed with the large proportion of boys and girls who, after returning to their reservations from Indian schools, fail to put into practice what they were taught at the schools. In too many cases these so-called 'returned students' not only do not show any progress, but actually go backward."[12] Brown was very defensive on this issue. While not denying that some former students were returning to the old ways, he placed the blame on the inadequate government resources. In response to a questionnaire, he stated: "I think we are trying to run our schools too cheaply. We are not willing to pay the salaries necessary to secure the best instructors." This comment highlighted the decline in the quality of instruction in Indian schools in recent years as government salaries failed to keep pace with professional standards. Brown was fully aware that many unqualified persons worked in the Indian service. His remark that better teachers would resolve the returned student problem seems naïve, however.[13] Still, if the government planned to stress graduation, employment opportunities, and good citizenship, the Phoenix Indian School would do its best to comply.

America's entry into World War I diverted attention from educational matters. With student life disrupted, the new course of study took a backseat to wartime production, and financial conditions grew worse. Indeed, the school faced a new set of challenges. Like everyone else in the nation, school employees and students became deeply involved in the 1917–18 war effort. The patriotism and bravery of Phoenix pupils ran deep, involving contributions on both the military and home fronts. Because most Indian schoolboys had received military training, they were willing, even eager, to enlist. Female students and younger boys did their part by keeping spirits high and war materials rolling.

The Phoenix school's young men were receptive to military service partly because the school had achieved a unique record before the war. As at other schools, boys had been receiving military-style training for years. In 1912, Arizona went one step further by organizing an all-Indian unit (Company F) of the state National Guard. Composed of former students residing in or near Phoenix and some of the older students, the company was the first such Indian militia unit in the nation. Superintendent Brown initially objected to student participation in the unit. He harbored no doubts as to their patriotism or courage, but feared enlistments would lead to "divided control of these young men" and disrupt educational activities. For this stance, the headmaster was labeled "un-patriotic and un-American" in some quarters.[14]

World and national events soon changed his mind. In the fall of 1915 miners in the copper towns of Clifton and Morenci, Arizona, went on strike. To avert violence, Governor Hunt called in the National Guard, Company F being the first unit activated. Although only a few schoolboys were apparently involved, Brown supported the decision to send Indians to Clifton. With Europe already at war and concern about radicalism rising at home, this was no time to appear unpatriotic. While Indian boys faced "the stones or bullets of striking miners," the superintendent publicly stated that the time had come to "fall in." No sooner had the copper strike been settled than the guard unit was called to more serious duty in response to Pancho Villa's raid near Douglas, Arizona, in the spring of 1916. On this occasion a greater number of schoolboys were involved, including some who had to leave campus just before graduation. Company F spent more than a year stationed at Naco guarding the border. They were not involved in any major action, but apparently skirmished with Mexican guerrillas on several occasions. The school did not forget its men in service. Pupils praised their comrades' patriotic courage, while the resulting publicity did a world of good for the school's reputation. Superintendent Brown again led the parade, suggesting that guardsmen be granted full citizenship on their return from duty. He also asked the government to furnish at least three companies of students with surplus Springfield rifles so they could improve their marksmanship after learning that Company F had gained a reputation for "the best drilled company in the regiment" but that its men could not "shoot a lick."[15]

The national guardsmen were still on the border when President Wilson declared war on Germany on April 2, 1917. Because of their noncitizen status, most young Indian men were exempted from military service. Large numbers came forward to volunteer, however. By July sixty-four Phoenix students and former students had entered the army or the navy. Brown proclaimed them "the finest and most capable of our students." Because of their training they were, in many instances, able to secure advanced ratings or positions as noncommissioned officers. Since government policy opposed the use of all-Indian companies, most of the volunteers were dispersed among various outfits. The one exception involved the soldiers of Company F. Upon returning from border duty in May 1917, most of them volunteered for the army. Preferring to remain together, they were assigned to a predominantly Indian company of the 158th Infantry, Fortieth Division. The unit arrived in France in August 1918. Several Phoenix boys reached the front lines and two were killed in action. At the end of hostilities, the 158th Infantry Indian band received the honor of playing at ceremonies marking the signing of the armistice. In all, students distinguished themselves in combat, helping to create a positive atmosphere that eventually resulted in the act of June 2, 1924, granting citizenship to all Indians.[16]

Students and employees who did not go to battle were expected to support the war effort. Less than a week after the declaration of war Commissioner Sells ordered Indian schools to increase agriculture production. With "a long pull, a strong pull, and a pull all together," he stated, Indians could "play a large and important part in the economic history of the nation during this period of war stress." Production of such commodities as wheat and potatoes, in particular, needed to be stepped up on school farms. Sells clearly intended the Indian's role on the home front to be strong and visible.[17]

Administrators at Phoenix met the challenge with enthusiasm. Brown wrote Sells that while potatoes did not grow well in the Arizona soil and it was too late in the season to plant more wheat, the school would produce all the surplus food it could. Employees and older students were called together, informed of the situation, and encouraged to fulfill their patriotic duty. One of the first official actions eliminated summer vacations for all male pupils, ordering instead that they take jobs on local farms "where they can do the most good." By the summer of 1917 every available schoolboy was working in the fields. So proud were the students of their record that they offered "to challenge any white high school in the United States in the matter of patriotic usefulness of its student body during the present summer." Indian students were mobilized to an even greater degree the following summer. Superintendents received instructions to leave no stone unturned in assuring that Indian labor be used to the best advantage. The Phoenix school responded by arranging for the employment of every boy who could be spared. Brown told the commissioner that "we are meeting with splendid cooperation on the part of our boys, and expect to insist that they shall work where they may be most effective in their efforts. . . . We shall refuse application for boys to do housework of any kind or to mow lawns or care for grounds when the owners are on vacation."[18] Unfortunately, concentration on war production drew attention and funds away from much needed campus maintenance and repair.

Students also supported the war by purchasing Liberty Bonds, raising money for the Red Cross and YMCA, and conserving food and other strategic goods. Staff members actively encouraged such activities, leaving students with little choice in the matter. Certainly there was pressure regarding Liberty Bonds and War Savings Stamps, a total of $36,173 having been invested by students and employees by the summer of 1918. Many pupils put their entire summer earnings into such deposits at the urging of school officials (who saw the school's patriotism measured in dollars). Other volunteer activities included producing Christmas boxes for soldiers in cooperation with the Junior Red Cross.[19]

Indian students had been so active in supporting the war effort that Commissioner Sells used their patriotism to denounce critics of federal policy. His 1918 annual report waxed eloquent on how recent policy had been sympathetic, humane, and practical. The Indian, he proclaimed, was recognized "as a man, the first and hyphenless American, possessing a quick intellect, a growing sprituality, an ardent love for his children, a brave heart, and fidelity to his promise until betrayed." Aside from life and health, the most important government concern had always been to teach the Indian to "use his brain efficiently and his hands skillfully." To Sells, the war effort had done much to brighten the future and assure ultimate assimilation.[20]

The Indian Office hoped wartime patriotism would enhance public and congressional support for Indian education. Yet the basic problems remained unchanged. The immediate postwar era therefore saw old policies perpetuated and several new difficulties emerge. All of these factors eventually produced ammunition for those who demanded a modification or end to nonreservation education.

Questions of school effectiveness and efficiency grew in intensity after 1918. Adding to the problem at Phoenix and other boarding schools was the even more ominous turn that financial concerns began to take during the war. It became increasingly obvious that inadequate appropriations were taking a heavy toll. The problem centered primarily on the formula used by Congress to finance education. For better than a quarter-century, the schools had received $167 per pupil a year, despite a continual rise in expenses. In 1915 the limit was raised to $200, but the total available money did not increase. As Brown explained to Arizona congressman Carl Hayden, "We have permission to use $200.00 per capita, but we do not have the $200.00." As a result, the school operated at a deficit for the first time in its history during the 1917–18 fiscal year. Had not Congress provided a supplemental wartime appropriation to financially strapped schools, Phoenix would have been forced to close its doors in March 1918, a disastrous eventuality. "It takes a long time to build up an efficient organization," Brown told Hayden, "especially when we are handicapped in the way of funds as we have been." Laid-off teachers might not be replaceable. Even more critical to ethnocentric educators was having to send children home three months early, turned loose in surroundings where "they would be exposed to every temptation."[21]

Requests for more money fell on deaf ears. In an atmosphere of wartime retrenchment, Congress seemed little interested in investing in federal Indian schools, particularly the off-reservation variety. In September 1918, Carlisle, the oldest and most famous nonreservation school, was closed (supposedly so that the buildings could be used as a military hospital) without a whimper of protest. A few months earlier, Congress passed legislation reaffirming that no more than two hundred dollars per student could be expended. Both Sells and Brown were irritated with the spending limit because it encouraged superintendents, struggling to secure the largest dollar amount possible, to overcrowd their schools. It also diminished the incentive to transfer students into public schools. Brown was particularly upset with the financial limitations because they flew in the face of quality education, undermining the goals of Indian policy and making it even more difficult to produce results. To remain within the budget, he protested, his school would have to dismiss instructors and abolish departments. In July 1918 the situation became so desperate Brown asked Sells to call a conference of superintendents to discuss their common problems, but nothing resulted. By 1919 the headmaster was reporting that expenses had increased 100 percent and programs were visibly suffering. The following year he closed the fiscal year without a deficit only by refusing to purchase supplies and allowing equipment to go unrepaired. With inadequate financial support, Brown was forced to witness the slow deterioration of his school. The facility needed new buildings, teachers demanded competitive salaries, and things seemed to be going downhill through neglect.[22]

Saving money became an obsession with Brown. One way he believed he could cut expenses was to reduce the number of runaways and desertions. The problem had continually worsened in recent years and cracking down on such activity promised to eliminate an unnecessary expense while simultaneously improving the moral environment of the campus. Brown was frankly horrified at what he considered the delinquent behavior of a few students. His request for new powers to deal with difficult cases was justified largely on economic grounds, though a puritanical element also entered the picture. Stressing that it cost large sums to capture and return runaways, he was further embarrassed by several recent inspection reports critical of school discipline. The superintendent therefore asked permission to increase campus security, construct a new guardhouse, establish reservation workhouses for chronic runaways, and send "deserters and incorrigibles" to the state reformatory without parental consent. Without waiting for a reply, he took matters into his own hands in April 1917 by turning two teenage female students over to Maricopa County for detention in the state reform school at Camp Grant. The girls were branded repeated deserters who made "automobile trips with dissolute Indian men, in some cases men with families." He hoped that such harsh punishment would have a preventive effect. If the state agreed to handle offenses committed off the reservation, it might prove effective in "checking or controlling the form of misconduct which it is well known constitutes our serious and most difficult problem," Brown remarked.[23] With that proclamation, a new disciplinary agenda went into effect. Corporal punishment returned, the jail was reopened, and a much more rigid atmosphere descended upon the institution. It is doubtful that any of this saved money, but it did cause plenty of trouble in the future.

With all his financial and disciplinary concerns, Brown never gave any thought to the prospect that his brand of assimilationist education might be in trouble. As the Phoenix school entered the critical third decade of the twentieth century, the stern schoolmaster presumed that things were returning to normal after the wartime confusion. The 1920 commencement ceremonies (the first since the war) seemed to confirm this impression. Public interest in Indian education appeared more intense than ever as a large group of spectators invaded the campus, inspecting classrooms and shops, listening to a band concert, and eagerly watching drill companies compete. Six students, all trained in a vocational skill, made up the graduating class. The lack of numbers, however, was made up with enthusiasm, and the *Arizona Republican* proudly proclaimed that the new course of study was a success and "the Indian school is fully up to the standard of other schools."[24] In this optimistic atmosphere, words of criticism from either the community or the Indians were still few and far between.

Though imperceptible to Phoenicians at the time, the entire scope of federal Indian policy was in for rough sledding in the 1920s. Nonreservation education would receive more than its share of criticism and in some respects become a symbol for all the failures of the assimilation program. One reason that effective opposition to the boarding schools had not emerged earlier was because the notion that assimilation, in whatever form, must eventually prevail continued to dominate the American scene. As late as 1920 any suggestion of deviating from this goal drew angry protestations from white reformers as well as such spokesmen for the Indian community as the acculturated members of the Society of American Indians. As long as these opinions held sway, any meaningful redirection of policy was impossible. During the 1920s, however, opposition to nonreservation schools grew in intensity, coinciding with the continuing neglect of these facilities that began during the Wilson administration, and the beginning of an effective crusade to discredit the old assimilationist policies. Thus institutions that were once bastions of the forced acculturation of the Native American population now headed down a path toward reform, reorganization, and even closure.[25]

The twenties actually began in a positive fashion for Superintendent Brown. In May 1920 he appeared before a touring delegation of the House Committee on Indian Affairs whose members were soliciting testimony in behalf of increased educational appropriations. Committee chairman Homer Snyder of New York complimented Brown on his handling of "one of the most progressive" government schools and intently listened to his opinions. Pleased with the recognition and opportunity to speak his mind, the superintendent flatly stated that increased funding was the best way to achieve results. Arguing that all deficiencies in the educational system were attributable to insufficient funds (a position shared by Commissioner Sells), Brown asked for as much money as possible. Though in general agreement with this request, Snyder reminded Brown that in order to get more financial support from a reluctant Congress, schools such as his would have to increase their productivity, particularly by demonstrating that more Indians were entering the work force and becoming useful citizens. As long as most Indians seemed to return "to the blanket," increased financial support would be difficult to obtain. Brown responded weakly that appearances were deceiving and in actuality very few students failed to benefit from their training. This plea, unsupported by facts, was apparently persuasive enough to squeeze a special appropriation of $5,000 from Congress in 1921 for some badly needed repairs.[26] Although grateful for the funds, Brown realized he needed much more, and to secure the future he must enhance the school's image as a successful pathway to civilization.

One convenient method of improving the school's image appeared to be increasing urban Indian employment and linking the school to these jobs. This scheme dovetailed with Brown's belief that the school was not being given enough credit for

Indian employment. As a result, the old outing system was phased out to make room for other Indians. In actuality, this move simply was confirmation that for some years nonstudent Indians had been providing an increasing percentage of domestic labor in Phoenix. By 1920 this change was so obvious that Brown proclaimed that the school no longer operated under the original system devised by Captain Pratt at Carlisle. In recent years, he stated, schoolchildren had been increasingly limited to working on weekends and during the summer, while nonstudents, many of whom were former pupils, made up the bulk of those sent out by the school. In essence, the school was turning into an employment agency, a trend Brown wished to enhance. Indeed, if all Indians employed in the Salt River valley were controlled by the school through its outing program, it promised to increase the institution's visibility as a major force in urban Indian employment. In June 1922, therefore, the school assumed formal responsibility for all Indians working in Phoenix. Under this system, employers seeking Indian women of any age were instructed to consult with the outing matron, who would procure the worker and make all necessary arrangements. Employers of Indian men were encouraged to turn to the school first and keep close track of all workers. As a consequence, the school began acting as an intermediary between employers and Indian labor. With this development, interest in student apprenticeships declined further. School officials were more concerned with finding urban employment for Indians, even those coming directly from the reservations. One inspector accurately remarked that the outing matron had become a social worker: "The amount of work done with individuals of school age is smaller than the amount done with adults and ex-students."[27]

The revamped outing system may have provided more jobs for former students and supplied the school with some favorable publicity, but it meant little in the long run as financial problems overwhelmed the institution, distorting everything else. Such troubles were aggravated by the return of Republicans to national office in 1921 under the administration of Warren G. Harding. The appointment of Charles H. Burke as Indian commissioner harmed Indian education while his ethnocentric policies helped give rise to the Indian reform movement of the mid-1920s.

Burke's administration (1921–1929) bred controversy primarily because he doggedly clung to old assimilationist ideas during a period of rapid change. His main educational goals were to get every Indian child enrolled in a school, to use public facilities as much as possible, and to improve the quality of instruction. Vocational training still seemed the best approach. To a degree, Burke supported the philosophy that day schools were more desirable than boarding facilities, but in general he regarded the major nonreservation institutions as the backbone of the government's assimilation effort. Unfortunately, he was reluctant to fight for increased appropriations, to challenge party leadership, or to admit the existence of serious flaws in the system. As a biographer has stated, "Despite criticism of overcrowding in the boarding schools and increasing evidence that children in those schools were not being adequately cared for, Burke refused to acknowledge the criticism or to ask for additional funds until the last years of his administration."[28]

Although Brown felt comfortable with most of Burke's ideas, he had to contend with the devastating effects of his policies. A major problem was created when the Indian Office decided to "put every eligible pupil in school." Despite laws requiring compulsory attendance, a survey published in 1922 showed that Arizona had approximately 7,500 Indian children not in school—by far the largest number of any state. Almost immediately after entering office, Burke launched a campaign to get these children into school. The resultant influx of new students overloaded the entire school system, and Brown was forced to take more students than he could care for. Average attendance for the 1921–22 fiscal year reached 789, although funds were provided for only 750 pupils. Maintenance and overcrowding problems multiplied. A federal inspector reported in

1923 that the girls' dormitories were extremely crowded, boys and girls were forced to use sleeping porches as dressing rooms, and there was no space for personal items.[29]

Operation of the East Farm Sanatorium, which came directly out of the school's budget, placed an additional financial drain on the institution. The success of the hospital in treating tuberculosis patients (primarily from the reservations) meant that the facility was caring for about eighty patients at any one time. At a cost of $1.27 per day per patient, the sanatorium used up a good portion of school resources. More than once Brown asked for a separate appropriation for the tuberculosis hospital, but the Indian Office persistently ignored these requests. The refusal to seek additional appropriations also meant that teacher salaries suffered. Brown issued annual pleas for increases, pointing out that in the decade following 1913 living expenses had risen 68 percent, leaving teachers' compensation grossly inadequate. Although hesitant to admit it openly, the superintendent knew full well that this condition was resulting in the loss of qualified teachers and a decline in the quality of education. At current salaries, good teachers could not be replaced, leaving the school with a disproportionate share of incompetent or ill-suited teachers.[30]

If all these problems were not enough, in 1922, Burke revised the course of study in an attempt to more nearly conform with public school curriculum. Intended to make it easier for Indian students to transfer to public institutions, this program, when combined with the effort to enroll more Indian children, put additional pressure on the Arizona school. Burke expected the public schools to absorb the excess pupils being forced into the system, but that did not happen in the Southwest. With the exception of Phoenix, Indians were not admitted to public schools in Arizona, no matter how hard the government lobbied. Still, Burke was committed to getting every child into school; and if public schools would not take them, the Indian service would have to make do. As he stated after a visit to the Navajo reservation: "It is a pitiful picture, and when it is realized that hundreds, possibly thousands, of these little children spend days, weeks, and months at such labor [tending sheep] instead of going to school as they should, it intensifies the feeling that the Government has not kept faith with these people." Consequently, more youngsters were crowded into the bulging boarding schools.

By 1925, 939 students were enrolled at Phoenix, the largest groups being Pima, Papago, Hopi, Navajo, and Apache. It was hoped that some of these children would transfer into public high school after finishing the tenth grade, but few showed any interest. Brown himself may have discouraged interest in advanced education with frequent expressions of his deep-seated belief that ten grades were "as far as the full blood Indian of the Southwest should be carried by the Government." Besides, he claimed, most graduates had reached twenty-one years of age, and "being men and women in physique and in the mating instinct, it is only the exceptional among them that seems likely to profit by further schooling." Hence only a few graduates were encouraged to go on to high school. Because younger students were reservation residents, they could not legally be enrolled in Phoenix schools.[31] Therefore, the effort to enroll Indians in public school failed in Arizona, leaving the government schools to shoulder an added burden.

Indirectly linked to the problem of overcrowding and underfunding was the continuing issue of discipline, punishment, and humane care of pupils, which began to attract especially unfavorable attention in the early 1920s. As noted previously, Brown took a tough approach to discipline, demanding that his matrons and disciplinarians rigorously punish all infractions. As a result, harsh punishment increasingly became a part of school life. Word of such treatment, although clearly confined to a relatively few pupils, soon reached the Indian community. As early as 1919, Mike Burns, a Yavapai activist at Fort McDowell, wrote to Dr. Carlos Montezuma that "old Bull Dog" Brown was jailing runaways on bread and water, putting them to work at hard labor, and beating some boys with baseball bats. Burns's call for an investigation never materialized, but the Yavapai continued to watch the school. In July 1923 he wrote Burke that Brown had initiated the practice of whipping pupils "for trifle doings." He complained that girls were whipped by both the matron and occasionally by a white male employee. From such "beastly punishment," Burns concluded, children became ill and some died. The Yavapai demanded that Brown be replaced and the punishment stopped. When informed of the complaint, the Phoenix headmaster called Burns to his office to discuss the matter. Under intense questioning Burns admitted that he had no concrete evidence that girls had been whipped, having heard of the alleged incidents from several runaways and a deceased former student. Brown thus brushed the complaint aside, maintaining that Burns harbored a personal grudge against the school.[32]

Brown's explanation may have satisfied Burke that nothing was amiss at Phoenix, but other events certainly raised questions about how the welfare of pupils was being protected. Just as Brown was responding to charges of whipping students, the Indian Office was compelled to investigate the conduct of outing matron Amanda Chingren. This episode originated with A. F. Duclos, the Pima agent, who wrote Burke that there were problems with Indian girls in Phoenix. He charged that Miss Chingren was out of sympathy with her charges, had a "nagging disposition," lacked tact and diplomacy, and tended to inflict punishment on the girls rather than instruct them. When confronted with the allegations, Chingren retorted with a moralistic defense; she was being criticized for being "over-zealous of their welfare to a degree that has not met with approval." The matron justified her conduct on grounds that everything she did had been directed at inducing her girls, both students and nonstudents, "to lead honorable and upright lives." Not satisfied with this reply, the office sent an inspector to the school in the fall of 1923. After interviewing employers and students, collecting a great deal of testimony, and analyzing the program, the inspector put together a picture of unsympathetic treatment, mental punishment, and a reign of fear. Still, she concluded, "there is nothing radically wrong except a lack of sympathetic handling of a most human question." Consistent with his reluctance to interfere with institutional operations, Burke issued a mild reprimand, expressing hope the situation might be corrected. Some of the collected evidence must have disturbed the commissioner, however. Witnesses stated that the matron frequently accused the girls of "having every buck on the reservation," that she played favorites, that she talked "awfully to the girls," and that she punished them for trivial offenses. She was also accused of sending girls to jails or reformatories as punishment for "immoral behavior."[33]

In September 1924 an accident occurred that cast even more doubt on the school's concern for its pupils. As part of the Defense Day celebration the school had agreed to send three companies of girls downtown for a parade. Because of a lack of usable vehicles, all 120 girls were loaded onto a single truck and trailer for the three-mile trip. The makeshift vehicle was so overloaded that as it turned the corner onto Van Buren Avenue several girls sitting at the rear of the truck fell to the ground and were run over by the trailer. Two young women died of head and chest injuries and several others were seriously hurt. Although purely accidental, the unnecessary deaths raised local concern. A coroner's jury laid the blame directly on school authorities. Brown, though not present at the loading, was judged indirectly at fault for the unsafe actions of his subordinates. The incident apparently caused considerable bitterness and recrimination among the staff. Brown refused to report the tragedy in the *Native American,* which was read by many Indian families and Indian service personnel.[34] This sad episode and the way it was handled did little to correct the growing image that school authorities were unable or unwilling to protect their wards.

Problems of finance, punishment, the ethnocentrism of federal educators, the general treatment of students, and a lack of useful results were by no means confined to Phoenix Indian School. Examples of the same conditions could be found just about anywhere across the West. The situation played directly into the hands of a group of new era reformers who burst onto the national scene in 1922. The movement to completely change the direction of Indian affairs started with the effort to defeat the Bursom bill. This legislation, which threatened to deprive the Pueblo Indians of their rights and considerable land, became a focal point for criticism of Indian policy, drawing a new kind of reformer into the debate and ultimately producing radical changes. In particular, John Collier rose to prominence as the spokesman for Indian reformers. In conjunction with the newly organized American Indian Defense Association, Collier set out to inform the public about the evils of the assimilationist approach. Through access to liberal magazines, this visionary and his friends demanded a wide variety of changes, charging that the Indian service was inefficient, insensitive, and headed in the wrong direction. One of the major issues involved education, with the nonreservation boarding schools drawing special attention. As Margaret Connell Szasz has rightly observed, as criticism of the Indian service intensified, "they began to identify the boarding school as the symbol of all the evils of the bureau education system." Writing for *Sunset* magazine in 1923, Collier criticized off-reservation education because it took young children from their homes and sent them to places "remote from home in order that they might never join their parents again." Using much of the rhetoric employed by Leupp and Lummis two decades earlier, he objected to the treatment of schoolchildren, the waste that came from their education, and the failure to achieve stated goals. This assessment, while based on existing conditions, considerably exaggerated the situation. But Collier was launching a crusade and would tolerate no contrary opinion. He concluded his article with a seething condemnation of the schools: "It is civilized, beautiful human life we are chopping to pieces at sizable cost to the taxpayer for the administration of the chopping process."[35]

From the reformers came a demand for action. In an obvious attempt to quiet some of the criticism, Interior Secretary Hubert Work called together a group of leading Indian experts in

May 1923 to discuss future policy. This group, known as the Committee of One Hundred, represented the great variety of opinions held in the country. Collier participated, as did representatives of Indian defense societies, noted ethnologists, members of the Board of Indian Commissioners, prominent assimilated Indians, and religious functionaries. It all added up to a curious mixture of old-guard assimilationists and cultural-pluralism reformers. Historian Lawrence C. Kelly has called the formal meeting of the group in December 1923 "the last stand of the assimilationist forces that had significantly influenced government policy since the late nineteenth century." Indeed, the committee was so diverse that few positive results could be expected, and the effort is generally regarded as a failure. Still, it pointed out the wide divisions of opinion between the old and the new, and left people like Collier more than ever determined to bring about radical change.[36]

Although discussion of education policy was overshadowed by other issues in the committee report, a number of items received consideration. In general, the group recommended an increase in federal appropriations to help secure qualified teachers and modernize facilities. Public schooling for Indian children received approval, as did the idea of bringing federal curriculum up to par with public institutions. To make the schools more effective, the committee suggested that a complete high school program be offered at major Indian schools and vocational training be more directly related to reservation conditions. Although the Indian Office acknowledged the usefulness of the report and even implemented a few of the suggestions, radical reformers were far from satisfied as the old system continued to limp along.[37]

As criticism of the nonreservation schools mounted in the years following the Committee of One Hundred report, conditions at Phoenix deteriorated, thereby giving more ammunition to reformers like Collier. The most difficult problems remained inadequate financial support, overcrowding, health, and discipline. Brown, finding himself the subject of increasing criticism, reluctantly spent most of his time and energy dealing with these issues.

During the four years following 1924, even more pupils were crammed into the school. By 1928 almost a thousand Indian youngsters were enrolled in a facility designed to accommodate seven hundred. To repeated requests for more funding, there was only a limited response. The Indian Office secured a few additional dollars, but the entire educational system needed far more financial aid than was provided. As a consequence, physical plants at Phoenix and elsewhere continued to deteriorate. Burke, constantly badgered by critics, was well aware of the problem. He noted in one circular that "the attention of the Office is repeatedly called to lack of ventilation in dormitories and toilets, to the promiscuous throwing of children's clothing on the floor and in corners. Overcrowding of Indian schools, particularly in the dormitories is a never ending source of criticism." Nevertheless, Burke refused to raise a fuss over appropriations. Instead, he encouraged superintendents to be more frugal. Such economies seldom worked. At Phoenix, Superintendent Brown found himself relying more and more on student labor to keep the institution in operation. Squads of student trainees, who should have been in the classroom, were put to work repairing buildings and machinery. Even so, each year the list of items needing repair grew longer. In addition, the campus was simply overcrowded. One inspector confided in 1925 that "the academic building, the diningroom and kitchen, and the domestic science department are inadequate in capacity for the needs of this school."[38]

The Indian Office continually reminded Brown to keep his enrollment in line with appropriations, but that was impossible. Even though the school stopped soliciting Papagos completely because of lack of space, parents persisted in bringing their children to Phoenix. With reservation schools either overcrowded or nonexistent, Brown felt compelled to enroll more pupils than he should have. Refusal appeared to condemn a child to a life of barbarism. In 1925 the headmaster explained his predicament to district supervisor E. H. Hammond, telling him the story of an old Papago man from Gila Bend who had recently shown up seeking admission for two young boys. Because the family lived a hundred miles from the nearest agency or school, Brown accepted the youngsters. "I cannot believe that you would have done differently had you been in my place," he told Hammond, "and there are many cases similar to this especially among the Papagos."[39]

Complicating matters even more was the decision to add the eleventh and twelfth grades to the curriculum. Partly in response to recommendations from the Committee of One Hundred, Burke adopted a policy modeled after the public school system, which usually operated on the basis of six elementary, three junior high, and three senior high grades. In 1926 three nonreservation schools—Chilocco, Albuquerque, and Salem— became full high schools. Phoenix followed suit the next year. The additional grades required several more teachers and pushed enrollment even higher as advanced students were retained for an additional two years. It was believed that the high school courses would benefit the Phoenix school, enabling it to compete with other nonreservation institutions and meet the increasing demand for high school graduates. The fact remained, however, that in 1928, Phoenix students ranged in grade from one to twelve.[40]

Overcrowding increasingly harmed student health. Epidemics of such diseases as measles, influenza, and whooping cough regularly swept the campus. In addition, tuberculosis continued to rear its ugly head. In 1925 the situation became so serious that Hopi parents demanded an investigation of the school's health program. In response to these concerns, the Bureau of Indian Affairs' chief medical supervisor visited the campus, reviewed sanitary procedures, and declared the conditions to be adequate. But, problems continued. Fortunately, the Indian Office encouraged staff members to be extremely careful regarding sanitation, and Brown initiated several programs to provide better health education, eliminate an unsatisfactory system of garbage disposal, and provide regular physical exams.

As a consequence, student health, though not especially good, was better than at most schools. One factor in keeping the school alert to potential health problems was Burke's personal sensitivity to the subject. He realized that schools were particularly vulnerable to charges of inadequate health care and went out of his way to neutralize critics on this issue. Thus Brown did what he could within the confines of his financial restraints. Some changes, such as providing a rest period for girls working in the sewing or laundry room, rotating chores, and eliminating hand-scrubbing of dishes, cost little or nothing to implement.[41]

Discipline also continued to attract attention. Brown put the best face on the matter, arguing that proper discipline promoted "self-control, promptness, and usefulness." The biggest problem for the ethnocentric administrator was what he considered moral delinquincy: sexual contact, runaways, and consumption of alcohol. Annual reports refrained from mentioning corporal punishment directly, yet it continued. Although such punishment was not unusual in the public schools of the day, federal school authorities were much more concerned with social offenses "on the part of these members of a primitive race whose moral standards have not reached the desired height." Besides taking what the superintendent described as the "usual measures," students whose conduct offended the staff were prohibited from participating in athletic, band, and social activities. Problems of contact between the sexes continued, with the school prohibiting anyone from graduating if they broke the code of moral conduct. Although Brown was clearly aware of the mounting criticism of the way pupils were treated, he continued to handle things in the same old way.[42]

Brown knew that the schools were being criticized because they attempted to destroy Indian culture. Yet here too he remained firm. Regarding a suggestion that traditional ceremonial dances be permitted at schools, he refused to make any concessions. Admitting that such dances were not necessarily immoral, he still refused to permit any "old-time Indian entertainment." Traditional ceremonies had been permitted once, lamented the superintendent, and it took several weeks before the pupils could again concentrate on "proper educational channels." Besides, he maintained with disdain, returned students seemed to have no difficulty in resuming their dances once they got home.[43] In short, the Phoenix Indian School was unwilling to make any concession to reform demands as long as it seemed possible to continue with the assimilationist policies that had long been in effect.

The exact degree to which Brown and his staff were aware of the rising sentiment for reform is difficult to ascertain. They could not have been oblivious to the intensified lobbying campaign of John Collier and others. Collier's constant criticism put the Indian Office on the defensive, and as the vocal reformer began to pay more attention to educational issues, the schools found it increasingly necessary to defend themselves. Nor would Collier relent. In the fall of 1926 he and Wisconsin Congressman James A. Frear made an extensive auto tour of the West in a quest for firsthand information. The pair spent some time in Arizona, visiting various reservations and apparently stopping briefly at the Phoenix school. Upon completion of the tour, Collier and Frear issued a stinging denunciation of Indian policy, criticizing the schools for kidnapping children, operating overcrowded and unhealthful facilities, and destroying the Indians' heritage. Given the fact that most of these conditions existed at Phoenix, it is interesting to note that Frear criticized the central Arizona school because it was a relatively decent place (which it certainly was compared to reservation schools). He charged the Indian Office with making Phoenix and a few selected schools showcases in order to offset the rising tide of criticism.[44]

Assistant Commissioner Edgar B. Meritt made a feeble attempt to defend the office from such criticism. In December 1926 he delivered a long speech deriding Congressman Frear to a group of Oakland, California, businessmen. He denied that children were being kidnapped, noting that the government had more voluntary students than it could handle. Meritt then went on to describe the federal school system as among the best in the United States. Quoting a member of the Board of Indian Commissioners, he went so far as to assert that "there are no finer [schools] in the country, public or private.... In educational theory and, in the larger schools, in equipment, none surpass and few equal them." That such statements were patently misleading was of no concern to Meritt. He was mainly interested in defending the bureaucracy against Collier. The assistant commissioner thus ended his talk with a quote from Burke that summed up the position of the Indian Office. "I cannot conceive of anything that would do more serious injury to the Indians than the campaign being waged by John Collier aided by Congressman Frear of Wisconsin," he concluded.[45] The battle over the future of Indian education was thus joined.

Unconvincing statements from government officials to the effect that current Indian policy was working only served to spur the reformers on. Consequently, Collier and Frear began to demand a thorough examination of Indian policy. In February 1927, Frear persuaded a Senate Subcommittee on Indian Affairs to consider launching a congressional investigation of the Indian Office. Frear and Collier were the star witnesses and they said a lot about education. They noted that boarding schools were crowded 38 percent beyond capacity, that health problems were severe, and that financial problems abounded. In one instance, Frear remarked that Navajos taken to Phoenix readily contracted tuberculosis because of the changed environment. Most of these conditions could be corrected, suggested the Wisconsin legislator, by constructing reservation day schools. Implied, but not specifically stated, was the belief that nonreservation boarding schools should be closed. It was largely a matter of philosophy to Collier and Frear. The old assimilationist approach was no longer acceptable. Frear summed it up for the subcommittee: "I think the school situation is indefensible, as it is carried out today. It is indefensible not to have some day schools on the reservation, not to have reservation schools where the Indians can be kept in touch with their parents. The theory is that by taking them away from their parents they will lose the Indian tradition and they will be changed in their life and prepared for a higher civilization. That may be open to question after you see what has been done."[46]

Collier wanted an immediate congressional examination of current practices. His tactics had their impact, although not exactly in the way envisioned. While Collier had been lobbying Congress, Interior Secretary Work, under considerable pressure, decided to launch an investigation of his own in hopes of quieting the criticism.[47] This survey would become known as the Meriam Report, and it produced a tremendous impact on Indian education. Phoenix would not escape the furor.

8
End of an Era

ON FEBRUARY 21, 1928, the Meriam Report was handed to Secretary of the Interior Hubert Work. Prepared by Lewis Meriam and a staff of experts working for the Institute for Government Research at the Brookings Institution, the report was entitled *The Problem of Indian Administration*. Some two years in the making, the lengthy survey provided a detailed review of nearly every facet of contemporary policy, analyzing administrative and financial conditions, Indian health, tribal economic status, the allotment system, family and community activities, legal difficulties, and, of course, education. The Meriam study presented the nation with a comprehensive, scientific evaluation of the Native American population, pinpointing problems and offering solutions. It was destined to have a far-reaching impact on American policy. Coming as it did at a time of substantial reform fervor, the report bolstered the demand for radical change. Activist John Collier, though distressed that the study tended to place more blame on Congress than on the Bureau of Indian Affairs, regarded it as a ringing condemnation of the whole system—a document that would force a dramatic redirection of Indian policy.[1]

The combination of the Meriam Report and a renewed assault on assimilation significantly affected the Phoenix Indian School in the years between 1928 and 1935, changing the institution's internal structure, subjecting it to embarrassing publicity, bringing to an end traditional ideas and programs, and nearly culminating in the school's closure. By the first years of the New Deal, the old program of assimilationist education was dead, and a new era in educational history had begun.

W. Carson Ryan, a highly regarded educator from Swarthmore College, wrote the education section of the Meriam survey. Long an advocate of progressive schooling, Ryan pulled no punches in condemning the current system and demanding a total change in direction. His narrative began: "The most fundamental need in Indian education is a change in point of view. Whatever may have been the official government attitude, education for the Indian in the past has proceeded largely on the theory that it is necessary to remove the Indian child as far as possible from his home environment; whereas the modern point of view in education and social work lays stress on upbringing in the natural setting of home and family life." With this in mind, Ryan presented a stinging criticism of the boarding schools, tackling just about every issue the reformers had brought forth over the past few years. Problems that school administrators knew from firsthand experience—overcrowding, want of resources, health, discipline, curriculum, and a lack of success—were addressed with such vigor that few readers could doubt that boarding school education was a disaster.[2]

While the Meriam Report faulted both reservation and off-reservation boarding schools, it came down hardest on the reservation facilities, which were admittedly inferior to the big urban institutions. The nonreservation schools, however, did not escape Ryan's fury. Anyone familiar with the recent administration of industrial education recognized the problems, but the report told a story of total incompetence and inhumanity on the part of the government. There is little question that the Meriam Report made the schools look worse than they were by playing up inadequacies and overlooking accomplishments. Still, there was more truth than exaggeration in the survey.

Ryan devoted considerable attention to such areas as health and overcrowding, relating them directly to insufficient congressional support. He revealed that many health problems were caused by substandard meals provided to students by administrators forced to feed youngsters on eleven cents per day for each child. Diseases like tuberculosis and trachoma flourished under such conditions. Overcrowding compounded the problem by squeezing more pupils into dormitory and toilet facilities than they were capable of handling, thereby promoting the spread of contagious disease. Such conditions could be corrected by proper funding, Ryan argued, as could the dilapidated state of the physical plants. The educator noted:

> Old buildings, often kept in use long after they should have been pulled down, and admittedly bad fire-risks in many instances; crowded dormitories; conditions of sanitation that are usually perhaps as good as they can be under the circumstances, but certainly below accepted standards; boilers and machinery out-of-date and in some instances unsafe, to the point of having long since been condemned, but never replaced; ... schoolrooms seldom showing knowledge of modern principles of lighting and ventilation; ... an abnormally long day, which cuts to a dangerous point the normal allowance for sleep and rest, ... have disastrous effects upon mental health and the development of wholesome personality.[3]

While not all of these conditions existed at Phoenix, many obviously did. Ryan urged that overcrowding be immediately ended, preferably by opening more day schools.

Boarding schools were additionally castigated for their noneducational use of student labor. Ryan remarked that children above the fourth grade ordinarily worked half a day, attending class for only a few hours. Much of this work supported the institution and could not legitimately be called occupational training. "The question may very properly be raised," noted the survey, "as to whether much of the work of Indian children in boarding schools would not be prohibited in many states by the child labor laws." Queries as to whether the welfare of Indian children could in any way be helped by the forced use of their own labor to support the schools were answered decidedly in the negative by Ryan and his colleagues.[4]

Questions about the competence of teachers and other school employees also attracted Professor Ryan's attention. Stating the obvious, he observed that the Indian service was handicapped by low salaries. Under such circumstances, adequate standards were difficult, if not impossible, to maintain. Many teachers were simply unfit for their work: "Although some of the non-reservation schools purport to be high schools, the qualifications of their teaching force do not entitle them to free and unrestricted recognition as accredited high schools." Better starting salaries would attract better teachers, thought Ryan, and monetary rewards for good teaching performance promised to revitalize existing Indian service personnel.[5] Something definitely needed to be done to upgrade the teaching force before any real educational progress could be made.

The controversial topic of discipline received particularly close scrutiny in the report. The Meriam staff did a great deal to document some of the harsh punishment meted out at Indian schools. Jails, confinement without food under unsanitary conditions, and a general inclination to deal with minor infractions by locking up students seemed to prevail. The desire to prevent contact between the sexes, moreover, led to unjustifiable restrictions that were not only humiliating but in some instances dangerous. At some locations, it was found, girls were locked up for the night, windows were nailed shut, and fire-escape doors were bolted, all in the name of morality. Such medieval practices could be eliminated, suggested the study, without endangering students' morals or increasing "instances of disaster."[6]

Despite this criticism, the Meriam Report concluded that nonreservation schools continued to be the "most prominent feature of Government Indian education." However, the old philosophy of removing Indian children from their traditional environment had no place in the modern world, and was unjustifiable. Young children, in particular, needed to remain close to home and family. There was no recommendation to immediately abandon the off-reservation schools, but their function needed to change: they "should be reserved for pupils above the sixth grade, and probably soon thereafter for pupils of ninth grade and above." Such alterations would leave Indian children with their parents during the formative years and convert nonreservation campuses into Indian high schools. Confining enrollment to advanced grades also promised to resolve overcrowding by reducing the number of children eligible to leave home.[7]

Additionally, the approach to education at these schools needed revamping. In direct reference to Phoenix and other large facilities, the report noted that such schools were "'institutionalized' to an extreme degree." Amid hundreds of students and an inflexible administrative structure, the child was ignored. Individual pupil needs demanded attention: "This will necessitate rooms for two to four students, for example, rather than the immense open dormitory system that prevails so generally; much more adequate health care than is now provided; smaller classes; less of the marching and regimentation that look showy to the outside visitor but hide real dangers." Neither could a curriculum that provided a uniform course of study and forced every student to do the same thing in the same way be expected to accomplish the desired end. Ryan instead recommended that each major school specialize in the vocational programs best suited to its abilities. Finally, in a remark that predicted future developments, he suggested that some schools be reserved for special types of pupils, notably mentally impaired, sick, delinquent, and maladjusted children who needed special treatment.[8]

In sum, the Meriam Report recommended a drastic change in the system. The old assimilation program had to be done away with. In its place the nonreservation schools were expected to become vocational high schools devoid of the regimentation and cultural immersion that had once been their trademark. Although the study failed to satisfy a number of interests and was deeply resented by old guard employees, Phoenix felt its full impact. Within five years almost all of its recommendations had been applied to the school.

The transition did not take place easily. With so much at stake, it is not surprising that charges and recriminations were exchanged, investigations demanded, longtime personnel replaced, and eventually a new regime installed. Because of the institutionalized nature of the old system and certain inevitable obstacles, it took time to make any noticeable headway.

Specifically, those who continued to favor forced acculturation fought to retain their way of doing things, resisting to the end the tidal wave of reform that eventually engulfed them.

Neither the Indian Office nor Superintendent Brown demonstrated great enthusiasm for the Meriam Report. Commissioner Burke had no political choice but to acknowledge that it made worthwhile suggestions; he promised to study it closely while claiming that a few of its recommendations were already in force. Rather than condemn his own office, Burke used the report to argue for more funding. The commissioner's annual report for 1928 thus concentrated on financial affairs, regretting that appropriations for school purposes had increased less than 20 percent in the past ten years. "Shortage of funds for the support of Indian schools makes it impossible to equip them adequately," he claimed.[9] Still, there was no indication that the government planned any significant changes.

Brown was even more emphatic. Editorializing in the pages of the *Native American*, he lashed out at critics of government policy, stating that neither the Meriam Report nor radicals like Collier gave the current system enough credit, preferring instead to emphasize the negative. "These critics make no effort to verify the contents of a damaging story," he complained, "nor to inquire as to the credibility of witnesses whom they quote. That magazines of good repute and men in high official positions will conduct so-called investigations in such a manner would be beyond belief did we not have the evidence before us." While agreeing that the report did document certain deficiencies, the Phoenix schoolmaster ventured a few suggestions of his own. He felt that most problems could be resolved by restricting government educational benefits to full bloods and increasing the congressional appropriation to $350 per pupil. "It is better to have $350 a year for the real Indian who needs it than $175 for faded ones who want it." Brown, of course, realized that such a plan benefited his school, which enrolled almost exclusively full bloods, at the expense of schools elsewhere. Then, in direct contrast to the Meriam Report suggestions, he added that should funding remain inadequate, enrollment ought to be curtailed by concentrating on the primary grades and leaving high school education to the states. Finally, he complained, the schools should not be blamed for a majority of the health and educational difficulties. Government programs and medical personnel were unwelcome among tribes where old prejudices and treatments prevailed. And, Brown noted in a comment reflecting his commitment to forced assimilation, "if we would lift a race from ignorance and disease, we must do many things which they do not want done."[10]

Regardless of such expressed sentiments, the Indian Office came under intense pressure to do something about the Indian schools. A confident John Collier, realizing he had the administration reeling, intensified his attack on the commissioner's office. Not content with the Meriam Report, Collier used his influence with Congress to focus attention on Burke, charging gross incompetence. The harried bureaucrat responded largely by making rash and unsupportable statements challenging the motives of his critics. His only concrete action came in regard to discipline. Concerned with public images, Burke had earlier ordered the abolition of school jails (January 3, 1928), stating that if confinement was necessary, "any spare room" would suffice. Now, on January 10, 1929, he went further by forbidding the use of corporal punishment in federal schools. This order struck down one of the most controversial aspects of educational policy, and when combined with the closing of school jails, seemed to put an end to what critics called "brutalizations conducted by principals and disciplinarians."[11]

The order displeased and angered the Phoenix headmaster, who was headed in the opposite direction. Indeed, in the fall of 1928 he had proposed that chronic deserters be incarcerated in the state reformatory until they reached age twenty-one. Shortly after Burke issued his ban on corporal punishment, Brown responded angrily, reporting that discipline had already suffered and several boys had "been dismissed who might have been saved." The superintendent frankly admitted his desire to preserve the independence of action formerly accorded school administrators. Let each chief administrator make decisions on the appropriate punishment, he suggested, while retaining proper safeguards against abuse. Brown's argument was based on the assumption that schools would become totally chaotic if administrators appeared weak. "We deal with a primitive race, with persons who often lack appreciation of the better reasons for good behavior," he concluded, asking that the Indian Office return to the former policy of permitting corporal punishment as long as it was not "cruel or degrading."[12]

Considering the way things had gone since the Meriam Report was made public, staff members at Phoenix were probably not too surprised when word reached them that a new commissioner had been appointed. Charles Burke had become such a liability that the incoming Hoover administration accepted his resignation in March, 1929. The new commissioner, Charles J. Rhoads, seemed to be just the opposite of his predecessor, the kind of person who would promote the changes suggested by the Meriam Report and demanded by Collier. The prominent Philadelphia businessman, a vice-president of Bryn Mawr College and staunch Quaker, had long been involved with Indian affairs, serving at the time of his appointment as the president of the Indian Rights Association. Rhoads was committed to reform and eager to get started. His choice of close friend and fellow Quaker Joseph H. Scattergood to serve as assistant commissioner strengthened the feeling that a new era lay just around the corner. So good did the prospect for change seem that even Collier was willing to hold his tongue. Although the reform leader would soon become disenchanted with Rhoads's businesslike approach and slow pace, historians of the period have concluded that Rhoads succeeded in implementing many of the Meriam suggestions, thus setting the stage for Collier's Indian New Deal.[13] Without doubt his administration left a significant impact on the Phoenix Indian School.

John Brown responded to the Rhoads appointment by ignoring it. Instead of contemplating future changes, the old-line administrator penned a tribute to former commissioner Burke. Yet there was no avoiding the fact that the Indian Office was preparing to alter the nonreservation school system. The first major directive arrived in July 1929, ordering the Phoenix school to immediately eliminate first- and second-grade pupils and phase out the third grade within a year. Reporting to reservation superintendents that "I regret the necessity for this action, but there appears to be no alternative," Brown sent twenty-eight pupils home, expressing hope they would eventually end up in public, mission, or day schools. At the same time, he redoubled his efforts to recruit students above the sixth grade and encourage admissions to public schools. Concerning the enrollment of Indian students in public schools, Brown made contact with the state superintendent of public education, who determined that Indian pupils could be admitted to local institutions on condition the government pay their full tuition cost. Because Rhoads generally favored such an arrangement, Brown eventually entered into an agreement with the state of Arizona which provided that the government would pay between thirty-five and fifty cents per day for Indian children enrolled in public schools. Although this did not dramatically increase public school enrollment (most of Arizona's Indian population lived far from public schools and were in no rush to attend such facilities), Arizona became one of the first states to agree to such a plan, thereby paving the way for the passage of the Johnson-O'Malley Act of April 1934, which confirmed the legality of such educational contracts.[14]

Curriculum also began to undergo noticeable change. In November 1929 the school was required to provide a list of the vocational classes it was best suited to offer and to improve the quality of instruction. Finding that many current instructors were unable to teach satisfactorily without close supervision, consultants were hired to work with shopmen in the preparation of courses. Although this seemed to improve the system for work training, Brown remained hesitant to do much with the academic department. "In general," he admitted, "it may be said that we favor the vocational or trades school for Phoenix, in preference to the academic high school with an industrial department." Rhoads, however, wanted to strengthen the academic program and insisted on improvements. One favorite proposal involved altering the old formula of half the student's time being spent at work training. The Indian Office opted instead for devoting three-quarters of the day to academics. Brown introduced the plan reluctantly, complaining that he had no funds to hire additional teachers and expressing the hope that a more traditional course of study could be devised. In a related move, the academic department was reorganized, giving it responsibility for all instruction, vocational as well as academic.[15] These changes gave some additional prestige to academic instruction, but they had little immediate impact on the basic curriculum. In the meantime, Rhoads continued his experiments with the proper balance between academic and vocational training.

Perhaps the most significant aspect of Rhoads's administration involved an increase in funding for Indian schools. On this point, at least, he and Brown saw eye to eye. Even with the onset of the Great Depression, which severely disrupted government projects, Rhoads managed to redirect funds into more useful channels, and after 1930 he secured substantially increased appropriations. The effects of this effort quickly became evident at Phoenix. Although only a few additional teachers were hired, big advances came in the more visible realm of health services. In December 1929 the school announced that in "keeping step with the constant growth of educational institutions in the valley," a new sixty-bed hospital would be erected on campus and a second unit added to the tuberculosis sanatorium. These additions promised to improve student health care as well as provide better treatment for nearby reservation residents who had no hospital facilities of their own. When the hospital was opened in the fall of 1930 it contained four wards, a dental clinic, modern sterilization equipment, electric lighting and refrigeration, and other up-to-date facilities. It thus became one of the best health care facilities in the Indian service. In another health matter, Brown, acting on orders, realized some success in improving the quality of food served to students by providing a more balanced diet and an abundance of vegetables, milk, eggs, and fruit collected from the school farm.[16]

Rhoads undoubtedly would have done even more were it in his power. Nevertheless, he made great strides toward modernizing the system and fulfilling the recommendations of the Meriam Report. Because Rhoads was a practical man, however, he hesitated to rush headlong into revisions without properly considering the consequences. His reluctance to act on emotion alone eventually created a rift with Collier, who approached the subject from a different philosophical viewpoint. Collier demanded instant gratification, and if it failed to come fast enough, or there was any hint of backsliding, he did not hesitate to lash out at the men in charge. Just such a circumstance developed in the spring of 1930 when the issue of discipline and punishment at Phoenix flared into a national scandal.

Trouble began in March 1930 when, after months of study, Commissioner Rhoads issued circular number 2666, which said, in essence, that certain forms of punishment would be permitted if necessary to maintain order. Although Rhoads did not regard the circular as sanctioning corporal punishment, it gave local superintendents wide latitude and allowed them to use "quiet rooms" and other devices, provided there was no physical abuse. His action apparently came in response to pressure from school superintendents like Brown who had continued to maintain that they could not keep discipline without effective punishments.[17]

On the surface the circular seemed harmless enough, but its publication incensed Collier and widened the split between him and the administration. The radical reformer regarded the circular as a step backward that sanctioned all forms of corporal punishment. He therefore decided to challenge Rhoads over the issue. In casting about for a method of bringing the matter forth, Collier latched onto several articles printed in the *Arizona Labor Journal*, a union newspaper. The stories maintained that Mrs. Elsie Schmidt, a tailor at Phoenix Indian School, and her husband, also a school employee (carpenter), had been fired on trumped-up charges because they dared to reveal campus brutality. Accompanying the story about the Schmidts was a list of severe punishments that allegedly had been inflicted in recent years, including the death in 1922 of one boy who had run away after supposedly being beaten into unconsciousness at the school. Collier used the story to denounce the new policy, demanding an investigation. Speaking as secretary of the Indian Defense Association in late April, the nationally known reform advocate charged "government brutality and injustice to the Indian," claiming that the commissioner's order permitted the return of flogging and imprisonment, and that schools like Phoenix had never, in fact, stopped the practice. The sensational nature of the allegations persuaded the Senate Subcommittee on Indian Affairs to hold a hearing on the Phoenix situation in late May 1930. Collier was the star witness.[18]

Even before the hearings convened, there was little doubt that corporal punishment had indeed continued at the Arizona school. Superintendent Brown, of course, favored such disciplinary measures and had apparently chosen to ignore the ban. Eventually word of this situation spread to the Indian Office, probably through some disgruntled employees, perhaps the Schmidts. The basic accusation was that head disciplinarian Jacob Duran and his assistants regularly struck children with their fists, beat them with leather straps, knocked them down, and kicked them. As a consequence, Rhoads had sent Supervisor Carl Moore to investigate in July 1929. Moore held long discussions with the Schmidts and other personnel before concluding that some employees were in fact prone to hasty action. Among the incidents that Moore reported was the severe beating of a boy who took a bath in violation of rules. The report contained evidence of numerous policy violations, but it was not conclusive. In the spring of 1930, therefore, Inspector H. H. Fiske was sent to Phoenix to provide a more complete examination. Fiske, however, was an old-guard Bureau employee and a friend of Brown, and spent most of his time looking into the activities of troublesome employees. Eventually

Fiske charged the Schmidts, who were foreign-born, with disloyalty and Bolshevik activity in an effort to embarrass the government. Brown, who had already recommended the dismissal of the Schmidts, concurred. Soon thereafter he found a pretext to fire the Schmidt couple and several other employees.[19] At this point (April 1930) the Schmidts went to the *Arizona Labor Journal*, and Collier became involved.

The Washington hearings brought a number of forces into play as the issue was emotionally debated. Newspapers had a field day as the Indian Office, represented by Rhoads and Scattergood, defended itself while Collier paraded forth a variety of sensational charges. Arizona Senator Carl Hayden led off the proceedings by defending the school's management, pointing out that all but 2 of the 106 employees stood squarely behind Superintendent Brown. Hayden also presented a resolution prepared by the employees' union denying that pupils were brutally treated or had died from their punishment, and "that other matters referred to are grossly distorted." The senator thus lent his prestige to the position that the allegations were raised by one or two employees who had performed unsatisfactorily and were published without sufficient verification.[20]

When Collier took the stand, he presented what he called "the record," admitting that he was not personally familiar with any of the events. Arguing that the Phoenix school's administration was guilty of brutal treatment, mismanagement, and retaliation against informants, he concentrated on the inspection reports of Moore and Fiske. Collier claimed to possess evidence of ninety-nine cases of "brutalizations and assaults," many attributable to Jacob Duran. Despite overwhelming evidence and Bureau instructions to Brown to cease such practices and dismiss guilty employees, the reform leader charged that the Fiske investigation had been a whitewash wherein the Schmidts were framed so they could be drummed out of the service. In fact, he stated, brutal punishment had been covered up, loyal and sincere employees dismissed, and the guilty allowed to escape entirely.[21]

Charles Rhoads finally testified on May 27, countering much of Collier's argument. He pointed out that most of the alleged abuses occurred years ago, that such activities were not presently taking place, and that the Schmidts were dismissed because they deliberately broke a quarantine, thereby endangering the health of nine hundred pupils. Rhoads did admit that the Fiske report concentrated on nonessentials and was unsatisfactory. He also promised that either he or Scattergood would soon visit Phoenix to review the matter with Brown and his staff. Finally, Rhoads issued a statement directly contradicting Collier's interpretation of the circular, saying that superintendents were never authorized to administer "brutal and degrading punishment," and if subordinates misunderstood the order, he would set them straight. Following this, Bureau chief inspector F. H. Daiker carefully reviewed the official record at Phoenix. He noted that only nine of the alleged incidents occurred after Burke's order of January 10, 1929. Many of the charges, moreover, were not sustained by supporting evidence. After these announcements, the hearing limped to an indecisive conclusion as Hayden objected that the hearings were not held in Phoenix, the subcommittee promised to visit Arizona, and matters were left without resolution.[22] Collier apparently thought he had made his point.

The sensational hearings blackened the reputations of Phoenix Indian School and Superintendent Brown. Indeed, Brown became discouraged, seeming to lose his enthusiasm and fire. Undoubtedly, his attitude changed because the Indian Bureau was in a state of transition, with the old guard being phased out. An example of this trend came in September 1930 when Commissioner Rhoads ousted the Bureau's director of Indian education, Hervey B. Pearis, replacing him with W. Carson Ryan. The appointment of Ryan, author of the Meriam Report's education section, temporarily quieted reform criticism of the Indian Office. Ryan firmly believed that school personnel, including superintendents, needed professional training. It took him only a short time to persuade Rhoads to initiate a complete reorganization of the Indian service. Basically stated, the reorganization of March 30, 1931, divided the Bureau into five sections, each controlled by a "professional" director. Education was headed by Ryan, and like the other four divisions, it stressed the hiring of college-trained personnel at higher salaries. Though older employees could not be fired, considerable pressure was exerted to ease them out. As a consequence, a new breed of professionally trained, socially minded educators came to dominate the Bureau's top administration. Their progressive ideas, to say the least, distinguished them from employees hired before the Meriam Report.[23]

Brown, meanwhile, continued to insist that the problems of Indian education could be rectified by a few simple changes and that the solutions offered by the reformers were far from novel. He remained convinced that the elimination of mixed-blood students would restore fiscal solvency, that the schools were doing much more than they were credited with, and that outsiders who did not understand practical operations would eventually ruin the system. He was also sure that boarding schools would be needed as long as "the Indian is regarded as a Federal responsibility." In one issue of the school paper, the headmaster summed up his discouragement by lamenting "let us not feel too sorry for ourselves, we 'old timers.' We are not the first nor shall we be the last to blaze trails or cut notches in the rocks of the mountain side for the feet of future climbers."[24]

The Phoenix superintendent was clearly fighting a losing battle to keep the old system alive. Adding to his frustration, the Indian Office began to take advantage of recent federal legislation lowering the retirement age for Indian school employees. The first to feel the effect was Amanda Chingren, the longtime outing matron who in many ways represented the repressive attitudes of the past. Under the new law Miss Chingren was ordered to retire early despite her appeal to remain in the service for two additional years. In the face of such administrative action, Brown refused to back down from his principles, continuing to act defiantly. On June 25, 1930, for example, he issued a staff memorandum on discipline. Regretting outside interference and the "drastic circular forbidding corporal punishment," he carefully permitted the continued use of corporal punishment. In response to the faddish argument that Indian parents did not punish their children, Brown defiantly answered that "if we are to use Indian standards of living and methods of character building, our whole system of education for Indians would seem to be unnecessary."[25] Independent action of this sort did little to endear him to his superiors.

Any chance Brown had of surviving vanished in April 1931 when the Senate Subcommittee on Indian Affairs held a series of hearings in Arizona as part of a continuing survey of conditions. The subcommittee met at Phoenix Indian School on April 17, 1931, with Arizona's entire congressional delegation as well as Assistant Commissioner Scattergood on hand. Although Collier was not present, his sentiments were well represented by Senators Burton K. Wheller, Lynn J. Frazier, and Elmer Thomas. The primary witness was John B. Brown, and the hearing centered on the effectiveness of nonreservation education.

Brown's performance under intense and often hostile questioning proved somewhat less than impressive. On the stand he appeared uncharacteristically ill informed, confused, and intimidated. Those who knew him well believed him to be totally discouraged, unable to convince the subcommittee that his school was doing an effective job. Much of the questioning dealt with why students could not find stable employment. When asked why, for example, with all the shops and vocational services, young Indian men and women were unable to secure decent work, Brown could only use the old argument that Indians were temperamentally unsuited to work without supervision. On several occasions he admitted that it was impossible to place many graduates and even his own institution refused to hire former students for advanced positions. Unfortunately, Brown's vacilating testimony combined with Senator Wheeler's penetrating questions to leave the impression that no pupil could find a job. At one point Wheeler queried the headmaster as to why the school's auto-mechanic course failed to produce a single qualified repairman. Brown lamely replied that distractions, lack of autos to repair, and various other difficulties seemed to cause the problem.

By the end of the day Wheeler was incensed, telling the witness that if a proper education could not be offered, none should be offered at all. "If you can not get Indians to sweep those floors as good as white people and can not get cooks over there who have been taught home economics," he informed Brown, "it is time to do away with home economics, it is time to do away with the Indian boarding schools altogether."[26] Assistant Commissioner Scattergood, repeatedly forced to come forward to correct Brown or clarify government policy, seemed relieved when the subcommittee moved on.

After his meek performance, Brown lost whatever support he might have had. At least one retired old-guard government employee wrote Senator Hayden complaining that the headmaster failed to stand up for his principles, particularly by failing to point out that Indians did not have "the ability to utilize this schooling in practical life equal to our own race." Most important, Brown had become a liability to the Rhoads administration, which was already seeking ways to replace old employees. It was thus no great surprise when on June 6, 1931, Brown publicly announced his retirement, effective July 1. His farewell message, published in the *Native American,* admitted that the years at Phoenix had not flowed "exactly as a peaceful river." Still, Brown remained committed to his own brand of assimilation and to the end he expressed no enlightenment.[27] His departure marked the dividing point between the old and new philosophies at Phoenix.

The school's new superintendent fit well into the new direction chartered by Rhoads. Carl H. Skinner, who took charge of the school in August, had served as the headmaster of several non-Indian schools before earning a doctorate in education at

Stanford University. More significantly, the young scholar possessed no prior connection with the Indian service; he was hired to modernize the facility, eliminate waste, ease out the old guard, and assure that the institution provided useful training. He quickly initiated a series of changes that demonstrated that a new era in Indian education had indeed arrived. His first move was more symbolic than real, but when classes opened in the fall of 1931, students and Phoenicians found the *Native American* discontinued and a new weekly magazine, the *Phoenix Redskin*, published in its place. Skinner informed readers that the new journal would confine itself to student affairs, avoiding the rambling discussions of policy matters so common under Brown.[28]

To a certain degree at least, the new school administrator continued the trend already in effect. Old-guard employees continued to be retired or transferred. Jacob F. Duran, for example, the head disciplinarian and chief figure in the flogging scandal of 1930, lasted less than five months before being sent to Tuba City, Arizona. Simultaneously, a new group of college-trained teachers were hired, giving the staff a more professional composition. Skinner also implemented new ideas that promised to improve the quality of education. In conformity with the progressive-education ideal of the Rhoads administration, one of his first tasks was to effectively reduce enrollment in order to provide more individual attention. In the fall of 1932 the school consequently announced plans to eliminate the remaining elementary grades, thus becoming a junior and senior high school. At the same time, enrollment, which then stood at eight hundred, would be reduced to 650. This reduction coincided with similar moves at other nonreservation institutions as the government attempted to convert all such facilities to high schools. In addition, although the half day of vocational training was restored in some areas, a new curriculum waited until the tenth grade before requiring pupils to specialize in a trade. Finally, in conformity with the new voluntary theme of off-reservation education, nearly all the pupils were permitted to return home for summer vacation. No pressure was placed on them to return the following semester, yet a remarkable 91 percent came back.[29]

Even though changes were taking place, critics of the Indian Bureau continued to complain about the slow and deliberate approach of the Rhoads administration. With the nation struggling through the worst of the Great Depression, the commissioner's office found it increasingly difficult to keep up the pace of reform, thus providing Collier and associates with even more ammunition. John Collier had always demanded a clean sweep, and his opportunity came with the election of Franklin D. Roosevelt in 1932 and the beginning of the New Deal. Roosevelt quickly named Collier head of the Indian Bureau. Thus the nation's leading Indian reformer, the man who had demanded so much from the outside, set out to complete his agenda. The Indian New Deal, with Collier at the helm, attempted to implement fully the Meriam Report while eliminating the assimilationist approach to Indian education. Collier relied heavily on his chief educational advisors, W. Carson Ryan and Willard W. Beatty, both educators in the progressive tradition, to carry out most of the program. Their main objectives were to provide students with more personalized attention, secure a qualified teaching staff, and pay more attention to Native American heritage. The Collier regime was also committed to opening more day schools and deemphasizing boarding facilities.

Several important developments occurred at Phoenix during the early years of Collier's administration. The most significant involved a continued decrease in enrollment and concentration on a high school program. Because of Collier's commitment to day schools, many new schools were constructed in Arizona, and older ones were improved. In particular, reservation education near Phoenix was expanded and upgraded. Both Salt River and Sacaton began offering junior high courses, making it possible to reduce the number of seventh- and eighth-grade pupils at Phoenix. Nevertheless, enrollment pressures remained high. Because the federal school system was simultaneously becoming more efficient, more children graduated from reservation schools to seek admission at Phoenix. In 1935, with his enrollment limited to 650, Skinner continued to receive applications from more students than could be accommodated. His main problem was with Collier, who felt the school should shrink even more. With the depression making funds scarce, and most of the Bureau's money going into the construction and staffing of day schools, considerable pressure was placed on Phoenix to cut back, and Skinner had no choice but to comply. As a consequence, in 1935 the number of pupils was reduced to five hundred, and the following year it leveled out at 425. To maintain the institution at that level, Skinner was forced to reduce seventh- and eighth-grade programs and pay more attention to the academic standards of those entering the school. Unfortunately, those refused admission had few educational alternatives and were prevented from completing their schooling—an unanticipated side effect of the emphasis on day schools.[30]

School financial problems also intensified during the New Deal. During 1934 and 1935 several teaching and staff positions, including that of assistant superintendent, were eliminated. Skinner realized these cutbacks harmed the effectiveness of his school, but he was in no position to do anything beyond complain. He did point out, however, that some of Collier's pet ideas caused unexpected hardships, mentioning, in one instance, that as the student body became older, children could not get half-price railway rates.[31] Budgetary problems also required the school to continue its reliance on student labor. Both Skinner and Collier disliked the practice, but they were overwhelmed by circumstances and forced to carry on one of the programs so heavily criticized by the Meriam study. Ironically, they quickly dragged out old justifications and applied them to the current situation. In 1934, for example, schoolboys from Phoenix were put to work full time building a day school at Salt River. In addition, all campus irregular labor and repair jobs were turned over to students. Skinner reported that, "while work done this way is naturally slower than when outsiders are employed, it has brought about a big saving in money and has given the boys the kind of training that they need."[32]

Curriculum changes were apparent during the New Deal period. The school, of course, remained committed to some form of vocational training, but academics became even more advanced. By 1935 a standard high school curriculum was offered that included four years of English, courses in general science and biology, history, economics, mathematics, and geography, plus a number of electives. Vocational training, in the form of shops offered in printing, auto mechanics, blacksmithing, masonry, carpentry, and printing, continued to be the mainstay of work training, while those interested in farming had an extensive agricultural program available. Girls were provided with the usual home economics courses. Despite the traditional nature of these industrial programs, there were some new wrinkles. One was that the point at which students needed to select a trade was pushed back to the junior year. It was also recognized that pupils would return to their reservations. Vocational training, therefore, was pointed much more in the direction of occupations that might be useful to reservation residents. Although Arizona was in the midst of the depression, Superintendent Skinner was able to boast that more graduates than ever were securing employment and that the success of former students in a reservation environment seemed to improve steadily. More were also going to college.[33]

Other major advances involved improving student social life, providing more personal attention, ending severe forms of regimentation, and easing the sense of alienation by permitting pupils to retain more of their cultural heritage. Although it would be an exaggeration to suggest that Indian youngsters were suddenly permitted to remain traditional Indians, Collier at least made some attempt to encourage appreciation of their native ways. He expected them to assimilate yet did not feel they had to give up their unique background. This attitude made itself felt at Phoenix in 1934 when the school began using Indian craftsmen to teach such traditional skills as pottery and basketmaking. At the same time, in an effort to assure religious freedom, compulsory attendance at religious services was eliminated. Although some pupils undoubtedly took advantage of this order to enjoy more leisure time, interest in socially oriented religious activities like the YMCA and YWCA appears to have continued at a high level. In another significant development, the academic department moved to introduce a semester of Indian history or anthropology. Meanwhile, the military regimentation so long a familiar part of student life was all but eliminated. The National Guard unit continued to function, but in general a great deal more individual freedom was permitted. Restraints on social contact between the sexes were also relaxed. School officials found, much to the amazement of old-time employees, that students responded well when entrusted with more responsibility. A merit-demerit system replaced most forms of punishment and seemed to work effectively. In general, then, the intense pressure of former years was reduced. In its place students were provided with more social activities. Extracurricular organizations flourished, and the athletic program, including intramural sports, was expanded to include almost every student.[34] As a consequence, the social, academic, and athletic life at Phoenix Indian School came to resemble that of a typical American high school.

New Deal programs could not eliminate many of the persistent problems of nonreservation education, however. Perhaps the most glaring problem remained the inability of the better students to find suitable employment. While Skinner boasted with some truth that more pupils were finding jobs on the reservations, the situation was tempered by the depression and a persistence of white prejudice. Of the nineteen boys who were graduated from the industrial division in 1935, for example, only one could find a permanent job (with the Indian service). Seven others remained at the school doing occasional labor, and the rest were forced to join various New Deal work programs. The situation was even more discouraging for females. Fairly typical of the problem was a case where a number of girls trained as nurses could find no employment because of an "over supply of white girls." Skinner proposed hiring them as "junior nurses" at the school hospital but was prevented from doing so by government regulations. Unfortunately, the superintendent received no satisfaction despite repeated requests to hire the former students. The Bureau's reluctance may have stemmed more from financial restraints than administrative opposition, but it still proved frustrating, especially since the regular staff was overworked while there was a plentiful supply of qualified Indian labor.[35]

Even with the changes and upgrading that followed the Meriam Report, the survival of the school was not guaranteed until 1935. Indeed, during the preceding fall rumors spread around Phoenix that the institution would in fact be closed. Though much of the speculation seemed to be based upon "the present fad for the expansion of day schools," it spread considerable fear among Phoenicians. For years local businessmen had taken the school and its sizable payroll for granted. Now, suddenly threatened with closure in the midst of depression and a desperate effort to keep the local economy alive, residents issued a cry of anguish. Fortunately, Senator Carl Hayden sprang into action as soon as the rumors reached his office. Writing to Collier, Hayden presented the commissioner with a memorandum purporting to show that "the school is being neglected whereas it should be built up and strengthened as an essential unit in the national system of Indian education." The Arizona politician pointed out that his state possessed the second largest Indian population, "practically all full bloods," with but one nonreservation boarding school. Admitting that day schools served the interests of younger children, Hayden argued that "adolescent boys and girls need training and supervision that they do not get at home." Finally, he concluded, the Indians of Arizona want the school.[36]

John Collier responded carefully, stating that he did not want to commit himself too definitely to a position that might have to be reversed, yet agreeing that the Phoenix school could not be closed in the foreseeable future. Acknowledging that his massive effort to construct day schools would have an impact on Phoenix, he nevertheless concluded that an advanced institution of that nature could not be replaced. "I am inclined to believe," he told Hayden, "that a distinctively vocational boarding school will be needed at Phoenix for some years." With that declaration, the school's future was assured.[37]

The Phoenix Indian School in the years following 1935 was considerably different from the institution that had developed and thrived on the theory of forced assimilation for more than forty years. Indeed, by the third year of Roosevelt's administration the transformation was virtually complete. Many of the staff members were professionally trained educators, harsh regimentation had all but disappeared, and the facility had become a vocational high school not unlike other such facilities across the country. It even assumed a new name—Phoenix Indian High School. These changes, to be sure, did not resolve the problems of Indian education, and in some ways they created as many difficulties as they solved. The education problems faced at Phoenix during the fifty years following 1935 belong to a different era of Indian education and government policy. Assimilationist education, in the sense envisioned by Thomas Morgan and the superintendents who ruled at Phoenix from 1891 to 1931, was gone forever.

9

Conclusion and Epilogue

IN 1889 Indian Commissioner Thomas J. Morgan wrote that "the Indians must conform to 'the white man's ways,' peaceably if they will, forcibly if they must."[1] His words, and the philosophy behind them, guided the Phoenix Indian School through the assimilation era. The history of the Arizona school during the years 1891 to 1931 indicates clearly the way assimilationist education worked in the field. It is the story of an institution that could neither claim success nor be classified as a failure. Those who judge by the goal of assimilation would conclude that the method of schooling forced upon Indian youngsters during this forty-year period simply failed. Students seldom merged into the mainstream of American society nor did they find adequate employment. Neither did the school improve the general condition of the Indian population. Such statements, as accurate as they may be, nevertheless fail to present a full picture of what happened at Phoenix Indian School.

Phoenix Indian School was operated by professional government administrators, trained in the Indian service and sympathetic to its goals. The superintendents were committed to assimilation and, each in his own way, attempted to make federal Indian education a success. There was nothing shameful about what they expected to accomplish. When given a measure of independence, they recorded some significant achievements. The headmasters built and operated a massive educational facility, brought thousands of Indian children into contact with white society, improved their intellectual skills, and prepared them to eventually assume leadership roles among their own people. School officials also served as conduits of information about local conditions and general policy matters. As the sole representative of the Indian Office in Phoenix, the superintendents had the added responsibility of assuring good community relations and the public acceptance of Indian education. They furthered the cause of assimilation, and despite the many obvious difficulties, some advance was made in that direction. These administrators were also much more competent than critics like John Collier would concede. Although much of the criticism of the Collier years was deserved, the entire system was moving, albeit slowly, in the right direction.

Phoenix Indian School was not an evil place, and some of its accomplishments were substantial. Although a majority of students received few material benefits from their school years, there were significant exceptions. A large percentage of Indian pupils, moreover, learned something about the larger world, generally valued their school experience, and tended to have fond memories. The spirit of camaraderie that developed under the system of strict discipline has remained with students trained during the assimilation era. Schooldays were no picnic, to be sure, but those who passed through the system have generally praised it. They learned English, how to keep track of money, and what to expect from American society. Even today, as memories dim and the survivors dwindle to a handful, the school experience still makes up an important part of their lives. Among the Hopis, the remaining members of the school band still hold reunions to play school tunes and remember the old days.[2] These proud people are right to feel they accomplished something by attending the white man's school. Additionally, they believe that the brand of education and strict discipline associated with the school developed moral character, a sense of responsibility, and integrity—qualities that seem painfully absent in later generations. On more than one occasion, a distinguished former student has expressed concern over the liberalized trend in Indian education prevalent in the past fifty years. They seldom complain or criticize what the government did for them; they feel that the schooling provided at Phoenix was, by and large, useful.

Of course, memories fade over the years. The positive memories of a few former students do not provide a good measure of the school's effectiveness. For all the good things that may have occurred on an administrative or individual level, the school was still considerably less than a roaring success. Perhaps the most obvious problem involved the idealistic belief of the era that assimilation could be accomplished through such a program. School administrators, moreover, never seemed to know how to prepare students for inclusion into the greater society. Despite great fluctuations in the definition of assimilation, the idea that vocational training was necessary remained constant. Work training therefore provided the main focus of the educational program, with academics always taking a backseat. Unfortunately, students were trained for jobs that theoretically existed in white society even though it was clear that former students preferred to return to the reservation. White prejudice and ethnocentric school administrators made it even more difficult to assure that trained students would be able to secure employment above the menial level. Although employment was usually available during this era, and young Indians who wanted work could find it, they were seldom able to secure permanent or meaningful jobs.

After 1900 the school simply failed to keep up with the times. Problems surfaced on the local as well as the national level. Congress, especially after World War I, neglected its responsibility for maintaining the school system. Appropriations were seldom adequate, forcing superintendents to overcrowd their schools, cut back on health care, and let buildings deteriorate. Phoenix felt the full impact of this national neglect. As a result, an institution that had been vital and up to date at the turn of the century degenerated into an inadequate campus by the 1920s, although it remained one of the best schools in the system.

School administrators shared the blame for not keeping up with the changing tempo of Indian education. Superintendents like John B. Brown were rooted in the assimilationist ideas of the late nineteenth century and were unable to adapt to new ideas. A program that required strict discipline and corporal punishment, a rigid moral code, and total separation from the home environment was outmoded by the third decade of the century, yet Phoenix and its sister institutions persisted in maintaining the old system. In so doing, they unwittingly played into the hands of unsympathetic reformers like John Collier. Collier's demands were not unreasonable and government educators knew full well that studies like the Meriam Report represented an accurate, if somewhat exaggerated, assessment of current problems. They could not, however, reconcile themselves to the fact that all this came from outside forces. As a consequence, their reluctance to cooperate only strengthened the cause of reform, especially since Collier and his friends were well versed in stirring up public opinion.

Indian education in the 1920s, as practiced at Phoenix Indian School, was not as inept as critics portrayed it. In fact, John Collier was often off base in his criticism of government employees. Yet his true-believer approach to reform and his use of sensationalism simply overwhelmed old-guard school personnel, who were exceedingly vulnerable. There was enough truth in Collier's charges to make it seem to the public that assimilationist education, after forty years, was a complete failure. The reform crusade painted a devastating picture, even though schools like Phoenix were making gains. Phoenix may not have been a failure, but it could not convince the public it was a success during the reform decade of the 1920s. Thus, to the end of the assimilation era, Indian education maintained an ambiguous status. Every positive feature seemed to be counteracted by a negative development. Added to this was the ethnocentrism and racism of the period, which ensured that no matter what was attempted, it would later be condemned. In the final analysis, the years of forced assimilation at Phoenix represent an honest experiment that can never be repeated. It was an attempt to deal with a national dilemma, and it must be understood in the context of its time. That it failed to solve "the Indian problem" was perhaps unfortunate, although that failure may have been a blessing in disguise for the preservation of the nation's Indian heritage.

In the fifty years following the advent of the Collier administration, the Phoenix Indian School has suffered as many, if not more, problems than it did during the assimilation era. John Collier's ideas proved no panacea, nor did they make the surviving nonreservation boarding schools more effective. As Phoenix Indian High School, the institution has served two basic functions since the mid-thirties. Its primary assignment has been to provide secondary schooling for Arizona reservation children. During the 1930s a large number of day schools were opened. High school construction, however, was much less prolific, leaving some areas unable to offer advanced schooling on the reservation. As a consequence, school-age Indian children continued to depend on Phoenix to complete their education.

The second significant trend in nonreservation education to affect the Phoenix school appeared in the 1930s and has continued to the present. This is the government's decision to place problem children in the institution. Disciplinary cases, handicapped youngsters, and slow learners have consequently come to represent an increasing percentage of the student body.[3] As a result, the school gained a reputation for housing misfits. This image was not helpful in attracting good, well-qualified students. As recently as 1984, the problem of such students dominated stories about the school with writers particularly noting that academic achievements were considerably below average, that harsh measures of discipline remained in use, and that the school had become a dumping ground for Indian children with "social problems."[4]

Compounding this situation were the substantial budget reductions during the New Deal as emphasis was placed on reservation schools. When the conservative reaction to the New

Deal set in at the end of World War II and a renewed attempt to provide formal education to large numbers of Indians developed, Phoenix found itself unable to handle the demand effectively. Yet when Congress suggested closing the school and using its resources elsewhere, Phoenicians again rose in protest. Closing the school, moreover, would have deprived many Indian children of a secondary education. Senator Carl Hayden, as he had done in the past, came to the rescue, pointing out that closure would create both welfare and educational problems for state government, which had no way of caring for the displaced students.[5] Again, local sentiment supported Indian concern, and the school continued to trudge along.

Meanwhile, enrollment began to rise. In 1945 the enrollment was increased from 425 to 550, and by 1949 the authorized level was 700. As had been past practice, most emphasis continued to be on some kind of vocational training. Yet there has been a more modern look to the process since the war. By the 1950s the Indian Bureau had given up on much of the New Deal idealism about reservation life, and once again the school looked toward securing employment for students within the white community. A 1952 article stated that "the Indian School now is simply preparing its graduates to earn a living in industry right here in the community, instead of returning them to the reservation where the economic outlook is bleak." Even at that late date, the vocational emphasis remained on manual labor.[6]

Exactly what the school should be expected to accomplish has continued to be a difficult problem and the subject of considerable debate. As the school entered the 1980s it again seemed out of step with modern education. The previous two decades witnessed a trend toward self-determination, including a return of the philosophy that the home environment is the proper place for schooling. Still, the Phoenix school continued along its usual path of serving Arizona tribes. As more and more high schools opened, the services of an urban, nonreservation institution appeared to become dispensable. With so many continuing problems, combined perhaps with a new Indian militancy that has attacked "colonial" institutions, the curtain seems destined to fall.

In 1982 the Reagan administration announced plans to close the school as part of a Bureau plan to phase out all off-reservation schools. The motivation for this action was the increasingly small clientele served by the school and the financial benefits to be reaped from closure. Momentarily, at least, the measure was defeated, primarily because two Arizona tribes, the Hopis and the Papagos, still had inadequate high school facilities. Yet the future was clear when the BIA later proposed to make the facility into a national vocational center. Representatives of several Arizona tribes responded that, although they recognized the need for more "high-school-level vocational programs," they wanted such services placed on the reservations. Perhaps because of its past history and current lack of success, one tribal official felt compelled to label the school a place of "cultural genocide."[7]

Government plans to close the school are still alive. A death blow may have been administered when a local periodical published an expose in 1984 of the school's dismal academic performance and harsh treatment of pupils. The sensational article focused on the 40 percent of students said to be attending for "social" reasons. Much like Collier's muckraking campaign in the late 1920s, the institution came out the loser, appearing to be a place of persistent brutality with no redeeming qualities. Exaggerated as the report was, it added fuel to those desiring closure. That the hundred-acre campus is located in the heart of central Phoenix and worth a small fortune has not been overlooked either.[8]

In 1987 the school was scheduled to cease operations within the next two years. The biggest controversy was over who would eventually own the property. Private developers, the city of Phoenix, and the Arizona tribes all thought that they should have the land.[9] During the first half of 1986 the issue heated up considerably when the Department of the Interior suggested swapping 128,000 acres of Everglades land owned by a Florida developer for the 105-acre school site. Under this agreement, the developer would have been able to use the valuable Phoenix site as he saw fit. Naturally, both the city of Phoenix and Arizona Indian leaders objected, moving to block any final disposition that did not take into account Indian interests or city concerns. Although the issues became more complex with each passing day, it was safe to say that the haggling would continue for some time.[10]

With the opening of two reservation high schools in 1987, the Phoenix school had for all practical purposes outlived its usefulness, and it seemed evident that it would not last until its centennial in 1991. Sometime in the late 1980s the institution will quietly fade away, lamented by few except some of the older Indians who remember it during its heyday. Arizonans, who more than once did everything they could to keep the school, now seem ready to see it destroyed for the same reason—financial benefit.

Notes

ABBREVIATIONS USED

AHF	Arizona Historical Foundation, Tempe, Arizona
AHS	Arizona Historical Society, Tucson, Arizona
ANSR	*Annual Narrative and Statistical Reports*
ASU	Arizona State University Library, Tempe, Arizona
BIC	Board of Indian Commissioners
CCF	Central Classified Files
CIA	Commissioner of Indian Affairs
FRC	Federal Records Center, Laguna Niguel, California
HEH	Henry E. Huntington Library, San Marino, California
IRA	Indian Rights Association
LR	Letters Received
LS	Letters Sent
NA	National Archives, Washington, D.C.
RG 48	Records of the Secretary of the Interior
RG 75	Records of the Bureau of Indian Affairs
SI	Secretary of the Interior
UNM	University of New Mexico Library, Albuquerque, New Mexico
U.S. Stat	*U.S. Statutes at Large*

1. INTRODUCTION: THE SWORD WILL GIVE WAY TO THE SPELLING BOOK

1. *Annual Report*, CIA, 1883, p. xxxviii.
2. A number of studies deal with early educational programs, although

215

a comprehensive study has yet to be completed. Among those to consult are Evelyn C. Adams, *American Indian Education: Government Schools and Economic Progress*; Alice C. Fletcher, *Indian Education and Civilization*, Sen. Ex. Doc. 95, 48th Cong., 2d sess. ser. 2264; Robert F. Berkhofer, Jr., *Salvation and the Savage: An Analysis of Protestant Missions and American Indian Response, 1787–1862*; Annual Report, CIA, 1844, p. 313.

3. There are several significant studies of the post–Civil War period. The most comprehensive is Francis Paul Prucha, *American Indian Policy in Crisis: Christian Reformers and the Indian, 1865–1900*. Others to be consulted are Robert W. Mardock, *The Reformers and the American Indian*; Henry E. Fritz, *The Movement for Indian Assimilation, 1860–1890*; Loring B. Priest, *Uncle Sam's Stepchildren: The Reformation of United States Indian Policy, 1865–1877*; Robert H. Keller, Jr., *American Protestantism and United States Indian Policy, 1869–82*; Frederick E. Hoxie, *A Final Promise: The Campaign to Assimilate the Indians, 1880–1920*.

4. Louis Morton, "How the Indians Came to Carlisle," *Pennsylvania History*, 29 (January 1962): 60–61; Robert L. Brunhouse, "The Founding of the Carlisle Indian School," *Pennsylvania History*, 6 (April 1939): 73. Good accounts of Pratt's career can be found in Elaine Goodale Eastman, *Pratt: The Red Man's Moses*; Richard Henry Pratt, *Battlefield and Classroom: Four Decades with the American Indian, 1867–1904*, edited by Robert M. Utley; and Everett A. Gilcreast, "Richard Henry Pratt and American Indian Policy, 1877–1906: A Study of the Assimilation Movement" (Ph.D. dissertation, Yale University, 1967).

5. David W. Adams, "The Federal Indian Boarding School: A Study in Environment and Response, 1879–1918" (Ed.D. dissertation, Indiana University, 1975), pp. 49–50; Pratt, *Battlefield and Classroom*, pp. 192–93; Gilcreast, "Richard Henry Pratt," pp. 16–29.

6. Pratt, *Battlefield and Classroom*, pp. 191–95; Gilcreast, "Richard Henry Pratt," p. 37; Helen W. Ludlow, "Indian Education at Hampton and Carlisle," *Harper's Magazine*, 62 (April 1881): 662, 666–67; Annual Report, CIA, 1878, pp. xliii–xliv; Annual Report, CIA, 1887, p. 3; Eastman, *Red Man's Moses*, pp. 64–65; David W. Adams, "Education in Hues: Red and Black at Hampton Institute, 1878–1893," *South Atlantic Quarterly*, 76 (Spring 1977): 159–76; [Helen W. Ludlow], *Ten Year's Work for Indians at Hampton Normal and Agricultural Institute*.

7. Adams, "Education in Hues," 169–72; Eastman, *Red Man's Moses*, pp. 64–67; Pratt, *Battlefield and Classroom*, pp. 213–18; Priest, *Uncle Sam's Stepchildren*, pp. 142–43.

8. Annual Report, CIA, 1880, pp. v–viii; Pratt to CIA, October 15, 1881, in Annual Report, CIA, 1881, pp. 185–94; Pratt to CIA, August 18, 1885, in Annual Report, CIA, 1885, pp. 214–21; Gilcreast, "Richard Henry Pratt," pp. 47–69; Ludlow, "Indian Education at Hampton and Carlisle," pp. 666–67; Ruth Shaffner, "Civilizing the American Indian," *The Chautauquan*, 23 (June 1896): 264. In addition to the works already cited,

general information on Carlisle can be found in Richard Henry Pratt, *The Indian Industrial School, Carlisle, Pennsylvania: Its Origins, Purposes, Progress and the Difficulties Surmounted*, introduced by Robert M. Utley; Thomas G. Tousey, *Military History of Carlisle and Carlisle Barracks*; and Pearl Lee Walker-McNeil, "The Carlisle Indian School: A Study in Acculturation" (Ph.D. dissertation, The American University, 1979).

9. O. B. Super, "Indian Education at Carlisle," *New England Magazine*, 18 (April 1895): 224; Pratt, *Battlefield and Classroom*, p. 283; Pratt to CIA, September 24, 1884, in *Annual Report*, CIA, 1884, p. 187.

10. Pratt to CIA, October 5, 1880, in *Annual Report*, CIA, 1880, pp. 179–80; Shaffner, "Civilizing the American Indians," p. 265; Pratt to CIA, October 15, 1881, in *Annual Report*, CIA, 1881, pp. 188–89; Josephine E. Richards, "The Training of Indian Girls as the Uplifter of the Home," *National Education Association Journal of Proceedings and Addresses, 1900*, pp. 701–5; Frances Willard, "The Carlisle Indian School," *The Chautauquan*, 9 (February 1889): 290; Robert A. Trennert, "Educating Indian Girls at Nonreservation Boarding Schools, 1878–1920," *Western Historical Quarterly*, 13 (July 1982): 276–78.

11. Carl Schurz, "Present Aspects of the Indian Problem" *North American Review*, 133 (July 1881): 1–24; *Annual Report*, CIA, 1880, p. vi; *Annual Report*, CIA, 1884, p. xix; Adams, "Federal Indian Boarding School," p. 65; Lillie G. McKinney, "History of Albuquerque Indian School," *New Mexico Historical Review*, 20 (April 1945): 109–38; Hoxie, *A Final Promise*, pp. 57–60.

12. Robert A. Trennert, "From Carlisle to Phoenix: The Rise and Fall of the Indian Outing System, 1878–1930," *Pacific Historical Review*, 52 (August 1983): 276–77; Gilcreast, "Richard Henry Pratt," pp. 106–51. A portion of the program at the western schools can be found in school reports printed in *Annual Reports*, CIA, 1884–1890.

13. *Annual Report*, CIA, 1885, p. cx; Report of Josephine Mayo, in *Annual Report*, CIA, 1886, p. 14; Education Circular #60 (December 20, 1901), NA, RG 75, Education Circulars; Gilcreast, "Richard Henry Pratt," pp. 111–12; Lewis Meriam et al., *The Problem of Indian Administration*, pp. 12–13, 375–76; Margaret Connell Szasz, *Education and the American Indian: The Road to Self-Determination Since 1929*, p. 20; Adams, "Federal Indian Boarding School," pp. 155–59; Trennert, "Educating Indian Girls," 278–79.

14. For biographical material on Morgan, see Francis Paul Prucha, "Thomas Jefferson Morgan," in Robert M. Kvasnicka and Herman J. Viola, eds., *The Commissioners of Indian Affairs, 1824–1977*, pp. 193–203; Prucha, *Indian Policy in Crisis*, pp. 294–305.

15. Supplemental Report on Indian Education, in *Annual Report*, CIA, 1889, pp. 93–114. Additional insights into Morgan's thinking can be seen in Francis Paul Prucha, ed., *Americanizing the American Indians: Writings of the "Friends of the Indian," 1880–1900*, pp. 239–59.

16. Supplemental Report on Indian Education, in *Annual Report*, CIA,

1889, pp. 93–104; Thomas J. Morgan, "The Education of American Indians," address before the Lake Mohonk Conference, 1889, in *Annual Report*, BIC, 1889, pp. 62–73; *Annual Report*, CIA, 1890, pp. viii–xi; Rules for Indian Schools, ibid., p. cliv; Frederick E. Hoxie, "Redefining Indian Education: Thomas J. Morgan's Program in Disarray," *Arizona and the West*, 24 (Spring 1982): 5–10; Hoxie, *A Final Promise*, pp. 64–65; Prucha, *Indian Policy in Crisis*, pp. 296–303; Adams, *American Indian Education*, pp. 54–58.

17. *Annual Report*, CIA, 1890, pp. viii–xviii; Rules for Indian Schools, ibid., pp. cxlvi–clxiv.

18. *Annual Report*, CIA, 1890, pp. x–xi.

2. AN OASIS IN THE DESERT

1. A dozen nonreservation training schools were opened during Morgan's four years in office. In addition to Phoenix, schools were established at: Santa Fe, New Mexico (1890); Fort Mojave, Arizona (1890); Carson, Nevada (1890); Pierre, South Dakota (1891); Fort Lewis, Colorado (1892); Fort Shaw, Montana (1892); Perris, California (1893); Flandreau, South Dakota (1893); Pipestone, Minnesota (1893); Mount Pleasant, Michigan (1893); Tomah, Wisconsin (1893).

2. Gilcreast, in his dissertation on Pratt, pp. 111–12, makes the point that one of Captain Pratt's major concerns about the western nonreservation schools was that they were indeed located in response to political pressures.

3. General background on the Pimas and Maricopas can be found in Edward H. Spicer, *Cycles of Conquest: The Impact of Spain, Mexico, and the United States on the Indians of the Southwest, 1533–1960*, pp. 118–51; Frank Russell, *The Pima Indians*, introduction by Bernard L. Fontana, pp. 19–34; Anna Moore Shaw, *A Pima Past*, pp. 1–89.

4. Spicer, *Cycles of Conquest*, pp. 148–49; Russell, *The Pima Indians*, p. 34; Keller, *American Protestantism and United States Indian Policy*, p. 35; Minnie A. Cook, *Apostle to the Pima Indians*, pp. 77–89; John M. Hamilton, "A History of the Presbyterian Work Among the Pima and Papago Indians of Arizona" (M.A. thesis, University of Arizona, 1948), pp. 18–54; Maxine W. Hagan, "An Educational History of the Pima and Papago Peoples from the Mid-seventeenth Century to the Mid-twentieth Century" (Ed.D. thesis, University of Arizona, 1959), pp. 120–25.

5. Address of the Lake Mohonk Conference, in *Annual Report*, BIC, 1883, p. 41; Roswell G. Wheeler to CIA, August 26, 1881, in *Annual Report*, CIA, 1881, p. 5; Wheeler to CIA, September 1, 1882, in *Annual Report*, CIA, 1882, p. 8; A. H. Jackson to CIA, August 14, 1884, in *Annual Report*, CIA, 1884, p. 6.

6. *Annual Report*, CIA, 1889, pp. 8–9; Report of the Superintendent of Indian Schools, September 5, 1889, in ibid., pp. 313–15; Report of the Superintendent of Indian Schools, September 11, 1890, in *Annual Report*,

CIA, 1890, pp. 246–48; "Daniel Dorchester," in Allen Johnson and Dumas Malone, eds., vol. 5, *Dictionary of American Biography*, pp. 375–76; Reverend Howard Billman, "Report on Papago, Pima Tribes," March 1890, Tucson Indian School Papers, AHS.

7. J. M. Lee to Assistant Adjutant General, February 1, 1890, NA, RG 75, LR, 17975–1890; Bill Reed, *The Last Bugle Call: A History of Fort McDowell, Arizona Territory, 1865–1890*, pp. 140–41.

8. Dorchester to CIA, March 20, 1890, NA, RG 75, LR, 9762–1890; Billman to E. H. Perry, March 30, 1890, Tucson Indian School Papers, AHS.

9. Dorchester to CIA (2 letters), March 25, 1890, NA, RG 75, LR, 9762–1890, enclosures 3 and 5; Redfield Proctor to SI, May 2, 1890, NA, RG 75, LR, 13762–1890; Reed, *Last Bugle Call*, pp. 140–41.

10. Wellington Rich to Morgan, May 7, 12, 1890, NA, RG 75, LR, 14799–1890 and 15223–1890. There is little information on Rich's early life. He was born in 1832 and moved to Nebraska in 1865. He served as a teacher and educator before joining the Indian service, apparently teaching at several Nebraska schools. He may have known Morgan, who worked at Nebraska State Normal School from 1872 to 1874. For a brief biographical sketch, see the entry under "Edson P. Rich," in vol. 2, *Omaha: The Gate City and Douglas County, Nebraska*, pp. 791–92.

11. Morgan to Rich, May 16, 17, 29, 1890, NA, RG 75, LS, Education, vol. 23.

12. Rich to Morgan, June 23, July 30, 1890, NA, RG 75, LR, 19509–1890 and 23619–1890.

13. *Arizona Republican*, August 12, 1890.

14. Rich to Morgan, August 15, 1890, NA, RG 75, LR, 26284–1890; Rich to CIA, August 5, 1891, in *Annual Report*, CIA, 1891, p. 555.

15. Rich to CIA, August 15, 1891, in *Annual Report*, CIA, pp. 555–56; Rich to Morgan, September 15, 1890, NA, RG 75, LR, 29491–1890. Official authority for the transfer of Fort McDowell did not actually come until October 1, 1890. See copy of General Orders #115, NA, RG 75, LR, 31753–1890.

16. Phoenix City Ordinance, May 30, 1881; James M. Barney, "Famous Indian Ordinance," *The Sheriff*, 13 (June 1954): 77; Shaw, *A Pima Past*, pp. 113–14; *Phoenix Daily Herald*, September 20, 1886, July 5, 1887, July 28, September 1, 1888, October 11, 1889; *Arizona Gazette*, July 3, 1886, December 16, 1887.

17. *Arizona Republican*, October 10, 1890. For background on the activities of local boosters, see Geoffrey P. Mawn, "Phoenix, Arizona: Central City of the Southwest, 1870–1920" (Ph.D. dissertation, Arizona State University, 1979), pp. 135–64; Bradford Luckingham, *The Urban Southwest: A Profile History of Albuquerque–El Paso–Phoenix–Tucson*, pp. 28–32; G. Wesley Johnson, *Phoenix: Valley of the Sun*, pp. 39–48; Richard E. Lynch, *Winfield Scott: A Biography of Scottsdale's Founder*, pp. 106–7.

18. Petition by citizens of Phoenix, October 2, 1890, NA, RG 75, LR,

35662–1890; Orlando Allen to Benjamin Harrison, October 29, 1890, NA, RG 75, LR, 36104–1890.

19. Prucha, *Indian Policy in Crisis*, p. 303; Morgan to R. V. Belt, October 13, 1890, NA, RG 75, LR, 32499–1890; *Arizona Republican*, October 10, 1890.

20. Morgan to Belt, October 13, 1890, NA, RG 75, LR, 32499–1890; *Arizona Republican*, October 12, 1890; Rich to CIA, August 15, 1891, in *Annual Report*, CIA, 1891, p. 557.

21. *Arizona Republican*, October 13, 1890; *Phoenix Daily Herald*, October 13, 1890.

22. Morgan to Belt, October 12, 13, 1890, NA, RG 75, LR, 32299–1890 and 32499–1890; Rich to Morgan (telegram), October 13, 1890, NA, RG 75, LR, 31687–1890.

23. *Arizona Republican*, October 14, 1890; *Phoenix Daily Herald*, October 14, 1890; *Arizona Daily Citizen* (Tucson), October 14, 1890; Rich to Morgan, October 14, 1890, NA, RG 75, LR, 32751–1890.

24. Orlando Allen to Harrison, October 29, 1890, NA, RG 75, LR, 36104–1890; Dorchester to Belt, October 28, 1890, NA, RG 75, LR, 37084–1890, enclosure 3.

25. John W. Noble to CIA, October 29, 1890, NA, RG 75, LR, 37084–1890. The impact of white squatters' claims on government decisions regarding the Indians during this period is discussed in Veronica E. Velarde Tiller, *The Jicarilla Apache Tribe: A History, 1846–1970*, pp. 101–8.

26. Rich to Morgan, December 18, 1890, NA, RG 75, LR, 39956–1890; Morgan to SI, December 29, 1890, NA, RG 48, LR, Indian Division, 9440–1890; Rich to CIA, August 5, 1891, in *Annual Report*, CIA, 1891, p. 557.

27. *Phoenix Daily Herald*, December 15, 17, 1890; *Arizona Daily Gazette*, December 17, 1890; Petition of citizens of Phoenix, December 16, 1890, enclosed in Rich to Morgan, December 18, 1890, NA, RG 75, LR, 39956–1890.

28. Rich to Morgan, December 18, 1890, NA, RG 75, LR, 39956–1890; Morgan to SI, December 29, 1890, NA, RG 48, LR, Indian Division, 9440–1890; Morgan to SI, December 29, 1890, NA, RG 75, LS, Education, vol. 28; Noble to CIA, December 30, 1890, NA, RG 75, Authorities, 25378–1890.

29. Rich to CIA, August 5, 1891, in *Annual Report*, CIA, 1891, p. 557; Rich to Morgan, January 1, 1891, NA, RG 75, LR, 1069–1891; Noble to CIA, February 19, 1891, NA, RG 75, LR, 6632–1891; *Phoenix Daily Herald*, January 9, 1891.

30. "Letter . . . submitting an estimate of an appropriation for an Indian school at or near Phoenix," *H. Ex. Doc.* 218, 51st Cong., 1st sess., ser. 2866; Memorial of Jerry Millay and others, January 9, 1891, NA, RG 75, LR, 1871–1891; Rich to Morgan, February 4, 1891, NA, RG 75, LR, 5521–1891; *Phoenix Daily Herald*, February 4, 1891.

31. Rich to Morgan, January 16, February 26, 1891, NA, RG 75, LR, 2809–1891 and 9092–1891; Hugh Patton to CIA, January 1891, NA, RG 75, LR, 3035–1891; *Annual Report*, CIA, 1892, vol. 2, p. 838. Patton's salary was $720 per year. He earned a good reputation among the Pimas and is frequently mentioned in Shaw, *A Pima Past*.

32. Rich to Morgan, March 19, 20, 24, 1891, NA, RG 75, LR, 11056–1891, 10649–1891, and 12286–1891; Rich to CIA, August 5, 1891, in *Annual Report*, CIA, 1891, pp. 557–58.

33. *Annual Report*, CIA, 1891, p. 558; Rich to Morgan, March 19, 1891, NA, RG 75, LR, 11506–1891; *Phoenix Daily Herald*, April 3, 1891.

34. Rich to Morgan, May 12, October 9, 1891, NA, RG 75, LR, 18387–1891 and 37314–1891; Rich to CIA, August 5, 1891, in *Annual Report*, CIA, 1891, p. 558; Rich to CIA, September 10, 1892, in *Annual Report*, CIA, 1892, pp. 654–55.

35. Rich to CIA, September 10, 1892, in *Annual Report*, CIA, 1892, p. 654; Rich to Morgan, July 13, 1891, January 14, 1892, NA, RG 75, LR, 24915–1891 and 2785–1892; Crouse to CIA, August 5, 1891, NA, RG 75, LR, 29462–1891; Quarterly Report of Indian Schools, Phoenix, September 30, 1891, FRC, Phoenix Area Office, Agency Box 239.

36. Rich to CIA, September 10, 1892, in *Annual Report*, CIA, 1892, pp. 654–55; Classification of Pupils, September 30, 1891, and Quarterly Report of Indian Schools, Phoenix, December 31, 1891, FRC, Phoenix Area Office, Agency Box 239; *Phoenix Daily Herald*, September 7, 1891; David S. Keck to Morgan, April 7, 1892, NA, RG 75, LR, 13592–1892.

37. *Phoenix Daily Herald*, September 3, 7, 24, 1891; *Arizona Republican*, December 9, 1891; Crouse to CIA, September 30, 1891, in *Annual Report*, CIA, 1891, p. 214.

38. Rich to Morgan, January 14, 1892, NA, RG 75, LR, 2785–1892; *Arizona Republican*, December 9, 1891.

39. Rich to Morgan, October 9, 1891, NA, RG 75, LR, 37314–1891; Dorchester to Morgan, March 1, 1892, NA, RG 75, LR, 8883–1892; Rich to CIA, September 10, 1892, in *Annual Report*, CIA, 1892, pp. 654–55.

40. Rich to CIA, September 10, 1892, in *Annual Report*, CIA, 1892, pp. 654–55; Rich to Morgan, April 23, 30, 1892, NA, RG 75, LR, 15867–1892 and 16754–1892; *Phoenix Daily Herald*, April 29, 1892; Descriptive Statement of Pupils Transferred to Phoenix Indian School, May 31, 1892, FRC, Phoenix Area Office, Agency Box 239.

41. Rich to Morgan, April 23, 1892, NA, RG 75, LR, 15867–1892; *Arizona Republican*, April 15, 30, 1892; *Phoenix Daily Herald*, April 15, 16, 29, 1892.

3. MARKING TIME

1. *Annual Report*, CIA, 1896, pp. 64–65; Gilcreast, "Richard Henry Pratt," pp. 190–211; Adams, *American Indian Education*, pp. 53–54.

2. Rich to Morgan, July 18, 1892, NA, RG 75, LR, 27120–1892; *Annual Report*, CIA, 1892, pp. 48–55.

3. Rich to CIA, July 1893, in *Annual Report*, CIA, 1893, pp. 403–4.
4. Ibid.
5. Rich to Morgan, July 18, August 16, 1892, NA, RG 75, LR, 27120–1892 and 30542–1892; Rules for Indian Schools, in *Annual Report*, CIA, 1890, pp. clvi–clx.
6. Rich to Morgan, April 23, 30, July 18, 1892, NA, RG 75, LR, 15867–1892, 16754–1892, and 27120–1892; Statement of Student Classification, March 31, 1892, FRC, Phoenix Area Office, Agency Box 239.
7. Rich to Morgan, July 2, 29, August 8, 1892, NA, RG 75, LR, 24151–1892, 27900–1892, and 20510–1892.
8. Billman to Morgan, September 5, 1892, NA, RG 75, LR, 33240–1892.
9. Rich to Morgan, September 23, 1892, NA, RG 75, LR, 35686–1892.
10. Belt to Rich, October 8, 1892, NA, RG 75, LS, Education, vol. 44; Morgan to Crouse, October 12, 1892, NA, RG 75, LS, Education, vol. 44; Prucha, *Indian Policy in Crisis*, pp. 313–14.
11. Rich to Morgan, August 16, 26, 1892, NA, RG 75, LR, 30542–1892 and 30959–1892; Crouse to CIA, May 12, 1893, NA, RG 75, LR, 18170–1892; Rich to CIA, July 1893, in *Annual Report*, CIA, 1893, pp. 403–4; *Phoenix Daily Herald*, January 24, 1893.
12. Crouse to CIA, May 12, 1893, NA, RG 75, LR, 18170–1893; Rich to CIA, July 1893, in *Annual Report*, CIA, 1893, pp. 403–4.
13. Crouse to CIA, May 12, 1893, NA, RG 75, LR, 18170–1893; George Allen to CIA, April 17, 1893, NA, RG 75, LR, 15255–1893.
14. Allen to CIA, March 31, April 17, 1893, NA, RG 75, LR, 13272–1892 and 15255–1893; Allen to CIA, July 19, 1893, and David Carruthers to Allen, July 13, 1893, in *Annual Report*, CIA, 1893, pp. 105–9.
15. *Annual Report*, CIA, 1902, p. 27; *Annual Report*, CIA, 1893, pp. 9–11; William T. Hagan, "Daniel M. Browning, 1893–97," in Kvasnicka and Viola, *Commissioners of Indian Affairs*, pp. 205–9. Even the Pima agent, Cornelius Crouse, who actively supported the Phoenix school, was upset by the constant recruiting. John W. Stewart, the superintendent of the Pima boarding school at Sacaton, was even more emphatic: "Another hindrance to learning English here, and indeed to our school work in general, is the frequent drafts made upon us for pupils for other schools.... This hinders the progress in English by depriving our weaker pupils of the benefit of contact with those who speak English more fluently." See Crouse to CIA, August 1, 1892, in *Annual Report*, CIA, 1892, pp. 214–17.
16. *Annual Report*, CIA, 1893, pp. 9–11; U.S. Stat., vol. 27, pp. 143, 628; Prucha, *Indian Policy in Crisis*, pp. 314–16.
17. Hall to CIA, July 31, August 19 (2 letters), 22, September 12, October 7, 1893, NA, RG 75, LR, 28367–1893, 30906–1893, 31316–1893, 31839–1893, 34749–1893, and 37757–1893; Hagan, "Daniel Browning," p. 207; Prucha, *Indian Policy in Crisis*, pp. 366–70. Hall's initial appointment was made August 1, 1893. See Frank Armstrong to Hall, August 1, 1893, NA, RG 75, LR, 28900–1893.

18. Rich to CIA, August 19, 1893, NA, RG 75, LR, 30906–1893; *Annual Report*, CIA, 1893, p. 19; Paul F. Faison to Hoke Smith, October 13, 1893, NA, RG 75, Reports of Inspection.

19. William M. Moss, Report on Phoenix Boarding School, March 28, 1894, NA, RG 75, LR, 12526–1894; Hall to CIA, September 19, 1898, NA, RG 75, LR, 43371–1898.

20. S. C. Burringer to CIA, August 22, 1893, NA, RG 75, LR, 31854–1893; Hall to CIA, December 18, 1893, NA, RG 75, LR, 47654–1893.

21. Moss, Report on Phoenix Boarding School, March 28, 1894, NA, RG 75, LR, 12526–1894; Hoke Smith to CIA, March 10, 1894, NA, RG 75, LR, 9947–1894; "Letter . . . transmitting estimate from the Secretary of the Interior of appropriation for the Indian School at Phoenix, Ariz.," *H. Ex. Doc.* 163, 53d Cong., 1st sess., ser. 3226; Hall to CIA, April 23, 1894, NA, RG 75, LR, 16048–1894; Adams, *American Indian Education*, p. 61. Hall was also upset because his salary was reduced from $1,800 to $1,500.

22. Hall to CIA, September 18, 1894, NA, RG 75, LR, 36860–1894; M. D. Shelby to CIA, November 3, 1894, NA, RG 75, LR, 43774–1894; "Want More School Room," *The Indian's Friend*, 7 (December 1894): 8; Report on Phoenix Indian School by C. C. Duncan, December 1, 1894, NA, RG 75, Reports of Inspection; Hall to CIA, August 10, 1894, in *Annual Report*, CIA, 1894, p. 370.

23. A. H. Heinemann to Superintendent of Indian Schools, April 12, 1895, NA, RG 75, LR, 16636–1895; Hall to CIA, September 12, 1895, January 11, 1896, NA, RG 75, LR, 38507–1895 and 2078–1896; Hall to CIA, September 14, 1895, in *Annual Report*, CIA, 1895, p. 360.

24. Report on Phoenix Indian School by P. McCormick, April 23, 1896, April 5, 1897, NA, RG 75, Reports of Inspection; Hall to CIA, September 1, 1896, NA, RG 75, LR, 34037–1896; Hall to CIA, September 1, 1896, in *Annual Report*, CIA, 1896, pp. 364–65; S. M. McCowan to CIA, July 15, 1897, in *Annual Report*, CIA, 1897, p. 344.

25. Report on Phoenix Indian School by P. McCormick, April 5, 1897, NA, RG 75, Reports of Inspection; Moss, Report on Phoenix Boarding School, March 28, 1894, NA, RG 75, LR, 12526–1894; Shelby to CIA, November 3, 1894, NA, RG 75, LR, 43774–1894; Heinemann to Superintendent of Indian Schools, April 12, 1895, NA, RG 75, LR, 16636–1895; Hall to CIA, August 10, 1894, in *Annual Report*, CIA, 1894, pp. 369–71; Sally J. McBeth, *Ethnic Identity and the Boarding School Experience of West-Central Oklahoma Indians*, p. 89.

26. Report on Phoenix Indian School by P. McCormick, April 23, 1896, April 5, 1897, NA, RG 75, Reports of Inspection; Hall to CIA, September 14, 1895, in *Annual Report*, CIA, 1895, p. 360.

27. Richards, "The Training of Indian Girls," 701–5; Trennert, "Educating Indian Girls," 280–81; Hall to CIA, August 10, 1894, in *Annual Report*, CIA, 1894, pp. 369–70; Hall to CIA, September 1, 1896, in *Annual Report*, CIA, 1896, pp. 364–65; Heinemann to Superintendent of Indian

Schools, April 12, 1895, NA, RG 75, LR, 16636–1895; Report on Phoenix Indian School by P. McCormick, April 23, 1896, NA, RG 75, Reports of Inspection.

28. Hall to CIA, July 7, 1897, in *Annual Report,* CIA, 1898, p. 357; Hall to CIA, August 10, 1894, in *Annual Report,* CIA, 1894, p. 370; Report on Phoenix Indian School by P. McCormick, April 5, 1897, NA, RG 75, Reports of Inspection; Superintendent of Indian Schools to CIA, December 23, 1895, NA, RG 75, LR, 51510–1895; *Arizona Gazette,* "Railroad Edition," March 12, 1895.

29. Crouse to CIA, May 12, 1893, NA, RG 75, LR, 18170–1893; Adams, *American Indian Education,* pp. 53–54; Hall to CIA, August 10, 1894, in *Annual Report,* CIA, 1894, p. 370; Hall to CIA, September 1, 1896, in *Annual Report,* CIA, 1896, p. 365; McBeth, *Ethnic Identity and the Boarding School Experience,* pp. 105–8.

30. Moss, Report on Phoenix Boarding School, March 28, 1894, NA, RG 75, LR, 12526–1894; Hall to CIA, April 11, 1894, June 16, 1896, NA, RG 75, LR, 14580–1894 and 23559–1896; J. Roe Young to CIA, August 27, 1895, in *Annual Report,* CIA, 1895, p. 23; McBeth, *Ethnic Identity and the Boarding School Experience,* pp. 108–11.

31. McBeth, *Ethnic Identity and the Boarding School Experience,* pp. 88–105; Adams, "Federal Boarding School," pp. 96–122.

32. Sara F. Gugle, *History of the International Order of the King's Daughters and Sons, Year 1886 to 1930;* Shaffner, "Civilizing the American Indian," p. 226. The King's Daughters were apparently introduced to the Indian schools by Merial Dorchester, wife of the superintendent of Indian schools. See Trennert, "Educating Indian Girls," p. 284.

33. Hall to CIA, August 10, 1894, in *Annual Report,* CIA, 1894, p. 371; Rich to Morgan, January 14, October 24, 1892, NA, RG 75, LR, 2785–1892 and 39108–1892; Hall to CIA, September 25, 1896, NA, RG 75, LR, 37735–1896.

34. Report as to employes [sic] connected with the Phoenix Indian School, December 1, 1894, NA, RG 75, Reports of Inspection; McBeth, *Ethnic Identity and the Boarding School Experience,* pp. 141–42; "She Would Go," *The Indian's Friend,* 7 (December 1894): 8.

35. Browning to Hall (copy), February 5, 1895, NA, RG 75, LR, 6682–1895; Hall to CIA, September 1, 1896, NA, RG 75, LR, 34037–1896. The school's budget for fiscal 1895–96, for example, was listed at $34,900, less any construction funds that might be available. See Hall to Hailmann, February 2, 1895, NA, RG 75, LR, 6451–1895.

36. Rich to CIA, July 1893, in *Annual Report,* CIA, 1893, pp. 403–4. There was a shortage of domestic servants in Phoenix at this time. Comments on this situation can be found in Mabel Hancock Latham Reminiscences, Hancock Family Collection, AHF.

37. Hall to CIA, August 10, 1894, in *Annual Report,* CIA, 1894, pp. 370–71.

38. Report on Phoenix Indian School by C. C. Duncan, December 1, 1894, NA, RG 75, Reports of Inspection; Shelby to CIA, November 3, 1894, NA, RG 75, LR, 43774–1894; Acting SI to CIA, [December 1894] NA, RG 75, LR, 48564–1894; Superintendent of Indian Schools to CIA, December 23, 1895, NA, RG 75, LR, 51510–1895; Report of Superintendent of Indian Schools, October 1, 1895, in *Annual Report,* CIA, 1895, p. 341.

39. Hall to CIA, January 16, 1895, June 16, 1896, NA, RG 75, LR, 3337–1895 and 23559–1896; *Phoenix Daily Herald,* June 18, 1896; Hall to CIA, September 1, 1896, in *Annual Report,* CIA, 1896, p. 364; Report on Phoenix Indian School by P. McCormick, April 5, 1897, NA, RG 75, Reports of Inspection.

40. Hall to CIA, August 10, 1894, in *Annual Report,* CIA, 1894, p. 369; Shelby to CIA, November 3, 1894, NA, RG 75, LR, 43774–1894; Hall to CIA, January 16, 1895, NA, RG 75, LR, 3337–1895; Heinemann to Superintendent of Indian Schools, April 12, 1895, NA, RG 75, LR, 16636–1895; Trennert, "From Carlisle to Phoenix," pp. 280–81.

41. *Phoenix Daily Herald,* June 1, 1893, June 8, 1894, August 1, December 23, 26, 1895, June 9, 11, 1896; *Arizona Daily Gazette,* June 8, 1894; Hall to Armstrong, June 9, 1894, NA, RG 75, LR, 22517–1894; Hall to CIA, September 1, 1896, in *Annual Report,* CIA, 1896, pp. 365–66.

42. *Phoenix Daily Herald,* February 18, 19, 20, 1896; Hall to CIA, September 1, 1896, in *Annual Report,* CIA, 1896, pp. 365–66.

43. Hall to CIA, April 3, 1897, NA, RG 75, LR, 13036–1897.

44. *Annual Report,* CIA, 1897, pp. 466–67, 557.

4. A SCHOOL FOR MANY TRIBES

1. Prucha, *Indian Policy in the United States,* pp. 252–55; James S. Olson and Raymond Wilson, *Native Americans in the Twentieth Century,* pp. 60–61; Hoxie, *A Final Promise,* pp. 190–95.

2. Adams, *American Indian Education,* pp. 61–62; Estelle Fuchs and Robert J. Havinghurst, *To Live on This Earth: American Indian Education,* p. 225; *Annual Report,* CIA, 1898, pp. 9–13; *Annual Report,* CIA, 1902, pp. 27–31; William A. Jones, "A New Indian Policy," *The World's Work,* 3 (March 1902): 1838–40; W. David Baird, "William A. Jones," in Kvasnicka and Viola, *Commissioners of Indian Affairs,* pp. 213–14. Jones continued to think of the reservation schools as providers for the nonreservation schools. This policy was confirmed in Circular #48 (February 13, 1901), NA, RG 75, Education Circulars.

3. Quote from Hoxie, *A Final Promise,* p. 145; Prucha, *Indian Policy in the United States,* pp. 259–60; Prucha, "Thomas J. Morgan," p. 198; Hoxie, "Redefining Indian Education," pp. 8–11; C. M. Woodward, "What Shall be Taught in an Indian School," in *Annual Report,* CIA, 1901, pp. 471–72.

4. *Annual Report,* CIA, 1898, pp. 6–7; Circular #3 (September 9,

1897), Circular #31 (August 5, 1899), NA, RG 75, Education Circulars; Baird, "William A. Jones," pp. 213–14; Diane T. Putney, "Fighting the Scourge: American Indian Morbidity and Federal Policy, 1897–1928" (Ph.D. dissertation, Marquette University, 1980), pp. 1–6.

5. *Portrait and Biographical Record of Arizona*, pp. 198–200.

6. McCowan to CIA, June 22, 1897, April 3, 1898, NA, RG 75, LR, 25419–1897 and 16534–1898; McCowan to CIA, July 30, 1898, in *Annual Report*, CIA, 1898, p. 352.

7. McCowan to CIA, June 22, August 2, 1897, NA, RG 75, LR, 25419–1897 and 32393–1897.

8. *Annual Report*, CIA, 1897, pp. 7–8; *Annual Report*, CIA, 1898, pp. 9–11; McCowan to CIA, May 7, 1898, NA, RG 75, LR, 22269–1898; Circular #3 (September 9, 1897), NA, RG 75, Education Circulars.

9. McCowan to CIA, July 30, 1898, in *Annual Report*, CIA, 1898, p. 352; McCowan to CIA, February 5, April 3, 1898, NA, RG 75, LR, 6148–1898 and 16534–1898; various Descriptive Statements of Children sent to Phoenix Indian School, 1897–1898, FRC, Phoenix Area Office, Agency Box 239.

10. McCowan to CIA, July 30, 1898, in *Annual Report*, CIA, 1898, pp. 352–53; McCowan to CIA, February 5, 1898 [telegram], NA, RG 75, LR, 6148–1898.

11. McCowan to CIA, August 14, 1897, NA, RG 75, LR, 34101–1897; Frank Conser to William N. Hailmann, April 19, 1898, NA, RG 75, LR, 19351–1898; John J. McKoin to CIA, June 30, 1898, in *Annual Report*, CIA, 1898, p. 351. McCowan was just as aggressive in recruiting advanced Pima students from Sacaton. When he found a few vacancies he immediately asked the commissioner to order the school superintendent, H. J. Cleveland, to transfer his best forty students to Phoenix. See McCowan to CIA, October 22, 1897, NA, RG 75, LR, 44857–1897.

12. McCowan to CIA, May 7, 1898, ibid., 22269–1898; McCowan to CIA; July 30, 1898, in *Annual Report*, CIA, 1898, pp. 352–53; *U.S. Stat.*, vol. 30, p. 589.

13. McCowan to CIA, June 8, 1898, NA, RG 75, LR, 27073–1898; James B. Alexander to McCowan, January 8, 1901, NA, RG 75, LR, 3069–1901; Hall to CIA, September 19, 1898, FRC, Sherman Institute Papers.

14. McCowan to CIA, July 31, 1899, in *Annual Report*, CIA, 1899, p. 384; McCowan to CIA, July 14, 1900, in *Annual Report*, CIA, 1900, p. 477; *Phoenix Daily Herald*, November 10, 28, 1898; Julian I. Williams, "Ten Days in Arizona," *Southwest Illustrated Magazine*, 2 (February 1896): 11–19; Frank Conser to CIA, January 3, 1899, NA, RG 75, LR, 1270–1899; McCowan to CIA, October 18, 1898, May 30, July 12, 1899, May 15, 1900, NA, RG 75, LR, 48088–1898, 25974–1899, 35613–1899, and 13844–1900.

15. Conser to CIA, January 3, 1899, NA, RG 75, LR, 1270–1899; McCowan to CIA, July 30, 1898, in *Annual Report*, CIA, 1898, pp. 353–54; McCowan to CIA, July 14, 1900, in *Annual Report*, CIA, 1900, p. 477;

Report on Phoenix Indian School by C. F. Nesler, April 6, 1898, NA, RG 75, Reports of Inspection; McCowan to CIA, July 12, 1899, NA, RG 75, LR, 35613–1899; *U.S. Stat.*, vol. 30, p. 589.

16. Petition of Pima, Maricopa, and Papago students, April 13, 1899, enclosed in H. S. Martin to CIA, nd., NA, RG 75, LR, 18457–1899.

17. McCowan to CIA, March 15, 1900, NA, RG 75, LR, 13844–1900.

18. Descriptive Statements of Children sent to Phoenix Indian School, FRC, Phoenix Area Office, Agency Box 239; Circular #54 (September 28, 1901), NA, RG 75, Education Circulars; McCowan to CIA, September 10, October 8, 1901, NA, RG 75, LR, 51148–1901 and 56793–1901.

19. McCowan to CIA, October 8, 1901, NA, RG 75, LR, 56793–1901.

20. Circular #55 (October 10, 1901), Circular #60 (December 20, 1901), NA, RG 75, Education Circulars; Jones, "A New Indian Policy," p. 1840.

21. McCowan to CIA, July 30, 1898, in *Annual Report*, CIA, 1898, p. 353.

22. Ibid., pp. 352–53; McCowan to CIA, July 14, 1900, in *Annual Report*, CIA, 1900, p. 477; Report on Phoenix Indian School by C. F. Nesler, April 6, 1898, NA, RG 75, Reports of Inspection; Circular #43 (September 19, 1900), NA, RG 75, Education Circulars.

23. McCowan to CIA, July 30, 1898, in *Annual Report*, CIA, 1898, pp. 352–53; McCowan to CIA, July 14, 1900, in *Annual Report*, CIA, 1900, p. 477; Reel to CIA, May 1, 1899, NA, RG 75, LR, 48170–1899.

24. Katie Pierson, "History of Phoenix Indian School" (unpublished manuscript, Arizona Collection, ASU), p. 186; McCowan to CIA, July 3, 1901, in *Annual Report*, CIA, 1901, pp. 523–25.

25. McCowan to CIA, July 30, 1898, in *Annual Report*, CIA, 1898, pp. 353–54; McCowan to CIA, July 14, 1900, in *Annual Report*, CIA, 1900, pp. 477–78; Report on Phoenix Indian School by C. F. Nesler, April 6, 1898, NA, RG 75, Reports of Inspection; *Phoenix Daily Enterprise*, July 6, 1898.

26. McCowan to CIA, April 25, 1898, NA, RG 75, LR, 20043–1898; *Arizona Republican*, January 15, 1900.

27. McCowan to CIA, August 3, 1897, NA, RG 75, LR, 32392–1897.

28. McCowan to CIA, March 15, 1900, NA, RG 75, LR, 13884–1900; Estelle Reel to CIA, May 26, 1900, NA, RG 75, LR, 31803–1900; *The Arizona Graphic*, 1 (September 30, 1899): 3.

29. [Estelle Reel], *Course of Study for the Indian Schools of the United States*, pp. 189–91. Similar statements can be found in the Report of the Superintendent of Indian Schools, November 12, 1902, in *Annual Report*, CIA, 1902, p. 395, and in *Annual Report*, CIA, 1900, pp. 30, 32.

30. *Arizona Republican*, January 8, March 11, 1901; McCowan to CIA, March 14, 1900, NA, RG 75, LR, 13553–1900.

31. *Annual Report*, CIA, 1896, p. 21; Report of Superintendent of Indian Schools, October 20, 1898, in *Annual Report*, CIA, 1898, p. 335; Circular #12 (May 2, 1898), Circular #15 (June 7, 1898), NA, RG 75, Education Circulars. The talks of distinguished visitors such as Hampton's H. B. Fri-

sell and Carlisle's Alfred J. Standing were printed in the separately published *Annual Reports,* Superintendent of Indian Schools, 1895 and 1896.

32. Report of Superintendent of Indian Schools, October 20, 1899, in *Annual Report,* CIA, 1899, pp. 445–47; Report of Superintendent of Indian Schools, August 20, 1900, in *Annual Report,* CIA, 1900, pp. 442–71; *National Education Association Journal of Proceedings and Addresses,* 1899, pp. 35–36.

33. Report of Superintendent of Indian Schools, October 20, 1899, in *Annual Report,* CIA, 1899, p. 447; *National Education Association Journal of Proceedings and Addresses, 1899,* p. 35; Richards, "The Training of the Indian Girl as the Uplifter of the Home," pp. 701–5.

34. McCowan to CIA, October 8, 1901, NA, RG 75, LR, 56793–1901.

35. Putney, "Fighting the Scourge," pp. 1–22; *Annual Report,* CIA, 1900, pp. 33–34; *Annual Report,* CIA, 1901, pp. 29–30; Circular #31 (August 5, 1899), Circular #46 (January 2, 1901), NA, RG 75, Education Circulars.

36. McCowan to CIA, July 30, 1898, in *Annual Report,* CIA, 1898, p. 353; Report on Phoenix Indian School by C. F. Nesler, April 6, 1898, NA, RG 75, Reports of Inspection.

37. McCowan to CIA, January 22, 1900, NA, RG 75, LR, 5185–1900.

38. *Annual Report,* CIA, 1899, pp. 641–42; Report on Phoenix Indian School by C. F. Nesler, April 6, 1898, NA, RG 75, Reports of Inspection; Genie A. Hunt to Indian Office [January 1901], NA, RG 75, LR, 2117–1901, enclosure #2; Petition of school employees relating to charges against S. M. McCowan, January 24, 1901, NA, RG 75, LR, 6372–1901, enclosure #1.

39. Report on Phoenix Indian School by Frank M. Conser, January 3, 1899, NA, RG 75, LR, 1270–1899; Estelle Reel to CIA, May 1, 1899, NA, RG 75, LR, 48170–1899; McCowan to CIA, December 26, 1900, NA, RG 75, LR, 324–1901; W. H. Gill to McCowan, December 18, 1900, NA, RG 75, LR, enclosure #1; Petition of school employees relating to charges against S. M. McCowan, January 24, 1901, NA, RG 75, LR, 6372–1901, enclosure #1.

40. McCowan to CIA, July 30, 1898, in *Annual Report,* CIA, 1898, p. 354; McCowan to CIA, July 31, 1899, in *Annual Report,* CIA, 1899, pp. 384–85; McCowan to Superintendent of Indian Schools, November 15, 1897, NA, RG 75, LR, 19213–1897; *Native American,* March 2, 1901.

41. McCowan to Superintendent of Indian Schools, November 15, 1897, NA, RG 75, LR, 19213–1897; *Daily Enterprise* (Phoenix), March 9, 11, 1899; *Phoenix Daily Herald,* February 22, 1898, November 29, December 1, 1900.

42. Hall to CIA, September 1, 1896, in *Annual Report,* CIA, 1896, pp. 364–66; *Native American,* March 12, 1904. There are many reports of sports activities in the *Herald, Enterprise,* and *Republican* after 1896.

43. Prucha, *Indian Policy in Crisis,* pp. 324–26; *Annual Report,* CIA,

1893, pp. 20–22; Report of Superintendent of Indian Schools, September 20, 1893, in ibid., pp. 392–96.

44. Hall to CIA, March 6, 1897, NA, RG 75, LR, 9448–1897; McCowan to CIA, April 17, 1899, NA, RG 75, LR, 19189–1899; McCowan to CIA, July 31, 1899, in *Annual Report,* CIA, 1899, p. 384; *Native American,* March 2, 1901; *Arizona Republican,* March 3, 9, 1901.

45. McCowan to CIA, July 14, 1900, in *Annual Report,* CIA, 1900, p. 478; *Arizona Republican,* January 3, 1900, January 8, 1901; *Daily Enterprise,* January 15, 1900.

46. McCowan to CIA, July 3, 1901, in *Annual Report,* CIA, 1901, pp. 523–25; *Arizona Republican,* April 20, 27, May 7, 8, 1901.

5. STABILITY IN AN ERA OF CHANGE

1. C. W. Goodman to CIA, March 3, 1902, NA, RG 75, LR, 14725–1902; Goodman to CIA, September 1, 1902, in *Annual Report,* CIA, 1902, p. 447; *Native American,* March 20, 1915.

2. School statistics accompanying Annual Report for fiscal year 1903, FRC, Phoenix Area Office, Agency Box 239; Statistics on degree of Indian blood of pupils enrolled at Phoenix, February 1, 1902, NA, RG 75, LR, [na]–1902; *Statistics on Indian Tribes, Agencies, and Schools, 1903,* pp. 155–56.

3. Goodman to CIA, March 3, 1902, NA, RG 75, LR, 14725–1902; Goodman to CIA, September 1, 1902, in *Annual Report,* CIA, 1902, p. 447; *Statistics on Indian Tribes, Agencies, and Schools, 1903,* p. 156.

4. Goodman to CIA, September 1, 1902, in *Annual Report,* CIA, 1902, p. 448; [Reel], *Course of Study for the Indian Schools,* passim.; Goodman to Superintendent of Indian Schools, September 5, 1902, NA, RG 75, LR, 54267–1902; Hoxie, "Redefining Indian Education," pp. 11–12.

5. *Native American,* December 20, 1902; *Arizona Republican,* December 26, 27, 28, 1902.

6. A. C. Tonner to Goodman, February 27, 1902, NA, RG 75, LS, Education, vol. 153; Goodman to CIA, April 11, 1902, NA, RG 75, LR, 22877–1902. See also William M. Raine, "The Government Indian School as a Promoter of Civilization," *World Today,* 4 (1904): 617.

7. Goodman to CIA, April 11, 1902, NA, RG 75, LR, 22877–1902.

8. CIA to Goodman, April 21, 22, 1902, NA, RG 75, LS, Education, vol. 156; Goodman to CIA, October 24, 1902, NA, RG 75, LR, 64577–1902.

9. Tonner to Goodman, June 13, 1902, NA, RG 75, LS, Education, vol. 158; Goodman to CIA, September 10, 1902, NA, RG 75, LR, 55054–1902.

10. Jones to Goodman, October 9, 1902, NA, RG 75, LS, Education, vol. 164; Goodman to CIA, October 24, 1902, NA, RG 75, LR, 64577–1902.

11. Reverend L. McAfee to James B. Alexander, November 18, 1902, NA, RG 75, LR, 1360–1903, enclosure #1; Jones to Goodman, October 9, December 8, 1902, NA, RG 75, LS, Education, vols. 164, 167.

12. Goodman to CIA, January 2, 1903, NA, RG 75, LR, 1360–1903.
13. Goodman to CIA, May 26, 1903, NA, RG 75, LR, 34373–1903; Richards, "The Training of the Indian Girl," pp. 702–4; *Native American*, February 27, 1904.
14. Jones to Superintendent, Riverside Indian School, October 30, 1903, Harwood Hall to CIA, November 16, 1903, FRC, Sherman Institute Papers.
15. Francis P. Prucha, *The Churches and the Indian Schools, 1882–1912*, pp. 58–62; Circular #62 (January 17, 1902), NA, RG 75, Education Circulars.
16. Goodman to CIA, May 17, 1902, NA, RG 75, LR, 30252–1902.
17. Tonner to Goodman, June 16, 1902, NA, RG 75, LS, Education, vol. 158; Circular #84 (November 1, 1902), NA, RG 75, Education Circulars.
18. Casimir Vogt to Goodman, March 28, 1902, enclosed in Goodman to CIA, May 28, 1902, NA, RG 75, LR, 32375–1902; Vogt to CIA, May 13, 1902, NA, RG 75, LR, 29724–1902; Tonner to Goodman, May 21, 1902, NA, RG 75, LS, Education, vol. 157.
19. Tonner to Goodman, May 21, 1902, NA, RG 75, LS, Education, vol. 157; W. H. Ketcham to CIA, May 19, 1902, enclosed in ibid.; Goodman to CIA, May 28, 1902, NA, RG 75, LR, 32375–1902; Tonner to Goodman, June 12, 1902, NA, RG 75, LS, Education, vol. 158; *Arizona Republican*, December 16, 1902.
20. Donald E. Parman, "Francis Ellington Leupp," in Kvasnicka and Viola, *Commissioners of Indian Affairs*, pp. 221–24; *Annual Report*, CIA, 1905, p. 1; Hoxie, *A Final Promise*, pp. 162–63, 198; Francis E. Leupp, "Indians and Their Education," *National Education Association Journal of Proceedings and Addresses*, 1907, p. 71. Leupp gave a preview of his Indian policy in "Outlines of an Indian Policy," *Outlook*, 79 (April 15, 1905): 946–50.
21. *Annual Report*, CIA, 1905, p. 3; *Annual Report*, CIA, 1906, pp. 12–16; Francis E. Leupp, *The Indian and His Problem*, pp. 156–57.
22. *Annual Report*, CIA, 1905, p. 43; *Annual Report*, CIA, 1906, p. 50; *Annual Report*, CIA, 1907, pp. 17–20; Leupp, *The Indian and His Problem*, pp. 135–37; *National Education Association Journal of Proceedings and Addresses*, 1907, pp. 1019–20.
23. Lummis first entered the debate when he published a series of six articles entitled "My Brother's Keeper," in *Land of Sunshine*, 11–12 (August 1899-January 1900). Then, between March 1902 and October 1903 he penned another series of articles and comments in *Out West*, 16–19 (March 1902-October 1903). A number of these essays have been collected in Charles F. Lummis, *Bullying the Moqui*, ed. with an introduction by Robert Easton and Mackinzie Brown.
24. William N. Hailmann, "Education of the Indian," *Monographs on Education in the United States*, 19 (1904): 942–43, 945–47.
25. *Annual Report*, CIA, 1905, pp. 46–47; *Annual Report*, CIA, 1906, pp. 52–55; Adams, "Federal Indian Boarding School," p. 244; *National*

Education Association Journal of Proceedings and Addresses, 1907, pp. 1020–21; Hoxie, "Redefining Indian Education," p. 16.

26. Putney, "Fighting the Scourge," pp. 78–93.

27. Circular #130 (January 15, 1906), Circular #156 (June 12, 1907), Circular #217 (June 2, 1908), FRC, Sherman Institute Papers. An especially good look at the recruiting activities of the Phoenix Indian School and the resultant expense is contained in Goodman to CIA, May 4, 1905, NA, RG 75, LR, 6459–1905.

28. Goodman to CIA, March 26, 1906, August 9, 1907, NA, RG 75, LR, 28633–1906 and 69605–1907; Leupp to Superintendent, Phoenix Indian School, August 22, 1907, NA, RG 75, LS, Education, Letterbook 634.

29. Goodman to CIA, August 31, 1905, in *Annual Report*, CIA, 1905, pp. 171–72; Annual Narrative Report, Phoenix, 1910, NA, RG 75, *ANSR*.

30. Estelle Reel to Harwood Hall, December 15, 1905, FRC, Sherman Institute Papers; Circular #80 (March 15, 1906), ibid.

31. Leupp, *The Indian and His Problem*, pp. 121–22, 140–41; *National Education Association Journal of Proceedings and Addresses, 1907*, pp. 1016–17, 1020. George Bird Grinnell, one of Leupp's closest advisors, strongly supported the outing system. See, for example, his somewhat uninformed article, "The Indian and the Outing System," *The Outlook* (September 19, 1903): 167–73.

32. Circular #123 (May 13, 1905), FRC, Sherman Institute Papers; Goodman to CIA, August 31, 1905, in *Annual Report*, CIA, 1905, pp. 171–72; Goodman to CIA, January 12, 1907, NA, RG 75, LR, 5390–1907; M. F. Holland to CIA, February 5, 1907, NA, RG 75, LR, 17284–1907.

33. Various monthly reports, 1905–1908, quarterly reports, 1907–1909, Outing Matron reports, 1911–1915, FRC, Phoenix Area Office, Agency Box 240; Annual Narrative Report, Phoenix, 1910, NA, RG 75, *ANSR*; *Native American*, January 18, February 8, 1908, March 26, 1910.

34. "Amanda Chingren," *Who's Who in Arizona, 1913*, vol. 1, p. 784; *Native American*, September 13, 1930; Amanda M. Chingren, "Arizona Indian Women and Their Future," *Arizona*, 2 (February 1912): 9–10; Outing Matron's report, 2d quarter 1911, FRC, Phoenix Area Office, Agency Box 240; Annual Narrative Report, Phoenix, 1910, NA, RG 75, *ANSR*.

35. Putney, "Fighting the Scourge," pp. 78–85; Circular #127 (August 14, 1905), NA, RG 75, Education Circulars.

36. *Native American*, March 30, April 6, 1907; Annual Narrative Report, Phoenix, 1913, NA, RG 75, ANSR; Aleš Hrdlička, *Tuberculosis Among Certain Indian Tribes of the United States*, Bureau of American Ethnology Bulletin, No. 42, pp. 25–26.

37. Hrdlička, *Tuberculosis Among Certain Indian Tribes*, pp. 22–26; Putney, "Fighting the Scourge," p. 96.

38. *Annual Report*, CIA, 1908, pp. 16, 23–24.

39. Annual Narrative Report, Phoenix, 1910, NA, RG 75, *ANSR*; *Annual Report*, CIA, 1908, p. 24; Circular #242 (September 30, 1908), Cir-

cular #246 (October 27, 1908), Circular #277 (February 4, 1909), NA, RG 75, Education Circulars; Etta Gifford Young, "Poor Lo—The Indian," *Arizona* (December 1913), 10; *Arizona Republican*, September 24, 1913; Annual Narrative Report, Phoenix, 1915, NA, RG 75, *ANSR*.

40. *Annual Report*, CIA, 1910, pp. 9–10; Annual Narrative Reports, Phoenix, 1910, 1911, 1912, NA, RG 75, *ANSR*.

41. Diane T. Putney, "Robert Grosvenor Valentine," in Kvasnicka and Viola, *Commissioners of Indian Affairs*, p. 233; Annual Narrative Reports, Phoenix, 1910, 1911, NA, RG 75, *ANSR*; Assistant Superintendent to Cato Sells, August 13, 1915, FRC, Phoenix Area Office, Agency Box 256.

42. Annual Narrative Reports, Phoenix, 1911, 1912, 1913, NA, RG 75, *ANSR*; Assistant Superintendent to Sells, August 13, 1915, FRC, Phoenix Area Office, Agency Box 256.

43. Annual Narrative Reports, Phoenix, 1912, 1913, 1914, NA, RG 75, *ANSR*; Assistant Superintendent to Sells, August 13, 1915, FRC, Phoenix Area Office, Agency Box 256.

44. Putney, "Fighting the Scourge," pp. 100–1; Dorothy Morse to Goodman, February 27, 1913, Goodman to Morse, March 8, 1913, R. C. Craige to Goodman, October 31, 1912, F.W.S. to Superintendent Ernest Stecker, November 26, 1912, FRC, Phoenix Area Office, Agency Box 257. There are many letters from prospective patients among the files of the Indian school.

45. Circular #150 (April 22, 1907), Circular #175 (December 3, 1907), FRC, Sherman Institute Papers; Annual Narrative Report, Phoenix, 1913, NA, RG 75, *ANSR*.

46. Annual Narrative Report, Phoenix, 1910, NA, RG 75, *ANSR*.

47. Roster of Graduates, nd., FRC, Phoenix Area Office, Agency Box 240; Annual Narrative Reports, Phoenix, 1911, 1913, 1914, NA, RG 75, *ANSR*.

48. Annual Narrative Reports, Phoenix, 1913, 1914, NA, RG 75, *ANSR*.

49. Annual Narrative Report, Phoenix, 1915, NA, RG 75, *ANSR*.

6. STUDENT LIFE

1. Annual Narrative Reports, Phoenix, 1916, 1918, NA, RG 75, ANSR; John B. Brown to CIA, September 1, 1917, NA, RG 75, CCF, Phoenix, 66595–17–820; Ella Lopez Antone interview, January 22, 1982; Anthony and Hazel Dukepoo interview, November 13, 1984. David Wallace Adams, "Schooling the Hopi: Federal Indian Policy Writ Small, 1887–1917," *Pacific Historical Review*, 48 (August 1979): 335–56, discusses the Hopi reaction to boarding schools in detail.

2. Peter Blaine interview, May 7, 1981; Brown to CIA, September 1, 1917, NA, RG 75, CCF, Phoenix, 66595–17–820; Helen Sekaquaptewa interview, March 26, 1985; Theodore Rios interview, May 16, 1974; Louise Udall, *Me and Mine: The Life Story of Helen Sekaquaptewa*, pp. 132–133. Polingaysi Qoyawayma, *No Turning Back: A True Account of a*

Hopi Girl's Struggle to Bridge the Gap Between the World of Her People and the World of the White Man, pp. 46–60, tells of her experiences upon being sent to Sherman Institute. Although more favorably inclined toward leaving home, she points out much of the general reservation sentiment.

3. Dukepoo interview, November 13, 1984; *Arizona Republican* quoted in *Native American*, January 2, 1904.

4. Antone interview, January 22, 1982; Shaw, *A Pima Past*, p. 132; Sekaquaptewa interview, March 26, 1985.

5. Adams, "Schooling the Hopi," 343; Udall, *Me and Mine*, pp. 134–35; *Native American*, January 2, February 6, 1904.

6. Shaw, *A Pima Past*, pp. 133–34; Dukepoo interview, November 13, 1984; *Native American*, February 20, 27, 1904, February 25, 1905, May 9, 1908.

7. Udall, *Me and Mine*, p. 135.

8. Young, "Poor Lo—The Indian," 4–5; *Native American*, May 9, 1908; Raine, "The Government Indian School as a Promoter of Civilization," pp. 616–17; Rios interview, May 16, 1974. Anna Moore Shaw, in *A Pima Past*, pp. 135–36, discusses her reaction to being moved from one work detail to another.

9. *Native American*, February 4, 1911; Udall, *Me and Mine*, pp. 136–37; Blaine interview, May 7, 1981; Shaw, *A Pima Past*, pp. 135–36; Antone interview, January 22, 1982.

10. Shaw, *A Pima Past*, pp. 135–36; Rios interview, May 17, 1974.

11. M. F. Holland to CIA, February 5, 1907, NA, RG 75, LR, 17284–1907; Brown to CIA, June 5, 1916, FRC, Phoenix Area Office, Agency Box 256; Cato Sells to Brown, April 28, 1917, FRC, Phoenix Area Office, Agency Box 256; Annual Narrative Reports, Phoenix, 1916, 1920, NA, RG 75, *ANSR*. Fourth-grade requirements quoted in Estelle A. Brown, *Stubborn Fool: A Narrative*, p. 228.

12. Annual Narrative Reports, Phoenix, 1915, 1919, NA, RG 75, *ANSR*.

13. Brown, *Stubborn Fool*, pp. 202–4; Udall, *Me and Mine*, pp. 138, 142; Shaw, *A Pima Past*, p. 137; Antone interview, January 22, 1982; Dukepoo interview, March 2, 1985; Annual Narrative Report, Phoenix, 1920, NA, RG 75, *ANSR*; *Native American*, May 3, 1919.

14. Raine, "The Government Indian School as a Promoter of Civilization," pp. 617–18; Young, "Poor Lo—The Indian," p. 4; Holland to CIA, February 5, 1907, NA, RG 75, LR, 17284–1907; Peter Blaine, Sr., with Michael Adams, *Papagos and Politics*, p. 23; Rios interview, May 16, 1974; Annual Narrative Report, Phoenix, 1917, NA, RG 75, *ANSR*.

15. Dukepoo interview, November 13, 1984; Blaine interview, May 7, 1981; *Native American*, April 28, 1906.

16. Quotes from letters home in the *Native American*, December 5, 1903, February 13, 1904. School policy on letters home was printed in the December 4, 1926, issue of the school paper. It said, in part, "a letter home from the boy or girl is an event of note. Friends and neighbors gather to

hear it read. If it contains a note of depression or discouragement this feeling is communicated to the group or village.... Hence we ask our students to write cheerful letters to the home folks. If there must at times be letter writers in a sadder tone or of a complaining nature we ask that they be sent to ... the 'Main Office.' "

17. *Arizona Republican*, December 29, 1902; Goodman to CIA, May 26, 1908 (2 letters), NA, RG 75, CCF, Phoenix, 36417–08–821 and Phoenix, 30089–08–821; Brown to Sells, April 17, 1917, NA, RG 75, CCF, Phoenix, 76512–16–806; Duncan D. McArthur to Goodman, May 24, 1905, Brown to CIA, January 2, 1918, FRC, Phoenix Area Office, Agency Box 257; Annual Narrative Report, Phoenix, 1917, NA, RG 75, *ANSR*.

18. Goodman to CIA, May 26, 1908, NA, RG 75, CCF, Phoenix, 36089–08–821; Brown to Sells, April 17, 1917, NA, RG 75, CCF, Phoenix, 76512–16–806; A. F. Duclos to Charles A. Burke, June 29, 1923, NA, RG 75, CCF, Phoenix, 91218–17–821; Brown to CIA, October 13, 1928, NA, RG 75, CCF, Phoenix, 51244–29–821; *Arizona Republican*, December 29, 1902, April 22, 1907.

19. *Native American*, April 11, 1908, April 22, 1911; Udall, *Me and Mine*, p. 137; Antone interview, January 22, 1982; Brown to Sells, April 17, 1917, NA, RG 75, CCF, Phoenix, 76512–16–806; *Arizona Star* (Tucson), March 31, 1917.

20. Philip Cassadore interview, February 5, 1980; Dukepoo interview, November 13, 1984; Blaine interview, May 7, 1981; Sekaquaptewa interview, March 26, 1985.

21. Dukepoo interview, November 13, 1984; Shaw, *A Pima Past*, pp. 253, 255–257; *Native American*, May 14, 21, 1904.

22. Shaw, *A Pima Past*, p. 134; *Native American*, April 4, August 27, September 3, October 1, 1905, February 13, 1926; *Arizona Republican*, June 19, 1903, October 14, 1909.

23. Annual Narrative Reports, Phoenix, 1920, 1921, NA, RG 75, *ANSR*; Report on the Phoenix Indian School by E. H. Hammond, April 24, 1925, NA, RG 75, CCF, Phoenix, 37108–25–806; *Native American*, June 5, 1926, June 4, 1927; *The New Trail*, vol. 2, pp. 67–74; Dukepoo interview, March 2, 1985.

24. Report on the Phoenix Indian School by E. H. Hammond, April 24, 1925, NA, RG 75, CCF, Phoenix, 37108–25–806; Rios interview, May 17, 1974; Dukepoo interview, March 2, 1985; Blaine, *Papagos and Politics*, p. 25; *Native American*, January 9, 16, 1904, January 11, 1908, January 22, 1910.

25. Annual Narrative Reports, Phoenix, 1919, 1920, 1921, NA, RG 75, *ANSR*; *Native American*, February 20, November 26, 1904, October 21, 1905, May 11, 1907, May 9, 1908, June 12, 1920, June 5, 1926; *Senior Class Annual, 1924*, pp. 14, 47; Dukepoo interview, November 13, 1984.

26. *Native American*, February 27, March 5, 1904, October 21, 1905, November 16, 1912, June 13, 1925, December 28, 1926; *The New Trail*, vol. 2, pp. 50–51.

27. *The New Trail*, vol. 2, pp. 45–46; *Native American*, March 10, 1906, February 17, 1912, January 18, 25, 1913, January 30, 1915.

28. Udall, *Me and Mine*, p. 138; Dukepoo interview, November 13, 1984; Blaine interview, May 7, 1981; Shaw, *A Pima Past*, p. 133.

29. Sells to Brown, September 30, 1916, Brown to Sells, October 7, 1916, NA, RG 75, CCF, Phoenix, 76512–16–806; Materials attached to Charles H. Burke to Amanda Chingren, December 5, 1923, NA, RG 75, CCF, Phoenix, 87833–23–824.

30. Sells to Brown, September 30, 1916, NA, RG 75, CCF, Phoenix, 76512–16–806; Annual Narrative Report, Phoenix, 1913, NA, RG 75, *ANSR*; Antone interview, January 22, 1982; Blaine interview, May 7, 1981; Dukepoo interview, March 2, 1985.

31. Most personal reminiscences mention romances and courtship. Among those to consult are Udall, *Me and Mine*, pp. 140–41, and Shaw, *A Pima Past*, p. 137. The same is true with such interviews as Dukepoo, November 13, 1984 and March 2, 1985, Antone, January 22, 1982, and Blaine, May 7, 1981. Porch climbing is mentioned in Brown to Sells, October 7, 1916, NA, RG 75, CCF, Phoenix, 76512–16–806.

32. Letters from Chingren file, NA, RG 75, CCF, Phoenix, 87833–23–824; Brown, *Stubborn Fool*, pp. 224–26.

33. Report of E. M. Sweet on the Outing System at Phoenix, July 15, 1916, NA, RG 75, CCF, Phoenix, 76513–16–806; Letters from Chingren file, NA, RG 75, CCF, Phoenix, 87833–23–824; Annual Narrative Reports, Phoenix, 1910, 1915, 1920, NA, RG 75, *ANSR*. Marriages among former students were sometimes reported in the *Native American*. See, for example, the January 21, 1905, March 24, 1906, and January 26, 1907, issues.

34. Annual Narrative Reports, Phoenix, 1910, 1918, NA, RG 75, *ANSR*; Dukepoo interview, November 13, 1984.

35. Udall, *Me and Mine*, pp. 136, 139–40; *Native American*, November 6, 1920.

36. *Native American*, October 9, 1920; Antone interview, January 22, 1982; Sylvia Laughlin, "Iron Springs, Arizona: Timeless Summer Resort," *Journal of Arizona History*, 22 (1981): 246.

37. Annual Narrative Report, Phoenix, 1920, NA, RG 75, *ANSR*; *Native American*, March 26, 1910, October 9, 1920, September 22, 1923; Rios interview, May 17, 1974.

38. Report of E. M. Sweet on the Outing System at Phoenix, July 5, 1916, NA, RG 75, CCF, Phoenix, 76513–16–806; Adelena O. Warren to C. H. Burke, November 8, 1923, NA, RG 75, CCF, Phoenix, 87833–23–806; miscellaneous correspondence in the Chingren file, ibid.

39. Antone interview, January 22, 1982; Blaine, *Papagos and Politics*, p. 25; Dukepoo interviews, November 13, 1984, and March 2, 1985; Rios interview, March 17, 1974; Udall, *Me and Mine*, pp. 142–43.

40. *Native American*, June 13, 1925, June 5, 1926; *Senior Class Annual, 1924*, pp. 8–13; *The New Trail*, 1930, vol. 2, pp. 19–24.

41. *Native American*, May 28, 1904, June 9, 1906, January 11, February 5, 1908, October 4, 1913, March 3, 1917, May 29, 1920; Annual Narrative Report, Phoenix, 1914, NA, RG 75, *ANSR*; Shaw, *A Pima Past*, pp. 141–42, 146–47.

42. *Native American*, September 24, November 5, 1904, March 25, 1905, December 1, 1906, May 4, 1907, June 15, July 6–13, 1912, February 1, 1913; Carl H. Skinner to CIA, January 28, 1933, FRC, Phoenix Area Office, Agency Box 251.

43. *Native American*, September 26, 1903, September 7, 1907; Annual Narrative Report, Phoenix, 1920, NA, RG 75, *ANSR*; correspondence regarding the case of Anna Moore, NA, RG 75, CCF, Phoenix, 91164–19–820.

44. *Native American*, November 28, 1903.

45. Ibid., September 26, 1903, January 16, May 7, 21, October 22, 1904, May 27, 1905, October 10, 1908, March 4, April 29, 1911, March 1, 1913; *Annual Report*, CIA, 1905, pp. 45–46; Dukepoo interview, November 13, 1984. Nearly every year after 1905 the school held a conference of returned students. Their comments were printed in the *Native American* and provide a good description of what returned students, both from Phoenix and other schools, were doing.

46. E. B. Meritt to Brown, August 8, 1916, FRC, Phoenix Area Office, Agency Box 255; Address of Commissioner Sells to Indian school employees, in the *Native American*, October 30, 1915; Annual Narrative Report, Phoenix, 1911, NA, RG 75, *ANSR*; *Native American*, December 1, 1906, May 18, June 29, October 12, 1907, April 26, September 20, 1913, May 15, 1915; Cassadore interview, February 5, 1980; Shaw, *A Pima Past*, pp. 151–54.

47. *Native American*, December 1, 1906, January 7, 1911, June 1, 1912, March 1, April 5, 1913; *Arizona Republican*, quoted in ibid., November 5, 1904.

48. "Indians of the United States," H. Rept. 1133, 66th Cong., 3d sess., 1920, pp. 8–9. See also Sells to Brown, April 28, 1917, FRC, Phoenix Area Office, Agency Box 255.

49. Memoranda on returned student problem, January 30, 1917, NA, RG 75, BIC, Reference Material, Tray 120.

50. Returned Student Survey, October 10, 1917, p. 3, ibid.

51. Ibid., p. 5; Reports of John B. Brown and Leo Crane, in Bulletin of Returned Students, nd. [1917], NA, RG 75, BIC, Reference Material, Tray 121; Sekaquaptewa interview, March 26, 1985; *Native American*, March 24, 1906, January 26, 1907; Qoyawayma, *No Turning Back*, pp. 72–73; Udall, *Me and Mine*, pp. 150–52.

52. *Native American*, November 6, 1909, May 22, 1915; Returned Student Survey, October 10, 1917, p. 15, NA, RG 75, BIC, Reference Material, Tray 120.

53. Richard H. Frost, "Pueblo Indian Returned Students: The Domi-

nance of Community Conservatism, to 1930" (Unpublished paper presented to the Lake Mohonk Conference, October 1983).

54. *Native American*, January 21, 1905, March 24, 1906.
55. Reports of Leo Crane and Frank Thackery, in Bulletin of Returned Students, nd., NA, RG 75, BIC, Reference Material, Tray 121.
56. Ibid.
57. Frost, "Pueblo Indian Returned Students;" Blaine, *Papagos and Politics*, passim.; Harry C. James, *Pages from Hopi History*, p. 204.
58. Report of Leo Crane, in Bulletin of Returned Students, nd., NA, RG 75, BIC, Reference Material, Tray 121.

7. EDUCATION UNDER DURESS

1. *Native American*, March 20, April 3, 1915.
2. Lawrence C. Kelly, "Cato Sells, 1913–21," in Kvasnicka and Viola, *Commissioners of Indian Affairs*, pp. 243–44; Hoxie, *A Final Promise*, pp. 204–6; *Annual Report*, CIA, 1914, pp. 5–8.
3. Annual Narrative Report, Phoenix, 1915, NA, RG 75, *ANSR*; *Native American*, June 6, 1931.
4. Materials relating to the 1915–1916 postcard controversy are in Dr. W. C. Gillespie to CIA, March 22, 1915, and other correspondence in FRC, Phoenix Area Office, Agency Box 256; *Native American*, October 30, 1915; *Arizona Republican*, May 7, 1916.
5. Superintendent to Mrs. James Gleason, May 15, 1916, Superintendent to Mr. Red Fox James, May 8, 1916, Superintendent to CIA, April 28, 1915, FRC, Phoenix Area Office, Agency Box 256; Annual Narrative Report, Phoenix, 1916, NA, RG 75, *ANSR*; *Native American*, November 27, 1915.
6. Mike Burns to Brown, May 27, 1916, Superintendent to Burns, June 2, 1916, [Brown] to CIA, July 5, 1915, FRC, Phoenix Area Office, Agency Box 256; E. B. Meritt to Brown, July 12, 1916, FRC, Phoenix Area Office, Agency Box 255; *Native American*, May 13, 1916.
7. *Annual Report*, CIA, 1916, pp. 24–25; Brown to CIA, June 14, July 8, 1915, February 10, 1916, FRC, Phoenix Area Office, Agency Box 256; Brown to CIA, November 20, 1916, and Meritt to Brown, December 4, 1916, NA, RG 75, CCF, Phoenix, 121186–16–820.
8. *Annual Report*, CIA, 1915, pp. 7–8; *Annual Report*, CIA, 1916, pp. 9–23; Superintendent to CIA, February 10, 1916, FRC, Phoenix Area Office, Agency Box 256; Adams, *American Indian Education*, pp. 62–63. In *A Final Promise*, pp. 204–6, Frederick Hoxie argues that the 1916 course of study marks the final stage in transferring control of Indian affairs from reformers to bureaucrats. While there are elements of truth in this assertion, the course of study was neither as radical nor as successful as Hoxie assumes and was done primarily to bolster a sagging public image.
9. Annual Narrative Report, Phoenix, 1916, NA, RG 75, *ANSR*; *Annual*

Report, CIA, 1915, p. 9; *Annual Report,* CIA, 1916, pp. 23–24; Superintendent to CIA, FRC, Phoenix Area Office, Agency Box 256; Brown to CIA, September 1, 1917, NA, RG 75, CCF, Phoenix, 66595–17–820.

10. *Annual Report,* CIA, 1917, pp. 9–14; Sells to Brown, April 28, 1917, FRC, Phoenix Area Office, Agency Box 255.

11. Annual Narrative Reports, Phoenix, 1916, 1917, NA, RG 75, *ANSR;* Superintendent to CIA, June 5, 1916, FRC, Phoenix Area Office, Agency Box 256; Superintendent to CIA, May 4, 1917, ibid., Agency Box 255.

12. *Annual Report,* BIC, 1917, p. 12.

13. Report of John B. Brown, in Bulletin of Returned Students, nd., NA, RG 75, BIC, Reference Material, Tray 121. See also Returned Students Bulletin #59, NA, RG 75, BIC, Reference Material, Tray 120.

14. *Native American,* November 13, 1915. See also W. Bruce White, "The American Indian as Soldier, 1890–1919," *Canadian Review of American Studies,* 7 (Spring 1976): 19, 24.

15. *Native American,* November 13, 1915, June 10, 1916, January 6, 1917; *Arizona Republican,* May 13, 27, 1916; Superintendent to CIA, August 3, 1916, FRC, Phoenix Area Office, Agency Box 256; Superintendent to CIA, May 4, 1917, FRC, Phoenix Area Office, Agency Box 255. The story of Ross Shaw's role is told in Shaw, *A Pima Past,* pp. 140, 142–43. See James R. Kluger, *The Clifton-Morenci Strike,* for a detailed account of the strike.

16. Annual Narrative Reports, Phoenix, 1918, 1919, NA, RG 75, *ANSR; Annual Report,* CIA, 1917, pp. 6–7; *Annual Report,* CIA, 1918, pp. 7–10; Sells to Carl Hayden, May 23, 1918, and various undated newspaper clippings in Carl Hayden Papers, ASU, Box 624, Folder 3; *Native American,* June 23, 1917, January 26, September 21, December 28, 1918; Shaw, *A Pima Past,* pp. 143–46.

17. Sells to Superintendents, April 12, 1917, FRC, Phoenix Area Office, Agency Box 256.

18. Superintendent to CIA, April 13, 1917, FRC, Phoenix Area Office, Agency Box 256; Superintendent to CIA, May 9, 1918, FRC, Phoenix Area Office, Agency Box 257; Annual Narrative Reports, Phoenix, 1918, 1919, NA, RG 75, *ANSR; Native American,* May 12, June 23, 1917, April 6, 1918; *Annual Report,* CIA, 1918, pp. 14–15.

19. Annual Narrative Reports, Phoenix, 1918, 1919, NA, RG 75, *ANSR; Native American,* December 1, 1917, January 26, March 9, April 6, 1918.

20. *Annual Report,* CIA, 1918, pp. 19–22.

21. Annual Narrative Report, Phoenix, 1918, NA, RG 75, *ANSR;* Brown to Carl Hayden, December 31, 1917, FRC, Phoenix Area Office, Agency Box 257.

22. *Annual Report,* CIA, 1918, pp. 32–33, 36–37; Brown to CIA, July 11, 1918, NA, RG 75, CCF, Phoenix, 59779–18–806; Annual Narrative Reports, 1918, 1919, 1920, NA, RG 75, *ANSR.*

23. Annual Narrative Reports, Phoenix, 1917, 1918, 1919, NA, RG 75, *ANSR;* Brown to CIA, January 2, 1918, FRC, Phoenix Area Office, Agency

Box 257; Brown to Sells, April 17, 1917, NA, RG 75, CCF, Phoenix, 76512–16–806; *Arizona Star*, March 31, 1917; *Native American*, May 12, 1917.

24. *Arizona Republican*, May 19, 1920.

25. Hazel W. Hertzberg, *The Search for an American Indian Identity: Modern Pan-Indian Movements*, pp. 68–69; Adams, "Federal Indian Boarding School," pp. 244–45; Adams, *American Indian Education*, p. 66.

26. "Indians of the United States," *H. Rept.* 1133, 66th Cong., 3d sess., 1920, pp. 8–9; Annual Narrative Report, Phoenix, 1921, NA, RG 75, *ANSR*; *Native American*, May 15, 1920.

27. *Native American*, January 10, October 9, 1920; Regulations Governing the Conduct and Service of Non-Citizen Indians in Phoenix and Vicinity, June 8, 1922, NA, RG 75, CCF, Phoenix, 87833–23–824; Report on Outing Matron Activities, Phoenix, Arizona, nd, NA, RG 75, CCF, Phoenix, 40642–25–824; Annual Narrative Report, Phoenix, 1922, NA, RG 75, *ANSR*.

28. Szasz, *Education and the American Indian*, p. 19; Lawrence C. Kelly, "Charles Henry Burke, 1921–1929," in Kvasnicka and Viola, *Commissioners of Indian Affairs*, pp. 252–53.

29. Annual Report, CIA, 1922, pp. 2–4; Report of Edna Groves, nd. [March 1923], NA, RG 75, CCF, Phoenix, 19964–23–806.

30. Annual Narrative Reports, Phoenix, 1922, 1923, NA, RG 75, *ANSR*; Kenneth R. Philp, *John Collier's Crusade for Indian Reform*, p. 82.

31. Annual Report, CIA, 1922, p. 5; Adams, *American Indian Education*, p. 66; Annual Narrative Reports, Phoenix, 1920, 1922, 1923, 1925, NA, RG 75, *ANSR*.

32. Mike Burns to Carlos Montezuma, April 11, 17, 1919, Carlos Montezuma Collection, ASU, Box 4, Folio 5; Burns to CIA, July 24, 1923, and Brown to CIA, September 28, 1923, NA, RG 75, CCF, Phoenix, 61544–23–820. For additional material on Burns, see Peter Iverson, *Carlos Montezuma and the Changing World of American Indians*.

33. A. F. Duclos to Burke, June 29, 1923, and Chingren to Burke, October 5, 1923, NA, RG 75, CCF, Phoenix, 91218–17–821; Adelena O. Warren to Burke, November 8, 1923, and Burke to Chingren, December 5, 1923, NA, RG 75, CCF, Phoenix, 87833–23–824. At this same time, the Indian Office ruled that "incorrigible Indian girls" could be turned over to state authorities by local superintendents. See John B. White to CIA, September 5, 1923, and Burke to White, September 22, 1923, NA, RG 75, CCF, Phoenix, 71229–23–821.

34. *Arizona Republican*, September 13, 1924; *Phoenix Evening Gazette*, September 12, 16, 1924; Miscellaneous reports on the incident, NA, RG 75, CCF, Phoenix, 70142–24–820; Pierson, "History of the Phoenix Indian School," p. 92.

35. Szasz, *Education and the American Indian*, pp. 13–15, 18; John Collier, "Our Indian Policy: Why Not Treat the Red Man as Wisely, as Generously as We Have Treated the Filipino?" *Sunset*, 50 (March 1923): 13–15, 89–93.

36. Hubert Work to Carl Hayden, December 4, 1923, Carl Hayden Papers, ASU, Box 619, Folder 13; Philp, *John Collier's Crusade for Indian Reform*, pp. 49–52; Hertzberg, *The Search for an American Indian Identity*, pp. 202–4; Lawrence C. Kelly, *The Assault on Assimilation: John Collier and the Origins of Indian Policy Reform*, pp. 288–93; John Collier, "The Red Slaves of Oklahoma," *Sunset*, 52 (March 1924): 95–100. In a recent study, Henry E. Fritz, "The Board of Indian Commissioners Versus John Collier and Lewis Meriam, 1923–1933" (unpublished paper presented to the Western History Association, October 1985), argues that assimilationist forces remained vigorous well after 1924.

37. *Annual Report*, IRA, 1923, pp. 40–41; Adams, *American Indian Education*, p. 66; Szasz, *Education and the American Indian*, p. 15; John Collier, "The Accursed System," *Sunset*, 52 (June 1924): 81.

38. Annual Narrative Reports, Phoenix, 1925, 1928, NA, RG 75, *ANSR*; Brown to CIA, November 3, 1927, and Circular #2397 (December 6, 1927), FRC, Phoenix Area Office, Agency Box 247; Report on Phoenix Indian School by E. H. Hammond, April 24, 1925, NA, RG 75, CCF, Phoenix, 37108–25–806.

39. E. B. Meritt to Brown, September 17, 1926, and Brown to E. H. Hammond, August 12, 1926, in NA, RG 75, CCF, Phoenix, 35047–26–806.

40. *Annual Report*, CIA, 1925, p. 6; *Annual Report*, CIA, 1926, p. 7; H. H. Fiske to CIA, March 21, 1927, NA, RG 75, CCF, Phoenix, 18443–27–806; Brown to CIA, November 2, 1927, FRC, Phoenix Area Office, Agency Box 247.

41. Annual Narrative Reports, Phoenix, 1925, 1926, NA, RG 75, *ANSR*; Report on Phoenix Indian School by E. H. Hammond, April 24, 1925, NA, RG 75, CCF, Phoenix, 37108–25–806; Circular #2397 (December 6, 1927), FRC, Phoenix Area Office, Agency Box 247.

42. Annual Narrative Reports, Phoenix, 1926, 1927, 1928, NA, RG 75, *ANSR*. That the Indian Office was well aware that critics intended to attack corporal punishment is evident in an undated memo in Carl Hayden Papers, ASU, Box 619, Folder 13.

43. Annual Narrative Report, Phoenix, 1926, NA, RG 75, *ANSR*.

44. U.S. Senate, *Survey of Conditions of the Indians of the United States*, pp. 2–6; "The Government's Handling of Indian Affairs," Address of Edgar B. Meritt before the Oakland Forum, December 1, 1926, p. 14, Carl Hayden Papers, ASU, Box 604, Folder 14.

45. "The Government's Handling of Indian Affairs,", pp. 14–15, 16a, Carl Hayden Papers, ASU, Box 604, Folder 14.

46. *Survey of Conditions of the Indians of the United States*, pp. 7–8, 40; Philp, *John Collier's Crusade for Indian Reform*, pp. 76–81.

47. The Meriam Report stemmed from several sources, including the Board of Indian Commissioners. See Fritz, "The Board of Indian Commissioners Versus John Collier and Lewis Meriam."

8. END OF AN ERA

1. Philp, *John Collier's Crusade for Indian Reform*, pp. 90–91.
2. Meriam, *The Problem of Indian Administration*, pp. 84, 346; Szasz, *Education and the American Indian*, p. 18; *Native American*, September 13, 1930.
3. Meriam, *The Problem of Indian Administration*, pp. 12, 314–39, 392–93.
4. Ibid., pp. 12–13.
5. Ibid., pp. 13, 347, 360.
6. Ibid., pp. 332, 577–79.
7. Ibid., pp. 402–4.
8. Ibid., pp. 33, 405–6.
9. *Annual Report*, CIA, 1928, pp. 1–4.
10. *Native American*, February 23, 1929.
11. Kelly, "Charles Henry Burke," p. 260; John Collier memo on flogging, May 15, 1930, and copy of undated circular abolishing jails [January 1928], enclosed in Mrs. Joseph Lincoln Smith to Hayden, April 15, 1931, Carl Hayden Papers, ASU, Box 623, Folder 6.
12. Brown to CIA, October 13, 1928, NA, RG 75, CCF, Phoenix, 51244–28–821; Annual Narrative Report, 1929, NA, RG 75, *ANSR*.
13. *Philadelphia Inquirer*, April 10, 1929; Lawrence C. Kelly, "Charles James Rhoads, 1929–33," in Kvasnicka and Viola, *Commissioners of Indian Affairs*, pp. 263–66; Szasz, *Education and the American Indian*, pp. 24–28; Philp, *John Collier's Crusade for Indian Reform*, pp. 92–96.
14. Brown to Superintendent at Truxton et al., July 31, 1929, Brown to Arthur C. Plake, July 25, 1929, and Brown to Agnes Lopez, August 8, 1929, FRC, Phoenix Area Office, Agency Box 246; Brown to CIA, January 20, May 5, June 14, September 20, December 16, 1930, February 5, 1931, FRC, Phoenix Area Office, Agency Box 255; W. R. Ashurst to Senate Committee on Indian Affairs, July 8, 1931, in U.S. Senate, *Survey of Conditions of the Indians in the United States*, part 17 (April 1931), pp. 8131–32; Szasz, *Education and the American Indian*, pp. 91–92.
15. Brown to CIA, January 8, February 12, April 28, 1930, FRC, Phoenix Area Office, Agency Box 255; Annual Narrative Report, Phoenix, 1930, NA, RG 75, *ANSR*.
16. Szasz, *Education and the American Indian*, p. 27; Annual Narrative Report, Phoenix, 1930, NA, RG 75, *ANSR*; Brown to CIA, July 17, November 13, 1930, FRC, Phoenix Area Office, Agency Box 255; *Arizona Republican*, December 29, 1929; *Native American*, February 14, 1931.
17. Circular #2666 (March 20, 1930), copy in Smith to Hayden, April 15, 1931, Carl Hayden Papers, ASU, Box 623, Folder 6.
18. Collier memo on flogging, May 15, 1930, in ibid.; *Arizona Labor Journal*, April 5, 19, 1930; unidentified newspaper clippings, May 4, 1930, in Carl Hayden Papers, ASU, Box 623, Folder 6.
19. Collier memo on flogging, May 15, 1930, in Carl Hayden Papers,

ASU, Box 623; U.S. Senate, *Survey of Conditions of the Indians in the United States,* part 8 (May 23 and 27, 1930), passim; Annual Narrative Report, Phoenix, 1930, NA, RG 75, *ANSR.* Brown's activities during this period are partly covered in Brown to CIA, April 9, 13, 24, June 10, 1930, FRC, Phoenix Area Office, Agency Box 255.

20. *Survey of Conditions of the Indians in the United States,* part 8, pp. 3015–23.

21. Ibid., pp. 3023–40; *New York Times,* May 23, 24, 1930; *Washington Star,* May 23, 1930.

22. *Survey of Conditions of the Indians in the United States,* part 8, pp. 3061–84; *New York Times,* May 28, 1930. Brown refused to admit that Collier and the Schmidts were right, and he spent the following year collecting evidence that the Schmidts had condoned unethical activities among students. His main charge was that the Schmidt's daughter was living with one of the male students and eventually bore an illegitimate child. The headmaster was eventually able to prove this, which perhaps explains why the matter was not pursued by the Indian Office. See Brown to CIA, December 23, 1930, April 8, 25, 1931, FRC, Phoenix Area Office, Agency Box 255.

23. *Native American,* September 13, 1930, April 11, 1931; *Annual Report,* SI, 1931, p. 83; Szasz, *Education and the American Indian,* pp. 29–30.

24. Annual Narrative Report, Phoenix, 1930, NA, RG 75, *ANSR; Native American,* January 17, 1931.

25. *Native American,* September 13, 1930; Brown to CIA, June 17, 1930, FRC, Phoenix Area Office, Agency Box 255; Brown memorandum of June 25, 1930, in *Survey of Conditions of the Indians in the United States,* part 17, pp. 8073–75.

26. *Survey of Conditions of the Indians in the United States,* part 17, pp. 8058–73, 8123, 8125–26; Charles L. Davis to Carl Hayden, July 16, 1931, Carl Hayden Papers, ASU, Box 623, Folder 8.

27. Davis to Hayden, April 21, July 16, 1931, Carl Hayden Papers, ASU, Box 623, Folder 8; *Native American,* June 6, 1931; *Arizona Republic,* June 28, 1931.

28. *Arizona Republic,* July 18, 1931; *Phoenix Redskin,* September 26, November 7, 1931.

29. *Phoenix Redskin,* January 2, 1932; Skinner to CIA, September 21, 23, December 14, 1932, FRC, Phoenix Area Office, Agency Box 255; *Arizona Republic,* November 20, 1932.

30. Skinner to CIA, January 27, 31, August 9, 28, 1933, FRC, Phoenix Area Office, Agency Box 251; Skinner to CIA, January 8, February 12, May 12, 1934, FRC, Phoenix Area Office, Agency Box 253; Collier to Hayden, January 18, 1935, Carl Hayden Papers, ASU, Box 626, Folder 5; Annual Narrative Report, Phoenix, 1934, NA, RG 75, ANSR.

31. Skinner to CIA, July 9, October 7, 1932, FRC, Phoenix Area Office, Agency Box 255; Skinner to CIA, February 4, 1933, February 28, 1935,

FRC, Phoenix Area Office, Agency Box 251; Skinner to CIA, July 23, 1934, FRC, Phoenix Area Office, Agency Box 253.

32. Annual Narrative Report, Phoenix, 1934, NA, RG 75, *ANSR.*

33. Annual Narrative Reports, Phoenix, 1934, 1935, *ANSR.*

34. Ibid.; Skinner to CIA, March 21, 1935, FRC, Phoenix Area Office, Agency Box 251.

35. Skinner to CIA, July 28, 1933, FRC, Phoenix Area Office, Agency Box 251; Skinner to CIA, February 21, March 7, 1934, FRC, Phoenix Area Office, Agency Box 253.

36. Hayden to Collier, memorandum, January 12, 1935, Hayden to Amanda Chingren, January 25, 1935, Carl Hayden Papers, ASU, Box 626, Folder 5.

37. Collier to Hayden, January 18, 1935, Carl Hayden Papers, ASU, Box 626, Folder 5.

9. CONCLUSION AND EPILOGUE

1. Quoted in Prucha, *Americanizing the American Indian,* p. 75.
2. Dukepoo interview, November 13, 1984.
3. Fuchs and Havinghurst, *To Live on This Earth,* pp. 222–45.
4. *New Times* (Phoenix), November 28-December 4, 1984.
5. Fuchs and Havinghurst, *To Live on This Earth,* pp. 227–28; Szasz, *Education and the American Indian,* pp. 108–90; *Phoenix Gazette,* May 7, 10, 1947.
6. *Arizona Star,* March 26, 1945; *Phoenix Gazette,* September 9, 1949; *Arizona Republic,* April 13, 1952.
7. *Arizona Republic,* March 23, September 18, 1982.
8. *New Times,* November 28-December 4, 1984.
9. *Arizona Republic,* April 10, 1985.
10. Ibid., May 23, 29, 30, June 15, 1986, January 1, 1987.

Bibliography

1. MANUSCRIPTS

Laguna Niguel, California. Federal Records Center.
   Record Group 75, Records of the Bureau of Indian Affairs.
      Papers of the Phoenix Area Office
      Sherman Institute Papers
Phoenix, Arizona. City Records Office.
   Municipal Ordinance File
Tempe, Arizona. Arizona Historical Foundation.
   Hancock Family Collection
Tempe, Arizona. Arizona State University Library.
   Arizona Collection
      Carl Hayden Papers
      Carlos Montezuma Collection
Tucson, Arizona. Arizona Historical Society.
   Tucson Indian School Papers
Washington, D.C. National Archives of the United States.
   Record Group 48, Records of the Secretary of the Interior.
      Letters Received
   Record Group 75, Records of the Bureau of Indian Affairs.
      Annual Narrative and Statistical Reports, M-1011
      Board of Indian Commissioners
      Central Classified Files, 1907–1930
      Education Circulars
      Letters Received, 1890–1907
      Letters Sent, 1890–1907
      Reports of Inspection, M-1070

2. FEDERAL DOCUMENTS

Fletcher, Alice C. *Indian Education and Civilization.* Sen. Ex. Doc. 85, 48th Cong., 2d sess., ser. 2264 (1888).

Hrdlečka, Aleš. *Tuberculosis Among Certain Indian Tribes of the United States.* Bureau of American Ethnology Bulletin 42. Washington, D.C.: U.S. Government Printing Office, 1909.
Indian Rights Association. *Annual Report.* Washington, D.C.: Government Printing Office, 1923.
"Indians of the United States." H. Rept. 1133, 66th Cong., 3d sess., 1920.
"Letter . . . submitting an estimate of an appropriation for an Indian school at or near Phoenix." H. Ex. Doc. 218, 51st Cong., 1st sess., ser. 2866 (1891).
"Letter . . . transmitting estimate from the Secretary of the Interior of appropriation for the Indian school at Phoenix, Ariz." H. Ex. Doc. 163, 53d Cong., 1st sess., ser. 3226 (1894).
[Reel, Estelle.] *Course of Study for the Indian Schools of the United States.* Washington, D.C.: U.S. Government Printing Office, 1901.
Statistics on Indian Tribes, Agencies, and Schools, 1903. Washington, D.C.: U.S. Government Printing Office, 1903.
Statutes at Large of the United States of America. Vols. 27, 30. Washington, D.C.: U.S. Government Printing Office, 1893, 1899.
U.S. Board of Indian Commissioners. *Annual Reports.* Washington, D.C.: U.S. Government Printing Office, 1883–1924.
U.S. Commissioner of Indian Affairs. *Annual Reports.* Washington, D.C.: U.S. Government Printing Office, 1878–1929.
U.S. Secretary of the Interior. *Annual Report.* Washington, D.C.: U.S. Government Printing Office, 1931.
U.S. Senate. *Survey of Conditions of the Indians of the United States.* Washington, D.C.: U.S. Government Printing Office, 1928–1931.
U.S. Superintendent of Indian Schools. *Annual Reports.* Washington, D.C.: U.S. Government Printing Office, 1895–1896.

3. ORAL INTERVIEWS

Antone, Ella Lopez (Papago), at Santa Rosa Village, Arizona, January 22, 1982 (interviewed by Kathleen Sands).
Blaine, Peter, Sr. (Papago), at Tucson, Arizona, May 7, 1981.
Cassadore, Philip (Apache), at Tempe, Arizona, February 5, 1980.
Dukepoo, Anthony and Hazel (Hopi), at Tempe, Arizona, November 13, 1984, and at Flagstaff, Arizona, March 2, 1985.
Rios, Theodore (Papago), at Sells, Arizona, May 16, 17, 1974 (interviewed by Kathleen Sands).
Sekaquaptewa, Helen (Hopi), at Scottsdale, Arizona, March 26, 1985.

4. NEWSPAPERS

Arizona Daily Citizen (Tucson)
Arizona Gazette (Phoenix)
Arizona Graphic (Phoenix)
Arizona Labor Journal (Phoenix)
Arizona Republic (Phoenix)
Arizona Republican (Phoenix)
Arizona Star (Tucson)
Daily Enterprise (Phoenix)
Native American (Phoenix)
New York Times
New Times (Phoenix)
Philadelphia Inquirer
Phoenix Daily Herald
Phoenix Evening Gazette
The Phoenix Redskin
Washington Star (Washington, D.C.)

5. BOOKS

Adams, Evelyn C. *American Indian Education: Government Schools and Economic Progress.* Morningside Heights, N.Y.: King's Crown Press, 1946.

Berkhofer, Robert F., Jr. *Salvation and the Savage: An Analysis of Protestant Missions and American Indian Response.* New York: Atheneum, 1972.

Blaine, Peter, Sr., with Michael S. Adams. *Papagos and Politics.* Tucson: Arizona Historical Society, 1981.

Brown, Estelle Aubrey. *Stubborn Fool: A Narrative.* Caldwell, Idaho: Caxton Printers, 1952.

Cook, Minnie A. *Apostle to the Pima Indians.* Tiburon, Calif.: Omega Books, 1976.

Eastman, Elaine Goodale. *Pratt: The Red Man's Moses.* Norman: University of Oklahoma Press, 1935.

Fritz, Henry E. *The Movement for Indian Assimilation, 1860–1890.* Philadelphia: University of Pennsylvania Press, 1963.

Fuchs, Estelle, and Robert J. Havinghurst. *To Live on This Earth: American Indian Education.* Introduction by Margaret Connell Szasz. Reprint. Albuquerque: University of New Mexico Press, 1983.

Gugle, Sara F. *History of the International Order of the King's Daughters and Sons, Years 1886 to 1930.* Np., 1931.

Hertzberg, Hazel W. *The Search for an American Indian Identity:*

Modern Pan-Indian Movements. Syracuse, N.Y.: Syracuse University Press, 1971.

Hoxie, Frederick E. *A Final Promise: The Campaign to Assimilate the Indians, 1880–1920*. Lincoln: University of Nebraska Press, 1984.

Iverson, Peter. *Carlos Montezuma and the Changing World of American Indians*. Albuquerque: University of New Mexico Press, 1982.

James, Harry C. *Pages From Hopi History*. Tucson: Univesity of Arizona Press, 1974.

Johnson, Allen, and Dumas Malone, eds. *Dictionary of American Biography*. New York: Charles Scribner's Sons, 1930.

Johnson, G. Wesley, Jr. *Phoenix: Valley of the Sun*. Tulsa: Continental Heritage Press, 1982.

Keller, Robert H., Jr. *American Protestantism and United States Indian Policy, 1869–82*. Lincoln: University of Nebraska Press, 1983.

Kelly, Lawrence C. *The Assault on Assimilation: John Collier and the Origins of Indian Policy Reform*. Albuquerque: University of New Mexico Press, 1983.

Kluger, James R. *The Clifton-Morenci Strike*. Tucson: University of Arizona Press, 1970.

Kvasnicka, Robert M., and Herman J. Viola, eds. *Commissioners of Indian Affairs, 1824–1977*. Lincoln: University of Nebraska Press, 1979.

Leupp, Francis E. *The Indian and His Problem*. New York: Charles Scribner's Sons, 1910.

Luckingham, Bradford. *The Urban Southwest: A Profile History of Albuquerque-El Paso-Phoenix-Tucson*. El Paso: Texas Western Press, 1982.

Ludlow, Helen W. *Ten Year's Work for Indians at the Hampton Normal and Agricultural Institute*. Hampton, Va., 1888.

Lummis, Charles. *Bullying the Moqui*. Edited and with an Introduction by Robert Easton and Mackenzie Brown. Prescott, Ariz.: Prescott College Press, 1968.

Lynch, Richard E. *Winfield Scott: A Biography of Scottsdale's Founder*. Scottsdale, Ariz.: City of Scottsdale, 1978.

McBeth, Sally J. *Ethnic Identity and the Boarding School Experience of West-Central Oklahoma American Indians*. Washington, D.C.: University Press of America, 1983.

Meriam, Lewis, et al. *The Problem of Indian Administration*. Baltimore: Johns Hopkins Press, 1928.

The New Trail. Volume 2—1930. Phoenix: U.S. Indian Vocational School, 1930.

Olson, James S., and Raymond Wilson. *Native Americans in the Twentieth Century*. Provo: Brigham Young University Press, 1984.

Omaha: The Gate City and Douglas County, Nebraska. 2 volumes. Chicago: S. J. Clarke Publishing Co., 1917.

Philp, Kenneth R. *John Collier's Crusade for Indian Reform, 1920–1954*. Tucson: University of Arizona Press, 1977.

Portrait and Biographical Record of Arizona. Chicago: Chapman Publishing Co., 1901.

Pratt, Richard Henry. *Battlefield and Classroom: Four Decades with the American Indians: 1867–1904*. Edited by Robert M. Utley. New Haven: Yale University Press, 1964.

———. *The Indian Industrial School, Carlisle, Pennsylvania: Its Origins, Purposes, Progress and the Difficulties Surmounted*. Edited by Robert M. Utley. Carlisle, Pa., 1979.

Priest, Loring B. *Uncle Sam's Stepchildren: The Reformation of United States Indian Policy, 1865–1887*. Lincoln: University of Nebraska Press, 1975.

Prucha, Francis Paul. *American Indian Policy in Crisis: Christian Reformers and the Indian, 1865–1900*. Norman: University of Oklahoma Press, 1976.

———, ed. *Americanizing the American Indians: Writings of the "Friends of the Indians," 1880–1900*. Cambridge: Harvard University Press, 1973.

———. *The Churches and the Indian Schools, 1888–1912*. Lincoln: University of Nebraska Press, 1979.

Qoyawayma, Polingaysi [Elizabeth Q. White]. *No Turning Back: A True Account of a Hopi Girl's Struggle to Bridge the Gap Between the World of Her People and the World of the White Man*. As told to Vada F. Carlson. Albuquerque: University of New Mexico Press, 1964.

Reed, Bill. *The Last Bugle Call: A History of Fort McDowell, Arizona Territory, 1865–1890*. Parsons, West Va.: McClain Publishing Co., 1977.

Russell, Frank. *The Pima Indians*. Re-edition edited by Bernard L. Fontana. Tucson: University of Arizona Press, 1975.

Senior Class Annual, 1924. Phoenix: U.S. Indian Vocational School, 1924.

Shaw, Anna Moore. *A Pima Past*. Tucson: University of Arizona Press, 1974.

Spicer, Edward H. *Cycles of Conquest: The Impact of Spain, Mexico, and the United States on the Indians of the Southwest, 1533–1960*. Tucson: University of Arizona Press, 1962.

Szasz, Margaret Connell. *Education and the American Indian: The Road to Self-Determination Since 1928*. Albuquerque: University of New Mexico Press, 1977.

Tiller, Veronica E. Velarde. *The Jicarilla Apache Tribe: A History, 1846–1970.* Lincoln: University of Nebraska Press, 1983.
Tousey, Thomas G. *Military History of Carlisle and Carlisle Barracks.* Richmond, Va.: Dietz Press, 1939.
Udall, Louise. *Me and Mine: The Life Story of Helen Sekaquaptewa.* Tucson: University of Arizona Press, 1969.
Who's Who in Arizona, 1913. Tucson: Jo Conners, 1913.

6. ARTICLES

Adams, David Wallace. "Education in Hues: Red and Black at Hampton Institute, 1878–1893." *South Atlantic Quarterly,* 77 (Spring 1977): 159–76.

———. "Schooling the Hopi: Federal Indian Policy Writ Small, 1887–1917." *Pacific Historical Review,* 48 (August 1979): 335–56.

Barney, James M. "Famous Indian Ordinance." *The Sheriff,* 13 (June 1954): 77.

Brunhouse, Robert L. "The Founding of the Carlisle Indian School." *Pennsylvania History,* 6 (April 1939): 72–85.

Chingren, Amanda M. "Arizona Indian Women and Their Future." *Arizona,* 2 (February 1912): 9–10.

Collier, John. "The Accursed System." *Sunset,* 52 (June 1924): 15–16, 80–82.

———. "Our Indian Policy: Why Not Treat the Red Man as Wisely, as Generously as We Have Treated the Filipino?" *Sunset,* 50 (March 1923): 13–15, 89–93.

———. "The Red Slaves of Oklahoma." *Sunset,* 52 (March 1924): 9–11, 94–100.

Grinnell, George Bird. "The Indian and the Outing System." *The Outlook,* 75 (September 19, 1903): 167–73.

Hailmann, William N. "Education of the Indian." *Monographs on Education in the United States,* 19 (1904): 939–65.

Hoxie, Frederick E. "Redefining Indian Education: Thomas J. Morgan's Program in Disarray." *Arizona and the West,* 24 (Spring 1982): 5–18.

Jones, William A. "A New Indian Policy." *The World's Work,* 3 (March 1902): 1838–40.

Laughlin, Sylvia. "Iron Springs, Arizona: Timeless Summer Resort." *Journal of Arizona History,* 22 (Summer 1981): 235–53.

Leupp, Francis E. "Indians and Their Education." *National Education Association Journal of Proceedings and Addresses,* (1907): 70–74.

———. "Outlines of an Indian Policy." *Outlook,* 79 (April 15, 1905): 946–50.

Ludlow, Helen W. "Indian Education at Hampton and Carlisle." *Harper's Magazine*, 62 (April 1881): 659–75.
Lummis, Charles F. "My Brother's Keeper." *Land of Sunshine*, 11–12 (August 1899-January 1900): 139–47, 207–13, 263–68, 333–35, 28–30, 90–94.
———. "Sequoyah League." *Out West*, 16–19 (March and November 1902, August, September, and October 1903): 297–302, 601–7, 207–8, 296–309, 419–23.
McKinney, Lillie G. "History of Albuquerque Indian School." *New Mexico Historical Review*, 20 (April 1945): 109–38.
Morton, Louis. "How the Indians Came to Carlisle." *Pennsylvania History*, 29 (January 1962): 53–73.
Raine, William MacLeod. "The Government Indian School as a Promoter of Civilization." *World Today*, 4 (1903): 614–19.
Richards, Josephine E. "The Training of Indian Girls as the Uplifter of the Home." *National Education Association Journal of Proceedings and Addresses*, (1900): 701–5.
Schurz, Carl. "Present Aspects of the Indian Problem." *North American Review*, 133 (July 1881): 1–24.
Shaffner, Ruth. "Civilizing the American Indian." *Chautauquan*, 23 (June 1896): 259–68.
"She Would Go." *Indian's Friend*, 7 (December 1894): 8.
Super, O. B. "Indian Education at Carlisle." *New England Magazine*, 18 (April 1895): 224–39.
Trennert, Robert A. "Educating Indian Girls at Nonreservation Boarding Schools, 1878–1920." *Western Historical Quarterly*, 13 (July 1982): 271–90.
———. "From Carlisle to Phoenix: The Rise and Fall of the Indian Outing System, 1878–1930." *Pacific Historical Review*, 52 (August 1983): 267–91.
"Want More School Room." *Indian's Friend*, 7 (December 1894): 8.
White, Bruce W. "The American Indian as Soldier, 1890–1919." *Canadian Review of American Studies*, 7 (Spring 1976): 15–25.
Willard, Frances E. "The Carlisle Indian School." *Chautauquan*, 9 (February 1889): 289–90.
Williams, Julian I. "Ten Days in Arizona." *Southwest Illustrated*, 2 (February 1896): 11–19.
Young, Etta Gifford. "Poor Lo—The Indian." *Arizona Magazine* (December 1913): 4–5, 10–11.

7. UNPUBLISHED MATERIALS

Adams, David W. "The Federal Indian Boarding School: A Study in Environment and Response, 1879–1918." Ed.D. disseration, Indiana University, 1975.

Fritz, Henry E. "The Board of Indian Commissioners Versus John Collier and Lewis Meriam, 1923–1933." Paper presented to the Western History Association, October 1985.

Frost, Richard W. "Pueblo Indian Returned Students: The Dominance of Community Conservatism, to 1930." Paper presented to the Lake Mohonk Conference, October, 1983.

Gilcreast, Everett A. "Richard Henry Pratt and American Indian Policy, 1877–1906: A Study of the Assimilation Movement." Ph.D. dissertation. Yale University, 1967.

Hagan, Maxine W. "An Educational History of the Pima and Papago Peoples from the Mid-seventeenth Century to the Mid-twentieth Century." Ed.D. dissertation, University of Arizona, 1959.

Hamilton, John A. "A History of the Presbyterian Work Among the Pima and Papago Indians of Arizona." M.A. thesis, University of Arizona, 1959.

Mawn, Geoffrey P. "Phoenix, Arizona: Central City of the Southwest, 1870–1920." Ph.D. dissertation, Arizona State University, 1979.

Pierson, Katie. "History of Phoenix Indian School." Unpublished manuscript, Arizona Collection, Arizona State University.

Putney, Diane. "Fighting the Scourge: American Indian Morbidity and Federal Policy, 1897–1928." Ph.D. dissertation, Marquette University, 1980.

Walker-McNeil, Pearl Lee. "The Carlisle Indian School: A Study in Acculturation." Ph.D. dissertation, The American University, 1979.

Index

Adams, F. Yale: 87
Albuquerque Indian Industrial School: 8, 13, 39–40, 60, 62, 177
Allen, George W.: 39–40, 62
American Indian Defense Association: 174, 193
American Red Cross: 132, 162–63
Antone, Ella: 139
Apache Indians: 81, 98, 171
Arizona Improvement Company: 19–20
Arizona National Guard: 116–17, 160–61, 203
Armstrong, Katie: 51
Armstrong, Samuel C.: 5–6

Beatty, Willard W.: 200
Belt, Robert V.: 22
Billman, Howard: 37
Blackwater, Charles: 29
Blaine, Peter: 123, 139, 148
Board of Indian Commissioners: 74, 94, 144, 159, 175, 180
Boy Scouts: 132
Brodie, Alexander O.: 87, 141
Brown, Estelle: 135
Brown, John B.: 114, 133, 136–37, 141, 209; attitude toward religion, 132; opinion of returned students, 143–44; background of, 150–51; activities as superintendent, 153–62, 164–73, 176–79; reaction to Meriam Report, 187–92; attitude on corporal punishment, 165–66, 171–72, 178, 188–89, 192–95; defends old guard, 195–97; resignation, 197–98
Burns, Mike: 171–72
Bursom Bill: 174

Camp Fire Girls: 132
Camp Grant: 165
Canfield, Bertha: 75
Carlisle Indian Industrial School: 13, 31, 47, 53, 63, 66, 82, 94, 96, 108, 114, 131, 153, 168; established, 5–9; athletic program at, 81; closed, 164

Catholic Holy Name Society: 131
Cheyenne Boarding School: 41
Chilocco Indian Industrial School: 8, 83, 85–86, 177
Chingren, Amanda: becomes school outing matron, 101; charged with misconduct, 172–73; retires, 196
Christy, William: 19–20, 23, 26
Civilization Fund: 4
Cleveland, Grover: 40, 43, 55
Clifton, Arizona: 160
Collier, John: 150, 182, 197, 207, 209–10, 212; leads Indian reform movement, 174–75, 188; criticism of Indian schools, 179–81; opposition to corporal punishment, 192–95; becomes Indian commissioner, 200–203; declines to close Phoenix school, 204–205
Columbian Exposition: 81–82
Commercial Club of Chicago: 82
Committee of One Hundred: 175, 177
Compulsory schooling: 59, 66–67, 169–70; see also Phoenix Indian Industrial School
Conser, Frank: 63
Cook, Charles H.: 13
Cook Bible School: 155
Crane, Leo: 145–48
Creighton, James M.: 28
Crouse, Cornelius M.: 28, 29, 38
Culbertson, M. K.: 38

Daiker, F. H.: 195
Deutch, Justin: 92–93
Dorchester, Daniel: 14–16, 18, 23–24, 31–32
Douglas, Arizona: 160
Dowawisnima, Helen (Sekaquaptewa): 118, 136–37, 145
Duclos, A. F.: 172
Duran, Jacob: 193–94, 199

Easchief, Oldham: 29

253

Fiske, H. H.: 193–94
Forest Grove Indian School: 8
Fort McDowell: 14–19, 20–21, 23–24, 26, 27
Fort McDowell Reservation: 98, 155, 171
Fort Marion: 5
Fort Mojave Indian School: 60, 63–64
Frazier, Lynn J.: 197
Frear, James: 179–80

Gates, Merrill E.: 74
Genoa Indian Industrial School: 8, 13, 39, 43, 131
Gila Crossing Catholic Day School: 92
Gila River Reservation: 13, 143
Gill, W. H.: 78
Goodman, Charles W.: 98; becomes school superintendent, 85; background of, 85–86; educational policies of, 86–87, 109–10; attitude toward outing system, 87–92, 100–101; religious policies of, 92–94; concerned about student health, 101–102, 105, 108–109; retirement, 111
Greater American Exposition: 82

Hailmann, William: 53, 96
Hall, Harwood: 33, 51; background of, 41; recruiting policies of, 42–46; educational philosophy, 46–49; develops outing system, 52–54; relationship with Phoenix, 54–56; dispute with McCowan, 63–64
Hammond, E. H.: 177
Hampton Institute: 5–6, 8, 13, 47, 82, 140–41
Harding, Warren G.: 169
Harrison, Benjamin: 23
Hatch, Frank C.: 27
Hayden, Carl: 164, 194–95, 198, 204, 211
Hayes, Annie: 140
Heyman, Ben: 71
Hopi Indians: 62, 113, 114–15, 139, 147, 157, 171, 207, 212
Hoxie, Frederick E.: 59
Hrdlička, Aleš: 102–103
Hunt, George W. P.: 154, 160

Indian Rights Association: 94, 189
Institute for Government Research: 182

Johnson-O'Malley Act: 190
Jones, William A.: 62, 66, 94, 95, 96; becomes Indian commissioner, 58; attitude towards Indians, 58–59; classification of nonreservation schools, 61; enrollment policies of, 66–67; favors vocational training, 68–69

Kachina, Vivian: 146
Keams Canyon Boarding School: 113
Kelly, Lawrence C.: 175
Ketcham, William H.: 94
King's Daughters: 50

Lake Mohonk Conference: 13
Lawrence (Haskell) Indian Industrial School: 8, 94, 114, 131, 150, 153
Lee, J. M.: 14–15, 17
Leupp, Francis E.: 99, 109, 124, 151, 174; becomes Indian commissioner, 94; background of, 94–95; educational philosophy of, 95–97; favors outing system, 100–101; concerned with Indian health, 101–105
Lummis, Charles F.: 96, 174

McAfee, Lapsley A: 90
McCowan, Samuel M.: 85, 156; appointed school superintendent, 57; educational philosophy, 57–58, 60; biases of, 60, 65–66; recruiting practices of, 61, 64, 66–68; expands campus, 64–65; favors vocational training, 68–70, 75–76; expands outing system, 70–73; supports staff development, 73–75; health concerns of, 76–77; advocates religious training, 77–78; relationship with Phoenix, 79–84; resigns, 83–84
McKinley, William: 57, 83
Manual labor schools: 4
Maricopa Indians: 12–13, 42, 43, 49, 81, 139
Martin, Ancil: 104
Meriam, Lewis: 182
Meriam Report: 150, 181, 182–205, 209
Meritt, Edgar B.: 179–80, 182
Mesa High School: 128
Mohave Indians: 39–40, 62
Montezuma, Carlos: 171
Moore, Anna: 115–16, 119, 127, 133, 134, 140, 141
Moore, Bill: 127
Moore, Carl: 193–94
Moore, Russell: 127
Morenci, Arizona: 160
Morford, N. A.: 22–23
Morgan, Thomas J.: 33, 37–38, 42, 55, 57, 157, 205, 206; becomes Indian commissioner, 9; background of, 9–10; educational philosophy of, 10–11, 14; favors school near Phoenix, 15–17, 23–25, 26, 34; visits Phoenix, 20–22; selects school site, 27–28; resigns, 40

INDEX

Murphy, Nathan O.: 20–23, 24
Murphy, William J.: 19–20, 23

Naco, Ariz.: 160
Nashville Exposition: 82
National Education Association: 9, 74–75
Navajo Indians: 156, 157, 180
Navajo Reservation: 170–71
New Deal: 183; Indian program of, 189, 200, 203
Noble, John W.: 24, 25

Office of Indian Affairs: 40–41, 59, 95, 148, 153, 154, 175, 177; organization of Education Division, 33–34; distinguishes among nonreservation schools, 61; encourages exhibits, 81–82; policy on outing program, 88–92; religious policies of, 93; vocational education policy of, 99–100, 156–57; attitude toward returned students, 144; compulsory schooling, 169–70; investigates Phoenix school, 172–73; attitude toward reform, 179–80, 194–98; reaction to Meriam Report, 187–92; *see also* names of various Indian commissioners
Outing System: 6, 8, 20, 72–73, 92, 100; *see also* Phoenix Indian Industrial School

Papago Indians: 42, 43, 49, 102, 113, 139, 148, 156, 157, 171, 176–77, 212
Patton, Hugh: 27, 29, 38
Pearis, Hervey B.: 195
Pehihonema, Hazel (Dukepoo): 139
Perris Indian Boarding School: 55, 73
Phoenix, Ariz.: 19–27, 29–31, 51, 81, 98–99, 128, 162, 212–13
Phoenix Indian Industrial School: 12, 33, 57, 85, 150, 182, 204-13; founding of, 21–26; acquisition of site, 21–28; use of West End Hotel, 22–28; vocational training at, 25, 46–47, 68–70, 99–100, 123–25, 158-59, 190, 202; construction at, 28–32, 38, 43–46, 65, 105, 191; women's education at, 32, 47, 91–92, 123–24, 202; enrollment and recruiting policies of, 35–40, 42, 606–64, 66–68, 110, 155–58, 199–201; student labor at, 37, 47, 118, 176, 201; description of campus, 45–46, 54-55, 64, 83, 86, 153; academic programs at, 46, 59, 99, 110, 119–23, 190–91, 200–202; discipline and punishment, 47–48, 50, 115–19, 125–26, 165–66, 171–72, 178, 188–89, 192–95, 196–97, 203; parental support of, 48–49, 113–14; student life at, 49- 50, 78, 112–49, 202; religious policies of, 50, 77, 92–94, 109, 131, 203; runaways from, 50, 92–93, 125–26, 165; outing program at, 50, 51–54, 70–73, 75, 87–88, 100–101, 136–38, 168; relationship with Phoenix, 51–55, 79, 133, 153–55, 211–13; school band, 55, 79, 116, 127–28; overcrowding at, 65, 76, 169–70, 176; staff training, 73–75; health concerns at, 76–77, 101–109, 118, 177–78, 191–92; athletic program, 81, 128–31, 203; *Native American*, 82, 139, 146, 154, 173, 187, 198–99; teaching staff, 86–87, 170; East Farm and Sanatorium, 86, 101, 105–109, 170; Indian arts and crafts at, 109–110, 202–203; language restrictions at, 109, 115; "de-Indianization," 114–15; tribal animosities at, 126–27; extra-curricular activities, 132–33, 203; dating and courtship at, 133–36; commencement, 139, 166; war effort of, 159–63
Phoenix Junior College: 128
Phoenix Union High School: 81, 131, 140
Pima Indians: 12–13, 42, 49, 81, 133, 139, 147, 157, 171
Polacca Day School: 114
Poston, Charles D.: 25
Pratt, Richard Henry: 4–8, 59, 74, 81, 95, 96, 100, 168
Public schools: 96–99, 110, 151, 156–57, 164, 170–71, 175, 190

Recruiting practices: 40–41, 67, 97–98; *see also* Phoenix Indian Industrial School
Reel, Estelle: 69, 72–73, 74, 86–87, 99
Rhoads, Charles J.: 198; becomes Indian commissioner, 189; implements Meriam Report, 189–92; dispute with Collier, 192–95, reorganizes Indian service, 195–96
Rich, Wellington: 33, 50, 51, 52; background of, 16, appointed school superintendent, 16–17; locates at Fort McDowell, 17–19; promotes Phoenix site, 21–23, 24–27; opens school, 28–29; enlists community support, 31; opens permanent facility, 32; educational philosophy of, 35–40; recruiting practices of, 40–41; replaced, 41
Richards, Josephine: 75
Rios, Theodore: 118
Roman Catholic Church: 92–94, 131

Roosevelt, Franklin D.: 200
Ryan, W. Carson: 183, 195, 200
Sacaton Indian Boarding School: 36, 38, 113
Saint John's Catholic Boarding School: 113
Salem Indian School: 117
Salt River Reservation: 78, 201
Santa Fe Indian Industrial School: 64
Santa Fe Railway: 128
Scattergood, Joseph H.: 189, 194, 197–98
Schach, Mrs.: 89–90
Schmidt, Elsie: 192–95
Schurz, Carl: 6
Sells, Cato: 133, 151–53, 156–58, 161–64, 167
Shaw, Ross: 141
Sherman Institute: 145
Skinner, Carl H.: becomes school superintendent, 198–99; implements New Deal program, 201–204
Smith, Hoke: 43
Snyder, Homer: 167
Society of American Indians: 132, 166
Student Health: 14, 15, 76, 97, 101–103, 108; *see also* Phoenix Indian Industrial School
Student labor: 9, 184; *see also* Phoenix Indian Industrial School

Sunderland, Edwin: 31
Szasz, Margaret Connell: 174
Taft, William Howard: 128
Tempe Normal School: 81, 128, 141
Thackery, Frank: 147
Thomas, Elmer: 197
Tonner, A. C.: 74, 88–89
Tucson Indian Mission School: 13, 36–38
Valentine, Robert G.: 105, 151
Vogt, Casimir: 93
Webb, George: 140
Wheeler, Burton K.: 197–98
White, Elizabeth: 145
Wilson, Woodrow: 151, 161, 166
Wolfchief, John: 140
Women's Christian Temperance Union: 132
Work, Hubert: 174, 181
Yankton Agency Boarding School: 16
Yavapai Indians: 98
Youhongva, Tony (Dukepoo): 114, 124, 136, 139
Young, J. Roe: 43
Young Men's Christian Association (YMCA): 78, 131, 162, 203
Young Women's Christian Association (YWCA): 50, 78, 131, 203